10th Anniversary Book
SELECTED ESSAYS
FROM THE
VIVEKANANDA INTERNATIONAL FOUNDATION

Contemporary: Economy

1

STATE OF THE ECONOMY: INDIA AND THE WORLD

S. Gurumurthy

Professor Roger Moser, who says India is a second home, was partnering with me in discussions today on employing technology which is already developed. This is a new area of development all over the world. Even before he went into the subject, he said, India must be more self-confident. A person who is a foreigner and who has made India second home, his first observation is that Indians must be more self-confident and India must be more self-confident. The necessity for reiterating what Mr Moser said will be to see that it runs through my presentation, including how we're handling current problems. Unless we understand where we are from, what are the problems and from where the problems are coming, we'll not be able to have clear, intellectual solutions for the problems.

India is a country with thousands of years of continuity. No other country has this continuity. Geography is existent, but culture hasn't been existent. As Swami Vivekananda said, a spider weaves its web where the Caesars ruled. The stones, buildings, pyramids are there but the thoughts, culture, language, literature, what bound the people at that time is no more there. He said if Veda Vyāsa came back to India, he would find traffic landmarks identified even today. That is the kind of change that the country has been able to adapt itself to. That is why it's a living civilization.

We have seen so many things happening and we have talked about recent things like colonisation, capitalism, socialism and globalisation. I have been having a helicopter look of the shelf life of all these ideas. Colonisation lasted for 200 years. Now it's abused as one of the worst happenings in the history of the world. It dominated the world, our minds, it left its imprint. Even today, we suffer from hangovers of colonisation. The colonisers feel guilty about colonisation. But the colonised people are not feeling sad that they were colonised. They revel in things that the colonisers left. It is a paradoxical phenomenon.

Capitalism came and exhausted itself in 100 years. Then came socialism that became irrelevant in 50 years. Then came globalisation which is irrelevant in 25 years. You can understand the shelf life of ideas which became so fashionable, powerful with an obsessive instinct; it becomes irrelevant in such a short time. We are gripped by thinking and impact which was foisted on us. It leaves us confronting what and who we are. When globalisation was hitting India like a tsunami, it was people like us who protested. An ex-serviceman said that people like you should be shot dead because you are preventing growth and development of India by opposing globalisation. You can't differ from mainline thought. That's the power of modernity. It makes itself so powerful that anyone who deviates from it has no right to live. That is the kind of imposition it brings.

Without this understanding about what is the state of the Indian economy and what are its solutions, we will never be able to understand how the Indian mind has been shaped by the policy making, intellectual, powerful, ruling, media mind over the last 100 years.

In 1853, Karl Marx wrote a couple of articles in the *New York Herald Tribune* in which he said that India is a very peculiar country. At that time, no one doubted the unity of India. Even Karl Marx said that India was a nation. It had one way of life; it had one kind of rule, though it had several rulers. But its economics was organised in terms of villages. For 2,000 years, the country's economy hasn't changed but there is such an intimacy between producer and consumer that there was very little exploitation. The only wrong thing with Indians was that they were worshipping cows and monkeys. That was his objection. He regarded us as a semi-barbaric society. So, this society must be demolished and the economic base must collapse, so that you are prepared for revolution. Without revolution, you cannot modernise. Indian society will never modernise because it's dipped in continuity. He said that the British are doing right by destroying the society. It's welcome destruction though it is painful, but it is pleasurable also.

Max Weber was the only brain in the world who linked philosophy, living style, society and collectivism to economic growth. All moved away from this position. He said that Protestant society moves faster because there is individualism and then there is enterprise and then there is entrepreneurship and then there is economic development. So, the modern economic model is aligned with protectionism. And Catholic society will not be able to catch up with such societies and he's right. America, Canada, New Zealand, England and Australia were all moving fast. If you look at France, part of Germany, Italy, Spain, they were all lagging. He was right as he spends 25 years studying this phenomenon. This is the origin of society and economics as a combined study. He wrote books on the religions of India and China in the 1950s. He said that these two societies would never grow because their religion makes them believe in karma and rebirth and no individualism. So, they will never grow in market and society. With frozen thoughts, they are condemned to live in abject poverty.

If the country must develop, it must give up its philosophy, way of life and relationship. In 1951, the U.N. prescribed it as a mandate for development of underdeveloped economies. That you must give up philosophy, way of life, otherwise you will be condemned to living in poverty. This is Western anthropological modernity which we internalised in public discourse, policy-making. A one-size-fits-all model not only in economics but also in society, cultures and value system. This is how we were progressing.

We adopted the socialist model. In 1978, when all the socialist nations were moving forward, and we weren't, then somebody asked Dr. Rajkrishna how was it that we are following the same socialist policies. He said we could have only a Hindu rate of growth because we are condemned to live in poverty with our thoughts. This was the implication. When this was the discourse going on in 1983, Paul Bairoch, one of the most well-known economic historians, brought out a book on the mandate given by the General Agreement on Tariffs and Trade (GATT) about the economic growth of 1750 and 1900 in which he made a disclosure that in 1750, India was number two in the economic development map, China was number one. America and England had a share of only two per cent in GDP whereas India had 24.5 per cent and China 34 per cent. This shook the world. Many French historians began saying let us admit we didn't have such good standards of living as China and India is 15th and 16th century and our prosperity is recently founded.

Then the Organisation for Economic Co-operation and Development (OECD) countries constituted a study in which Angus Maddison, after 18 years of research, came out with his magnum opus—*The World Economy: A Millennial Perspective*—in which he said that for 1,500 years, India had been the leading economic engine of the world. In the 16th century, India and China became equal. In the 17th century, India rose above China. In the 18th and 19th centuries, both were overtaken by others. If this research was available, would Karl Marx and Max Weber have written like they did? There are studies that show it's these two great men who influence the Indian academia, education system, public discourse and policymaking. We decided that we couldn't generate our ideas. Importing goods can be stopped once you import ideas. This is where Indians were caught in a Catch-22 situation of being the largest society. One-sixth of humanity is India. We didn't develop the faculty of our own thinking and that's where we as a nation suffer today. Otherwise, you will be saying we are in mess but what is the cause? Where has our thought pattern been interfered with so powerfully that even to think differently we need to look here and there. Whether I will be misunderstood if I think differently is the lack of confidence into which Indians have fallen. We must recover from it.

You had two opposite parallels of Marxism and capitalism which ruled the world for 25-30 years. Communism collapsed. The global order was seen as based only on free market and liberal democracy. Francis Fukuyama even wrote a book and said that these institutions have established themselves as the final victor as West over the rest. It's best for the rest to follow the West. This became the Bible of globalisation. We were mandated into globalisation because of our wrong policies which we followed for 25 years in the name of "command economy" which destroyed Indian enterprise. Indian enterprise dominated the world. In Greco-Roman literature, in the Roman parliament it was discussed that Indian traders were looting the Roman Empire. All their gold was disappearing. There were 300 ships floating around the waters carrying goods from India and carrying nothing back. This was the kind of economic impact we had over the world. But colonisation, capitalism, communism, globalisation in succession made us feel that we cannot do anything. We must wait for others to tell us what we should do. That is how we accepted globalisation.

Francis Fukuyama wrote another book in 1994 in which he said that family-based societies are different from individual-based societies. This was a book on how Asia was different as China was rising and when Japan, Korea and Taiwan had already risen at that time. He said that individualism-based societies are losing out and family-based societies are rising. *The Economist* magazine commented that he earlier spoke about the end of history and he was now talking about the end of economics. If you write a book on the success of family-based societies in economics, then you are talking about the end of economics. This is where globalisation began as the all-pervasive and the dominant idea. India, if it has to develop, will have to only go through globalisation and that it cannot make a local variation. This was the thought against which we fought for the last 25 years.

President Trump came to power in America. Many of us have not followed very minutely on what was the discourse in America and the world when Trump was contesting the elections and he was a candidate. Then Lawrence Summers, economic advisor to Clinton, said that Trump would cause a market crash and throw the world into recession. The election was going to take place in November-December and he said it in June. Citigroup said that a Trump victory would mean global recession and the first gift could be another financial crisis. The *Washington Post* said that Trump would destroy the world economy. Former Chief of the International Monetary Fund (IMF) predicted recession for 18 months from which the world cannot recover. After the election, there was the prognosis that Trump may win. Paul Krugman, a Nobel Laureate, said that there would probably be a global recession with no end in sight. After Trump won, the U.K.-based *Independent* magazine wrote, "Trump's first gift to the world—another catastrophic financial crisis."

After Trump came to power, the dollar index rose by 5.6 per cent in one month, the highest in 14 years. It shook America and the world. On the third day of his power, he terminated the Trans-Pacific Partnership of 12 nations. On the seventh day, he said these people should not send refugees to America. In June, Trump withdrew from the climate accord. He said he had to make America strong. The country which drove the very process of globalisation said that no one's interest is important, the collective interest of all is important. That country said my interest is important. It is Americanism which is important. We have to factor it in if we want to decide what we want to do. He took on traditional allies of America. He said Russia should be brought back in G8, which had been removed after it occupied Crimea.

Trump was working with a plan and was correcting the distortions for America. See the results he produced—the dollar rose by 5.6 per cent. The stocks rose by 38 per cent in 22 months, a historic rate of return for America by any standards. Tax savers became rich because of it. Trump promised a 3.5 per cent GDP growth when the whole world was expecting that he would destroy the American and global economy. Trump achieved a growth of 3.1 per cent in the second and third quarter after he came to power. He achieved a GDP growth of 4.2 per cent in the second quarter of 2018 and 3.5 per cent in the third quarter. Trump stopped the experts from commenting on his policies. He is creating 223,000 jobs per month. The unemployment rate has come down to 3.8 per cent, which is an 18-year low. The entire expertise of the world failed against the policymaking of Trump.

The entire American media converge on a particular day to write the same editorial in all newspapers. I have never seen newspapers behaving in a converged manner against an individual. India also joined the chorus. Instead of discussing Trump's initiatives for America and its impact on India and the world, we are conducting discussions whether Trump is right in America or not. This is a completely misdirected discourse of a slavish nation. When Moser said that Indians have to grow self-confidence, we should know how we should participate in this discourse. We never know that we can differ from other American newspapers as we don't have self-confidence. Trump said that they are wrong. Thus, he established that a determined leader could prove the economic thinkers wrong.

There are two situations in which economists and economics have let down the world. In 2008, all the economists were saying that everything was good. Former Federal Reserve Chair Alan Greenspan wrote a book in 2007 that everything was hunky dory. After that, there was a catastrophic collapse. The *Economist* magazine wrote a cover story that the economic theory had melted away and that the arrogant economic expert has been beaten to shyness and shame. The same thing was repeated when all the experts said the Trump would fail. However, Trump lifted America and even the global economy is doing well. Trump hit China in a big way. No American President stood against China except Trump. China retaliated saying that they have $1.8 trillion in the U.S. Treasury. Trump replied, "Sell it. Who are you going to sell it to?" If you invest in a wrong company, it is not that the company benefits, but the country is also in trouble. America has sold securities to the world to the extent of $11 trillion. Everyone is saddled with securities, including Japan . India has $150 billion invested in dollars. The dollarisation of the world is something about which the world has to think but we are not thinking.

How to get out of this? We have already started doing it. However, there is no discourse. When the government is doing it, then there is not a single editorial talking about it. When the petrol price goes up, the dollar value depreciates which will partly compensate for the oil prices. But this has stopped from 2015. This is because America allowed American oil companies to export oil. They began producing so much oil that their imports came down by 23 per cent in 2016. They began exporting oil. There is no trouble for America from the rise in crude prices. This is a complete shift from the 1950s when America feared the rise in oil prices, it always feared the fall in dollar value. Now, the negative co-relation between the dollar and oil has become a positive co-relation between them. In the last three years, not only have crude prices gone up but also dollar prices, which is a double-whammy for oil-importing countries which are dollarised in their economy. This has enabled Trump to take strong action against Iran. America is one of the top three oil producer and the largest oil producer this year. Trump is not bothered about oil prices because of the shift in co-relation between oil and the dollar, a subject which is ignored in Indian discourse. Our idea is how to find fault with the government. Our idea is politics.

A 30-year settled relationship between China and America has been broken and reversed and China is running for cover. China was a country which was feared, as to how price levels would be maintained and standard of living continued had become the factory for America and the world. If it produced 100 units, they consumed only 46 and exported the balance. They were over-dependent on globalisation and never expected Trump to come.

There is no functioning universal economics theory today. America has been incurring Current Account Deficits from 1976 until today. They have incurred $11 trillion Current Account Deficit (CAD). Any other country incurring CAD, economic theory says, the value of the currency should go down, so the trend will reverse. They will be exporting rather than importing. Instead of dollar value going down during the period, it appreciated 330 per cent, completely giving the lie to the theory of economics. America printed $4.5 trillion between 2008 and 2014. They issued digital currency and saved the local economy, funded the global economy and no one said the U.S. Fed was wrong in doing it. But if any other country had done it, they would say it would die of inflation. We have given up the right to print our own currency by Fiscal Responsibility and Budget Management (FRBM) law. The Government of India has given up the right to print the Indian rupee.

The Indian rupee is expanded only when the dollar comes to India and when the RBI acquires the dollar, it prints Indian rupees and gives it to the banking system. There is no other way the Indian rupee is generated today. If there is dollar inflow, Indian rupee supply will increase. If $30 billion goes out of India, then the Indian rupee supply will be withdrawn. Has anyone evaluated the economic consequences of it? The Government of India cannot borrow from the RBI by firing its securities. That the Centre should not borrow excessively is understandable but it should not borrow at all is not understandable. We pleaded with the Centre, after which they constituted a committee in 2015 to amend the FRBM law which was passed in 2002 when the world thought that there should be no printing of currencies and that the market will take care of the whole thing. It has become outdated economics because the U.S.A. itself has printed $4.5 trillion.

Japan began printing $40 billion every month from October 2015. Today they have increased the size of printing to $70 billion per month. Have we ever discussed this in the context of India? It is not necessary that if they print we should also print. But if we need it, can we print today? There is the liquidity problem. Can the Government of India say it will give you Rs. 100,000 crore worth of government securities, you give us the cash. The Government of India cannot do it because it has passed a law giving up that power. Our economists will say that the printing of currency is wrong. You cannot give it to politicians and it should be with the Reserve Bank of India (RBI). The central bank will only print currency when the dollar comes in. Can you have national economics based on the inflow of foreign exchange? These are the issues which will decide the state of the economy in India and the solutions which we need to find.

Trump is clear that he is no more for globalism but for 'Americanism'. He has also decided that the USA will not print the dollar any more and that it would withdraw the dollar from circulation. The USA began withdrawing $40 billion from circulation every month from October 2018.

On the one hand, the dollar is needed more and more and on the other America is withdrawing it from circulation so that its value goes up. America is happy with the rise in dollar value. However, Indian economists are thinking that the lower rupee value will benefit exporters. The dollar value was 45 and now it is 70. Exports have not picked up with the fall in dollar value, but the economy is continued with a lower rupee value as it is a philosophy for us. The imports into America will become cheaper as the dollar appreciates. Trump has a solution for it: levying import duty so that the goods will not be cheap. If things go according to his expectations, he will impose 25 per cent duties from January on $500 billion imports of China. No one knows what will happen to China after that. China has established factories for America.

The foundation of globalisation has been shaken. Multilateralism has been de-legitimised. If Trump does it, every country will do it. Trump has unilaterally imposed duties on aluminium, steel imports from European Union (EU) and Canada. You may find fault with Trump, but he has given growth to America. Whether he is there or not after 2020, Americans can never give up Trump's policies. Any President will find it difficult not to follow the policy because if consequences are difficult, he will have to take responsibility, so the Trump phenomenon will last beyond Trump. Do you see Indians discussing these subjects? There is a complete failure of economic intellectualism in India.

There are two kinds of polarised economics. America withdrawing the dollar and Japan printing the yen. America is raising interest rates, while Japan is looking for negative interest rates. People are forced to spend but they are not spending. In a family-based society, people don't spend as much as the government wants it to spend. In America, people spend. These are culturally different situations. So, we have a world monetary order in which one country is printing currencies and distributing them free. They are investing 5 lakh crore in our high-speed railway at 0.1 per cent interest for the next 50 years because they print the money. On the other hand, you have America withdrawing the dollar, raising interest rates and the IMF and the World Bank can't do anything. They are onlookers today. They are only rushing to help countries that are in distress. They have become a distress lending institution and are no more the world's monetary authority.

The IMF was constituted to find a common currency for the world. It has failed in its main objective. The dollar became the main currency. First, it was backed by gold and then to have common currency to trade between anybody. So, the dollar became a necessity and that become the strength of the dollar. The USA, which held the responsibility for the world, is withdrawing from that central position. We need to have an extensive discussion on how it will affect the world and India.

Phoney money decides the value of money. Phoney money had brought about the downfall in the world economy in 2005. The real money in 2010 was $6 trillion, while the phoney money was $600 trillion. This is money built on money which had no relevance to the real economy. The world GDP is $90 trillion. The phoney money is $900 trillion. This is generated by the financial system which will invest in a country and withdraw the money. This is not real money, but it will decide the fate of nations. Now, we have crypto currencies. These are private currencies. There are about 100 private currencies in Japan. You can create it and circulate it among yourselves. These private currencies are based on actual trade. There is a group of people admitted into a club. They began investing, trading, which is going through a supercomputer. The demand and supply based on the actual transaction will decide the price. Nobody has control on it. There is an attempt to get it regularised in India.

Geopolitics has never been so complex as it is today. Trump is fighting with his own trusted friends. He is calling Canadian Prime Minister a liar. There is instability in the Western bloc. The USA and Russia are friends in one place and are fighting in another. Europe says it will have its own army, but they will need NATO also. This kind of a situation has never been witnessed after the Second World War. Globalisation is now a matter of the past, and the World Trade Organisation (WTO) is in the ICU. Nobody even talks about it. These were all obsessions 20 years back. The shelf life of all these newly-created institutions, which were fashionable at a particular time, loses relevance because they are not founded on firm foundations of collective behaviour. You can't have a ruling elite saying that we will have globalisation from today onwards without the people wanting it. Trump has found out that American people don't want globalisation.

Geopolitically influenced global economics will be the future. The 2+2 model, in which the VIF is engaged in a big way, is not only about economics but also about security. It will not only be the finance secretary but the defence secretary will also be in the discussions. We are not going to build economic alliances, we are going to build security, civilisational, social, political alliances and more. This was unheard of 5-10 years back. A new model of international relations is developing. We are only talking about NPA, recapitalisation of banks.

There is no towering thinking mind. Everybody is looking through one particular window, but the nation doesn't consist of 10 windows but one building. We need to have a very comprehensive thinking model. There was a time when Japan used to build roads which they will not use. They build only to give employment to people. That was the economics that Japan followed. Then China followed expecting airports and eight-lane roads to be used in future. But there is no future. There is a chaotic situation in monetary, trade, economic and political relationships in the world. India is too big a country to be pushed over today. There is some awakening in India. We have gained strength, become militarily strong and have atomic power. The Indian passport has become a respectable document today. The world recognises the worth of India.

In an unstable world, how do we handle our situation? I will take you to 1999-2004, 2004-2014 and 2015 onwards. Unless we understand this, the state of economics cannot be understood, and we cannot grasp solutions for it. I will give you figures of 1999 to 2004 and 2004 to 2010 which is supposed to be the best periods for India with 9.8 per cent GDP growth. Foreign exchange reserves spiked from $140 billion to $340 billion. This is supposed to be the golden period of the Indian economy. In 1999-2004, GDP growth was 5.4 per cent. In 2004-10, it was 9.8 per cent. Prices were at 4.8 per cent in 1999 and 6.8 per cent in the next six years. Stock prices rose by 32 per cent in 1999-2004, then 311 per cent in the next six years. Gold prices rose 38 per cent in the first five years, 320 per cent in the next six years. Land prices rose 21 per cent in the first five years, 221 per cent in the next six years. Jobs generated were 60 million in the first five years and 2.7 million in the next six years.

This is the period of destruction of the Indian economy. In this period, foreign exchange spiked from $140 billion to $310 billion and was transformed into rupees. The banks were saddled with money. Y.V. Reddy (then RBI Governor) said not to allow this money to come in because you will not know how to use it. We want that to be taxed, but the finance minister said the whole world wants to put money in India. The money came in the stock market, transformed into rupees, became bank deposits. If the bank has deposits, it has to lend. But there were no borrowers. The Government then brought down the import duty of capital goods to zero and made the banks lend. As a result, bank deposits went to 20 per cent from 12 per cent. Credit went up to 27 per cent from 15 per cent. We imported capital goods which we did not need. All this money went to China. We had a trade deficit of $125 billion with China in 14 years, which is equal to three times China's defence expenditure and five times India's defence expenditure. This is because we allowed money which we did not need to come in and which was converted into rupees. We did not know how to use it, banks were asked to lend it, for which customs duties were brought down and that money is the non-performing asset (NPA) of today.

I challenge anybody to deny this fact. Raghuram Rajan admitted that excessive lending took place at that time which became bad debt. The RBI at that time was headed by the topmost macro-economist, Y.V. Reddy; he was called by the U.S. Fed and he addressed all the governors. The U.S. Fed had said that if Y.V. Reddy was the U.S. Fed Chair, the world economic meltdown would not have taken place. He advised stopping this money from coming in, but our government didn't follow his advice. The money that came in became NPA today, and this government began grappling with it.

During this period, revenue deficit went up by Rs. 16 lakh crore in five years and tax cuts were Rs. 3 lakh crore per year. So, this money was given to spend the foreign exchange which we had received. During the 10-year UPA period, oil imports were $515 billion and capital goods imports were $585 billion. In the NDA, capital goods imports were $10 billion. For the first time, and only in the NDA period for two years we have a current account surplus of $25 billion. That is why India was seen as a rising power. Everything was reversed as we were getting free flow of money. The phoney money unbacked by production and investments turned the economy into NPAs and saddled it on this government. The only fault of this government is that it did not come out with a white paper stating what had happened.

Asset prices rose because of high denomination currencies. In just 18 months prior to demonetisation, 500-rupee and 1000-rupee notes were Rs 4.8 lakh crore, which funded gold and real estate prices. What had taken place in 2008 in America due to subprime lending could have happened due to high denomination currency in India. The Indian economy could have collapsed if demonetisation hadn't happened. It was a corrective. The people should be congratulated as they stood in queues to collect money as they put faith in the government that they did the right thing. Nobody welcomed this and said that there will be riots. Even the Supreme Court said there will be riots. So many people died of heart attacks and still people weren't rioting. Then came the Goods and Services Tax (GST). Two powerful reforms—one is corrective and the other is reformative. I don't think any other government would have taken this measure. There is no reasoned appraisal of government actions. You can find fault. Opposition parties can do it as they can point out wrongs even when there is nothing. But what about the media and the intellectuals? They are doing what the American media did when Trump was coming to power.

We need to understand that we are a bank-driven economy and not a market-driven one. In America, 75 per cent of the money comes from the stock market. In India, only 3 per cent of savings goes into the stock market. We are not the only fools. The Japanese invest 9 per cent of savings in stocks. 51 per cent of Japanese savings are held in bank deposits. The depositor has to give money to the bank to keep the money. Still 51 per cent of savings of the Japanese are invested in bank deposits. The most modern instruments are traded in the Japanese stock market. But mostly foreigners trade in them. This is the character of a family-based society. Therefore, in India, banks are the lifeline. But Indian banking policies are based on the American model in which the stock market is the prime mover and the bank is the subordinate player. In India, the bank is the main player. So, if you restrict the banks, then you are restricting the economy and the flow of funds into the economy.

There are certain norms prescribed for banks that you need to have so much capital. The Basel Institution which created this model laid down rules that applied to commercial and international banks, but not for banks that are not internationally active. We do all kinds of activities, but still, the same Basel norms are imposed on all banks.

In Japan, there are internationally active banks and domestic banks. For internationally active banks, the norm is eight per cent and for domestic banks, it is four per cent. In India, for both, it is nine per cent. I don't know where this nine per cent was caught up by the regulator. We are doing more than what the Basel wants and so the banks have less money to lend. These are all the things which don't have discourse in India. There are only four internationally active banks in India. All the others are domestic banks. They need not have eight per cent capital. But they are also forced to have nine per cent capital because some people think that the IMF feels happy if we have nine per cent capital. We create problems for ourselves where they do not exist and you are praised for it all over the world. The same thought guides us and we are not independent.

A saint in Kanchipuram, who guided my life, issued a statement on 15 August 1947 and said, "We have become free, now we can become independent." We do not have original thinking even today. This government has taken far-reaching original steps by a $75 billion swap with Japan. The dollar-rupee relationship has been working against the rupee for the last several decades. Now, we are moving towards the yen. We are having $147 billion in foreign exchange in terms of dollars. The Government is probably well-advised in thinking that we should move more towards the yen because it has a natural hedge against the dollar and is running a current account surplus with America and has a $1 trillion investment in American securities. Therefore, our financial, investment, trade partner must be Japan. But our mind is hooked to America. America is not wrong, but it is not appropriate for us. We should think of an alternative umbrella. Even if a solution is available, your mind is blocking it. America is necessary for many geopolitical purposes, but it is not necessary that we should have this kind of dollarised integration with them. Even America will not mind it. But you are not a free thinker.

We have been following the wrong import policy of having capital goods imports exceeding oil imports. We need to go in for heavy import restriction. We have to cut down the CAD, trade deficit in the next one year otherwise we will continue to accentuate this problem on which all the institutions will have to work together. If an import restriction is made, the media will say India is moving away from free trade. Your newspapers have nothing to do with reality. They do not understand any of the implications of what is happening in the world. The FRBM law needs to be amended. We have to align the NPA rules to Basel norms and no more. This should be looked upon as a bank-driven economy.

India lacks credit for the Micro, Small and Medium Enterprises (MSME) sector today. Without understanding the MSME sector, you will not understand the Indian economy. We see stock markets and say India is at the top of the world. All the listed companies put together contribute only five per cent of India's GDP. The entire corporate sector listed and unlisted put together constitute 15 per cent of India's GDP. It is the MSME sector which contributes 50 per cent of India's GDP and 90 per cent of India's employment. The Economic Census 2014 says that the number of people employed in non-formal enterprises is 128 million whereas the entire corporate sector, including the government, employs only 12.8 million employees. It is the MSME sector which was hit by both demonetisation as well as GST. It is this sector which has been robbed of credit. In any other country, this would have collapsed. They are surviving because of community support. They cannot survive for long. When the government said this sector should be funded, the media said the government is now working against the independence of the Reserve Bank.

So, a sector which is driving India and constitutes 70 per cent of India's exports, 90 per cent of employment, 50 per cent of GDP of India, is starved of money. Once the money is released, the growth rate will pick up along with consumption, investment and savings. It will not be the top-down economy as the stock market coming and flooding the economy which it did between 2004 and 2010.

A new thinking is needed. An India-centric thinking is needed. We should not be ideological in thinking. We have to be rooted to the ground. We should ensure that a proper discourse takes place in Delhi because this is where action is.

(*Swaminathan Gurumurthy is an internationally acclaimed economist, writer, academic and activist. A Visiting Faculty and Distinguished Professor in various institutions, he is also the Chairman of the VIF. The speech was delivered by Shri S. Gurumurthy at the VIF at New Delhi on 15 Nov 2018*)

*

Contemporary: Foreign Policy

2

INDIA'S PAKISTAN AND CHINA POLICIES MUST BE BASED ON REALISM, NOT HOPE

Satish Chandra

India's relations with Pakistan and China have been deeply troubled for several decades. With Pakistan, this has been the case since its inception and with China since the 1960s. We have disputed borders with both countries and have been engaged in four hot wars with the former and one with the latter. These troubled relationships are not of India's making. Indeed, India has left no stone unturned to establish peaceful and harmonious ties with both countries and towards this end has made many concessions.

Some of the notable concessions made to Pakistan by India may be listed as: payment of Rs. 55 crore in January 1948 on account of division of assets even while under attack by the former in Kashmir, non-pursuit of its claims vis-a-vis Pakistan for non-payment of the pre-Partition debt of Rs. 300 crore, giving Pakistan 80 per cent of the flows of the Indus Basin rivers along with over 62 million pounds sterling for building canal works under an overly generous Indus Waters Treaty, returning to Pakistan the 5,386 square miles of its territory captured in the 1971 conflict without exacting a quid pro quo, obtaining concurrence of Bangladesh for the return of nearly 93,000 Pakistani prisoners-of-war held in India under the joint India-Bangladesh Command, facilitating Pakistan's re-entry into the Non-

Alignment Movement (NAM) in 1979 and into the Commonwealth in 1989, unilaterally according Most Favoured Nation (MFN) treatment to Pakistan, and most recently under the United Progressive Alliance (UPA) Government, giving up its opposition to the European Union's move to allow duty-free entry to Pakistani textile manufactures at the cost of its own textile exports.

As with Pakistan, so too with China India's foreign policy has been excessively conciliatory. Some instances of such an approach that readily come to mind are the adoption of the 'One China' policy and extreme caution exercised in developing ties with Taiwan, ardent promotion for the end of China's isolation and expansion of its links with the Third World, refusal to countenance the possibility of securing a permanent seat in the UN Security Council in the 1950s and insistence that the seat should instead first be given to China, renunciation of India's special rights in Tibet along with the recognition that Tibet is an autonomous part of China, the failure to expose China for its hegemonic tendencies and for its breach of innumerable understandings with us, and the timidity shown in expanding the role of the USA, Japan, Australia and the India Quadrilateral or 'Quad'.

Given the extraordinary moves made by India to befriend Pakistan and China, it is prima facie perplexing that relations with both countries are at such low ebb. While Pakistan seeks to bleed India through a 'thousand cuts' and openly uses terror as an instrument of foreign policy against it, China uses its leverages to undermine India's rise through a variety of means like opposition to our joining the Nuclear Supplier Group (NSG), pressure on our borders with Tibet by delaying its settlement and making unwarranted intrusions and claims, adoption of a 'string of pearls' strategy on our periphery to constrain us, disregarding our legitimate sovereignty concerns by pushing ahead with the China-Pakistan Economic Corridor (CPEC), etc. To make matters even worse, Pakistan and China have been colluding against us for decades with the former being nothing short of the latter's proxy to keep India in check. In this context, it should not be forgotten that at the core of the Sino-Pak relationship are their military ties and at the core of their military ties is the support provided by China to Pakistan to enable it to emerge as a nuclear armed state.

In devising appropriate policies towards Pakistan and China, it is imperative to understand their respective motivations and why, despite all our endeavours, they continue to have an adversarial relationship with us.

As far as Pakistan is concerned, anti-Indianism is a part of its DNA. Having failed to evolve a firmly rooted and unifying sense of identity, Pakistan has found value in anti-Indianism as a glue to hold the country together. This has metamorphosed into a search for parity with India leading it to become a security state with daunting democratic and development deficits. The Pakistani Establishment, with its strong military core, has consistently promoted the demonization of India as a means to perpetuate itself in power, to justify high levels of defence spending to maintain national unity. In these circumstances, no matter what concessions India makes, Pakistan will persist with its machinations against it. Indeed, Parvez Musharraf in a speech in Karachi in April 1999 admitted that even if the Kashmir issue was resolved, problems with India would persist.

China's approach to India is the product of its past mindset, whereby its norm is a natural dominion over everything under the heavens. Hence its quest for Super Power status. It has already become a regional hegemon unable to countenance multi-polarity in Asia. This, inevitably, places it on a collision course with India with its Pavlovian urge to undermine the latter's rise by all possible means. In these circumstances, China's antagonism to India, though not as deep rooted as that of Pakistan, is nevertheless fundamental and impossible to erase or even mitigate. The situation is further exacerbated by the fact that it disputes our entire border with Tibet and has claims on Arunachal Pradesh. The latter constitutes a part of China's so-called "lost territories" like Taiwan or the South China Sea islands, which it is committed to recover. Brutally put, until and unless, India does not kowtow to China on all issues of import to it like the CPEC, give up its strategic autonomy, and meekly accept whatever crumbs it is offered in terms of a border settlement, amicable ties with it are not in the realm of possibility.

In view of the foregoing, India's ties with Pakistan and China have a bleak future. Placatory moves are uncalled for and could even be perceived as signs of weakness. India, instead, needs to pursue hard-headed and sustained policies aimed at undermining these countries to the extent possible and deter them from moving against us. The Modi Government is on the right track by pursuing firmer policies vis-a-vis Pakistan and China than those attempted in the past.

With Pakistan, the free hand given to the Army to respond to cross-border infiltration, the surgical strikes, non-resumption of the composite dialogue process, highlighting of human rights violations committed by Pakistan in Baluchistan and elsewhere as well as in Pakistan Occupied Kashmir (PoK), the sustained and vigorous projection of Pakistan as a terrorist state, the endeavours to move towards full utilisation of Indus Waters in accordance with our Treaty rights, etc., are steps in the right direction. The following additional measures could also be considered:

1. The campaign to project Pakistan as a terrorist state may be intensified so that international sanctions are imposed on it, which inter alia, lead to suspension of military and economic assistance as well as targeted actions against the Inter Services Intelligence (ISI) and military officials by way of travel and financial restrictions.
2. Confidence Building Measures (CBM) like grant of MFN status to Pakistan must be terminated, not only to hurt Pakistan but also to carry conviction with the international community about the depth of our concerns on its export of terrorism.
3. An Act of Parliament may be passed declaring Pakistan a terrorist state, and placing restrictions on our grant of any special facilities to it like the MFN, reducing the size and level of our diplomatic presence in that country, etc.
4. While speeding up the maximisation of use in India of the Indus Waters Treaty, notice should be served on Pakistan for renegotiation of the Treaty under which we get only 20 per cent of the waters while having 40 per cent of the catchment area.
5. Pakistan's fault lines must be ruthlessly exploited in Baluchistan, Sindh and Khyber Pakhtunkhwa. Towards this end, we should carry

out a relentless campaign against the human rights violations perpetrated by Pakistan in these areas. We should also evolve a considered refugee policy in keeping with our traditions under which we should provide asylum to all who wish to flee from Pakistani tyranny.

6. We should highlight the atrocities being committed by Pakistan in the areas of Jammu & Kashmir under its illegal occupation and reach out to the Kashmiris residing there.
7. We should not hesitate to resort to covert strikes to take out terrorist elements and their supporters in Pakistan.
8. Contingency plans for surgical strikes should be developed expeditiously so that following another 26/11, which is always a possibility; these can be undertaken within a matter of hours.

The Modi Government's firmness in dealing with China is reflected in its exemplary handling of the Doklam crisis and its principled and steadfast opposition to the CPEC. Nevertheless, much more needs to be done. The following are some specific moves that could be considered as part of a get tough policy vis-a-vis China:

1. Relentless pressure should be maintained for an early settlement of the boundary dispute and, in particular, on the need to evolve a common understanding on the alignment of the Line of Actual Control.
2. Appropriate counters to Chinese pinpricks such as border intrusions, stapled visas, arming of Pakistan, People's Liberation Army's (PLA) presence in Pakistan Occupied Kashmir, opposition to India's quest for membership of the NSG and blockage in the UN of the listing of Masood Azhar as an international terrorist should be evolved and exercised.
3. The intensification of our ties with the USA and military exercises with it on land, air and sea, as well as with other regional players like Japan, Australia, etc., must not only be continued but also strengthened as a hedging strategy. Additionally, we should encourage these countries to conduct air and land exercises with our forces in J&K and Arunachal Pradesh. The Quad should be

invigorated with regular meetings held at a higher level for an all-encompassing dialogue on security, economics, environment and connectivity related issues. Ties with countries on China's periphery that feel similarly threatened by it like Vietnam, South Korea, the Philippines, Indonesia, etc., should be assiduously invigorated, including by provision of military assistance.

4. Much as the PM did in his interaction with the Persons of Indian Origin (PIO) parliamentarians recently in Delhi, we need to expose the hegemonic and grasping nature of China in juxtaposition to India's cooperative and non-threatening outlook. This should become a regular feature in all our interactions in the region and extend also to the other harsh truths about China, like its genocide in Tibet and Sinkiang, the environmental degradation that it has wrought and the plans it has on the use of waters to the detriment of the lower riparians.

5. We should also consider playing the Tibet and Sinkiang cards through the prism of human rights. Disaffected elements who seek asylum may be accorded the same. In order to play the Tibet card, it is imperative to maintain close links with the local Tibetan community, to make known our empathy for them, to gradually distance ourselves from our recognition of the Tibet Autonomous Region (TAR) as a part of China, to prepare for the post-Dalai Lama situation, and to ensure that the Karmapa is critical of China's moves against Tibetans.

6. Expression of sympathy for the Uyghur's who have been victimized by China in much the same manner as the Tibetans is not only a suitable riposte to its role in Kashmir and CPEC, but it would also immeasurably improve India's standing in the Muslim community at home and abroad. It will also shatter Pakistan's efforts to project itself as the champion of Islam the world over.

7. Finally, our economic and commercial links with China need to be reconfigured. These currently work in China's favour and are detrimental to our interests at multiple levels. At the most superficial level, our enormous $50 billion trade deficit with China is a drain

on our balance of payments situation and is of major benefit to China. Indeed, in just one year it effectively finances the CPEC! The situation is, however, much more insidious. Cheap imports from China are destroying our industries in many areas ranging from active pharmaceutical ingredients to telecom. They are also resulting in an unhealthy dependency on China. In order to reverse this dangerous trend and wean ourselves away from the opiate of cheap Chinese imports, we need to ensure the success of the 'Make in India' campaign. This would most effectively be accomplished by the revival of our traditional pride in *Swadeshi* together with a policy designed to speedily create a much friendlier industrial environment which enables our manufacturers to compete with the best in the world in terms of quality and price. Creation of such an environment will demand adoption of policies which promote innovation, technology transfer, lower input costs, and required infrastructural necessities. These remedial steps should be accompanied by the curbing of Chinese imports through a variety of measures where possible like countervailing duties, non-tariff barriers, etc. China's investments and projects in sensitive sectors should also be eschewed.

The contention that such a tough approach towards Pakistan and China will provoke retaliation does not hold good as they are already doing their worst. Furthermore, there are limits on how far China would wish to engage in adventurism vis-a-vis India given the fact that this would set it back by decades in its quest for parity with the USA which is its overriding long-term objective.

In conclusion, it goes without saying that the proposed more muscular approach towards Pakistan and China must be accompanied by a series of measures designed to rapidly upgrade our comprehensive national power.

(A career diplomat, Satish Chandra served as India's Permanent Representative to the UN Offices in Geneva and later as High Commissioner to Pakistan. He, subsequently, went on to head the National Security Council Secretariat and was the Deputy National Security Advisor. He is the Vice Chairman of the VIF)

*

Contemporary: Defence

3

ARIHANT TO INDIA'S DEFENCE: NUCLEAR TRIAD PROVIDES CREDIBLE STRATEGIC DETERRENCE

General N.C. Vij, PVSM, UYSM, AVSM

Monday, 5 November 2018, was indeed a red-letter and historic day in the history of India's security paradigm when a visibly proud Prime Minister Narendra Modi declared the completion of a maiden 'deterrent patrol' by INS Arihant, India's first indigenously built nuclear ballistic missile submarine. This has added maritime strike capability to the land and air-based delivery platforms of nuclear weapons, thus completing the nuclear triad. Arihant has very thoughtfully been named as it means, 'Slayer of the Enemy'.

It is well known that India is confronted with a very challenging security environment. We have none too friendly neighbours who are also nuclear powers, along our western, northern and north-eastern borders. Furthermore, in the Indian Ocean, Chinese submarines are constantly prowling round the year. It is believed that they have deployed seven to eight submarines, alternating between nuclear and conventional, under the guise of anti-piracy patrols since 2013.

The PM had Pakistan in mind when he stated that INS Arihant was an open warning to the enemies of India who follow the policy of nuclear blackmail blatantly. Pakistan's effort to promote terrorism under the umbrella of nuclear blackmail is a case in point. They better have a second thought now.

A nuclear submarine provides to India the capability to hide its ballistic missiles at sea for long periods and provide an assured Second Strike capability to hit back at the enemy, should the land and air delivery systems be neutralised. The biggest advantage of the Submersible Ballistic Nuclear Submarine is that the sea is an opaque medium which makes the SSBN the most survivable leg of the triad. It is insulated from surprise attack scenarios. Presently, the SSBN has been equipped with a missile system with a range of 750 km but it will gradually be upgraded to missiles with ranges up to 4000-5000 km and even MIRVs (multiple independently targetable re-entry vehicles), if necessitated.

The deterrence patrol was conducted after due validation of all related concepts during the extensive trial phase. Very significantly, the successful deployment of Arihant with nuclear weapons has also established the efficacy of the robust command and control structure under strict political control whilst adhering to stringent safety mechanisms. Regular and unhindered communication from the National Command Authority (NCA) to the SSBN is critical for assuring the success of Second Strike capability especially when we have a No First Use nuclear doctrine. Various layers of communication have been developed indigenously which provide redundancy and enhance survivability. They have proved their battle worthiness.

INS Arihant is the first SSBN of the advanced technology vessel programme which was started in the early 1980s aimed at developing indigenous SSBN design and construction capability. It was commissioned on 25 August 2016. Being the first of its class, exhaustive harbour and sea trials were undertaken by the Navy and its designers. Due to its complexities, the programme was regularly and closely monitored at all stages by the executive council of the NCA under the NSA and the Chief of the Naval Staff, with the PM being regularly briefed at all stages of the exercise.

A very high degree of technological sophistication has been achieved incorporating state-of-the-art technology which meets global standards. It is genuinely indigenous as not only the steel but also various other critical equipment have been fabricated indigenously with the active participation of PSUs and private industry, besides the shipyard. Design features are innovative and software-based stability and motion control systems have been indigenously developed. These controls are vital during the firing of a ballistic missile because of its heavy downward thrust and three dimensional effects on stability. The construction incorporated very high and stringent safety standards, which have been tested under extreme weather and operating conditions, thereby ensuring high survivability. Underwater noise has been minimised. Miniaturisation of nuclear power plant has been achieved by the Department of Atomic Energy and calls for deep appreciation of the herculean effort on the part of the Indian Navy and the scientific community. We are very happy that our Navy has now been equipped with this very potent capability.

Arihant is the largest submarine built in India till date. It is over 110 metres long and displaces 7500 tonnes (6000 tonnes on surface and 7500 tonnes when dived). To ensure round-the-year vigil by Continuous At Sea Deterrence, at least one SSBN requires to be deployed at sea at all times, requiring a total of at least four to five submarines. Work for that is already in progress. The second submarine was launched last year and is slated to become operational by 2020. By 2022 we are likely to have four submarines, the last two will be larger and with a higher displacement. The ecosystem in the private and public sectors that has been built as a result of the construction of these SSBNs will have tremendous spinoff benefits for indigenous submarine building.

Operationalisation of these SSBNs will further strengthen our stated approach towards achieving peace and stability in the region. Even at the cost of repetition, it is necessary to emphasise that we remain committed to our stated nuclear doctrine of No First Use. These strategic assets for us are only for deterrence. India's long-awaited nuclear triad is now fully operational and provides us with a 'credible strategic deterrence'. What a great Diwali gift to the nation!

(Gen. Vij was the 21st Chief of the Army Staff of India (2002-05). He is remembered for many notable improvements in operational and administrative systems in the Army. He was the Director General of Military Operations (DGMO) during the Kargil operations in 1999. After superannuation, he was the Founder Vice Chairman of the National Disaster Management Authority in the rank of Cabinet Minister for five years. He was the Director of the Vivekananda International Foundation (2014-17).

*

4

INDIA'S STRATEGIC CULTURE: NEED FOR AN INDIAN NARRATIVE

Arvind Gupta

ABSTRACT

This paper argues that as India takes its place in the comity of nations, there is a need for it to build its own narrative on contemporary issues. In order to do so, India should delve into its ancient culture, which is a deep reservoir of knowledge and wisdom. It is possible to build a narrative which combines tradition with modernity. The paper further seeks to refute the perception that India lacks a culture of strategic thinking.

India's Vision

As India rises politically and economically in the comity of nations, a question is being asked: What is India's vision for the world; how can India contribute to world peace and stability; how will it deal with the tremendous socio-economic and political turbulence that the world is facing due to globalisation? The conflict between modernity and tradition is becoming sharper. Western values of materialism and individualism are leading to atomisation of society and its institutions. How will India navigate these choppy waters? These questions are valid and are being discussed increasingly at academic seminars, conferences and in literature. However, the answers are not clear. Many observers continue to remain unconvinced that India has a coherent story to tell the world.

The Chinese have unfolded their world view through a series of official documents, presidential addresses and pronouncements followed by roadmaps. Even though it is a communist state, China is laying claims on Buddhism. In contrast, India has tremendous cultural attraction and soft power, but this is not being used for national interest under a well thought out strategy.

As India grows and reclaims its place in the comity of nations, there is a need for India to build its own narrative on contemporary issues. People want to understand as to what has India to offer by way of new ideas and concepts in an interconnected world. After independence, India tried a big economy model for economic growth and development. Since 1991, India has introduced the capitalist market model. However, the Indian economic model which is based on traditional social capital has yet to win global recognition. India cannot yet claim to have offered an alternative to existing theories. Not having an Indian narrative can be detrimental to national interest.

Western countries have for long shaped the global narrative for several centuries. The Western influence is so dominant that Indians have been accused of having been enslaved by Western culture. This must change. China, a rising power, is delving deep into its past and building its grand narrative based on Confucianism, tailored to modern needs. The Russians also have a narrative of Russia having been a saviour of Europe in the last one thousand years. Indians have so far not made a serious effort to build a strategic narrative which is based on their culture and values. Very often, Indians, influenced by Western values and material advancement, are defensive about their own culture. Culture must inform the Indian narrative for it to be convincing.

At the turn of the 20th century, India saw a powerful nationalist movement in favour of the indigenous or *swadeshi*. Many eminent Indian thinkers (Vivekananda, Rabindra Nath Tagore, Aurobindo, Sister Nivedita, M.K. Gandhi and K.M. Munshi, amongst many) have emphasised the need for Indian history to be written from the Indian perspective. Vivekananda wanted Indians to take pride in Hinduism and its universal values and in their culture. He was of the view that on that basis alone will new India arise and awaken. Rabindra Nath Tagore talked about the need for writing the history of India from the Indian perspective. In his address to students and teachers in 1903 titled 'The History of Bharatvarsha,' he said, "By not viewing Bharatvarsha from Bharatvarsha's own perspective...we get demeaned ourselves...what our ancestors did, this we do not know, therefore we do not know what we ought to aim for".

Likewise, K.M. Munshi stressed the need for writing Indian history by Indians. He wrote, "The central purpose of a history must, therefore, be to investigate and unfold the values which age after age have inspired the inhabitants of a country develop their collective will and express it through the manifold activities of their life. Such a history of India is still to be written." He lamented that the histories written of India decried the Hindu social system, ignoring the fact that the very same social system developed the tenacity that armed the people to "survive catastrophic changes for millennia." The strong social system developed in India over a long period imparted to Indian society the resilience and capacity to withstand the changes.

Anand Coomaraswamy was an ardent cultural nationalist who saw culture as a vehicle for national awakening. He lamented that Western culture had vulgarised Indian culture and that the Indian education system had no place for Indian culture. Indian students coming out of the Indian education system were strangers in their own land. He also criticised the British for neglecting Indian culture. Philosopher K.C. Bhattacharya talked about the need for 'Swaraj in Ideas.' More recently, S. Gurumurthy has been a strong supporter of the role of Indian culture in developing an Indian model of economic development. The prevalent notion of secularism has prevented Indians from being proud of their culture. Gurumurthy quotes Daya Kishan Thussu, Professor of International Communication and Co-Director of the India Media Centre at the University of Westminster in London, from his book, *Communicating India's Soft Power: Buddha to Bollywood*: "In a nutshell, the distinctive characteristics of India's soft power is based on its traditions of public reasoning and religious tolerance, its culture of argumentative heterogeneity and philosophy of peaceful coexistence;" and further, "Secular India is afraid of opening the locker of ancient India fearing that the pseudo secular foundation of Indian secularism will crumble." Rajiv Malhotra, an Indian-American scholar, argues that Western scholars, who are aware of the superiority of Indian thought, are engaged in imbibing ideas from Hindu culture without acknowledgment in their own culture and sanitising them by stripping them of their religious and philosophical context.

The situation may be changing. The Government is conscious of the Indian approach to development. A Cabinet Resolution of 2015 by which the NITI Ayog was set up talks about the need for finding "own strategy of growth," It says, "The new institution has to zero in on what will work in and for India. It will be a 'Bharatiya approach to development'." The resolution quotes Mahatma Gandhi, Tiruvalluvar, Deen Dayal Updhyaya, Sankara Deva and Ambedkar in the text. In this connection, the concept of "Social Capital" which encompasses the collective will of the people manifested through family, caste, community and mutual association is mentioned. Social capital reduces the reliance on the state to provide social security and thus unburden it.

The truth, however, is that we have failed to develop an Indian approach to resolving Indian problems. Even our history has been written and interpreted in the Western framework. Western writers wrote the earlier history of India. Their benchmark was European history and historical standards. Some of them made great efforts to learn Sanskrit and other Indian languages in order to learn about India. Laudable as their efforts might have been, their Western biases were visible. On the one hand, they made laudatory references to Indian culture, and extremely derogatory on the other. The context of Indology studies of that time was colonialism. Europeans saw themselves in the superior role of civilizers and educationists. They failed to appreciate the variety and depth of Indian philosophy and its richness because these ideas differed from the Western ideas rooted in materialism. Missionaries tried to preach their religion in the process helping the colonial rulers. Macaulay wanted to churn out an army of English-speaking *babus* who would propagate and defend the values of the British Raj.

The result of all this activity was that the history of the Indian people written by Europeans was one-sided, with the ulterior motive of undermining Indian culture and propagating Western cultural and material superiority. The effort was to enslave the Indian mind by inculcating in the Indians a sense of inferiority vis-a-vis what was regarded as a superior Western culture. It is regrettable that even in post-independent India, there have been few efforts to base Indian policies on Indian culture. The result is that our minds remain enslaved, in awe of the Western civilisation and its material achievements.

India has been an unbroken and flourishing civilisation for more than 5,000 years. No other civilisation can claim such long continuity. The present-day, Greeks, Egyptians and Romans have little in common with their respective ancient civilisations. On the other hand, Indians relate to their ancient civilisation very well. This is a remarkable fact. Understanding how Indian civilisation has survived so long is a matter of great significance. It has contributed significantly to the world culture in philosophy, sciences, religion architecture and literature. Ancient Indian treatises like the *Vedas*, the *Upanishads* and the epics like the *Mahabharata* and the *Ramayana* are a fund of ideas. India's soft power is undisputed. Clearly, India has the possibility of delving deep into its past and look for ideas which can be useful today. Some people hold the view that looking to a long gone, though glorious, past for solving contemporary problems is a futile and regressive exercise. But this need not be so. The present has been built on the foundations of the past. The past cannot be ignored as it holds lessons for today and tomorrow. A synthesis of cultural past and modernity is perfectly possible.

The reality, however, is that many Indians of today's generation, including the educated ones, have precious little knowledge of what India was. They do not have the knowledge of Sanskrit and other classical languages in which these texts were written or spoken. Western education has also decried Indian culture as mumbo-jumbo and inferior to Western culture. This has created a sense of inferiority among Indians about their past. Most Indians do not take pride in their heritage and are quite oblivious of it. This manifests in the great deal of insensitivity of the public and the government towards the archaeological sites that are disappearing fast due to neglect and ignorance. The disappearance of ancient languages, dialects and entire cultural eco-systems should be a matter of great concern for all Indians.

India has given birth to some of the world's major religions like Hinduism, Buddhism, Sikhism, Jainism, etc. The followers of Christianity, Islam, Zoroastrianism, Judaism, etc., also live in India without any coercion or constraints. Unlike the principal monotheistic religions of the world, the Hindus have been tolerant in their approach to religion, having accommodated and assimilated many sects. The culture and religions of the vanquished have been taken into the mainstream Hindu religion. This inclusiveness is a unique aspect of Indian culture. Hinduism has a lot to contribute by way of ideas. Religions like Buddhism and Jainism arose as a reaction to orthodoxy in Hinduism and yet the Hindus relate positively to these religions. Ancient Hindu thought holds, *Ekam Sat, Vipra Bahudha Vadanti* that is, "Which exists is one: Sages call it by various names." Such an understanding allows for the existence of multiple approaches to the ultimate truth, which is one.

In the last century-and-a-half, India has produced many thinkers who argued and contributed to the renaissance of Indian culture. This process must continue. The tolerance of the Hindus comes from the fact that the core of Hindu religion is strong. At the core lies the belief that divinity is reflected in every human being. Thus, there is a spiritual connection between every individual. That is why Hinduism has survived for so long. It is a confident religion. There is a long tradition of self-reflection, self-correction and assimilation of ideas from other schools of thought. Some people resent this tendency in Hinduism to assimilate external influences as in their view this dilutes the very essence of the Hindu religion. Others feel that the core of Hinduism is strong and assimilation has only helped the religion to survive and flourish and maintain the essential unity of the different sects of the religion.

The unique Hindu qualities of tolerance and assimilation have been noted by many Western scholars. Scholars note that there has been an unbroken continuity in Indian civilisation since 3000 BCE at least. A wide variety of faiths is encompassed within the Hindu religion which respects reason, debate and scholarship. It is, therefore, natural that rather than depending for ideas only in Western scholarship, one can turn to this ancient but vast repository of knowledge and wisdom for identifying universal ideas which may provide guidance for solving today's problems. The Chinese are turning to the texts written in the era of Warring States, roughly contemporaneous with Kautilya, for ideas for their foreign policy and security. Why cannot India, which has much wider sources to draw upon, do the same?

Sources of Indian Thought: The Indian Narrative

The ancient Hindu texts are a rich source of ideas. The universalism of some of the Indian thinking is striking and has impressed modern philosophers and thinkers. The *Vedas*, *Brahmanas* and the *Aranakyas* provide the foundation of ancient Indian thought. A brief description follows.

Vedas* or *Samhitas: These are the most ancient specimens of Vedic literature. They go back to at least 1100 BCE or even earlier. There are four *Vedas* or *Samhitas*—the *Rig Veda*, *Sam Veda*, *Yajurveda* and *Atharaveda*. Their teachings are considered eternal. They deal with a variety of topics ranging from deep philosophical questions about nature and the universe to rituals and ceremonies.

Brahmanas: These are commentaries on the *Vedas*. They discuss the meaning of the various concepts propounded in the *Vedas*. They also go into the recensions of the Vedas. Each of the *Brahmanas* is associated with one of the *Samhitas* or its recensions.

Aranakyas: These are associated with the Vedas and the Brahmanas. They deal with rituals, ceremonies and their interpretations. Some of them have philosophical discussions as well.

Upanishads: These are philosophical works of great significance. The teachings of the *Upanishads* provide the basis of Hindu thought. They speculate over the concept of *atman* (soul), *brahman* (the absolute), what is the origin of the universe, etc. Of a vast Vedic corpus, the *Upanishads* have left a deep impact on Hindu thought. They are also called *Vedantas* or the end of the *Vedas*, or the last chapters of the *Vedas*.

Vedangas: They represent the additional fields of study and include many sciences such as phonetics (Śikṣā), poetic metre (Chandas), grammar (Vyākaraṇa), etymology and linguistics (Nirukta), rituals and rites of passage (Kalpa), time keeping and astronomy (Jyotiṣa). They have influenced the various schools of Indian philosophy.

Upvedas: Several technical works are included such as archery (Dhanurveda), associated with the *Rigveda*; architecture (Sthapatyaveda), associated with the *Yajurveda*; music and sacred dance (Gāndharvaveda), associated with the *Samaveda*; medicine (Āyurveda), associated with the *Atharvaveda*, drama and dance, etc.

Puranas: The *Puranas* are a vast repository of myths, legends, genealogies and lore. There are 18 *Maha Puranas* (Great Puranas) and 18 *Upa Puranas* (Minor Puranas), with over 400,000 verses. They are considered *Vaidika* (congruent with Vedic literature). The *Bhagavata Purana* has been among the most celebrated and popular texts in the Puranic genre. Though mixed with mythology, the *Puranas* give a glimpse of ancient Hindu India.

Epics: The *Ramayana* and the *Mahabharata* are the most celebrated epics of Hindu culture. They have a venerable place in the average Hindu's daily life and influence his or her thoughts deeply. Their importance cannot be overstated. The key takeaways from the *Mahabharata* are fight for rights; good prevails over evil; wars have to be fought after planning. The *Ramayana* lays out the conduct of the king, his subjects, the opponent, the principles of war, etc. Wars for a just cause must be fought; high personal moral standards are a must; good will prevail over evil.

The *Bhagwad Gita* is the finest jewel of Indian thought. Though a part of the *Mahabharata* in the form of a dialogue between Krishna and his friend and disciple, Arjuna, the *Bhagwad Gita* has universal messages for the individual relating to his or her conduct. The importance of Karamyoga (Action), Jnanyoga (pursuit of knowledge) and Bhaktiyoga (devotion and surrender to God) has been underlined. The *Bhagwad Gita* has provided guidance to countless generations. Some of the greatest thinkers in India and outside were influenced by the *Bhagwad Gita*. It distils the basic message of the *Vedas* and the *Upanishads*.

Schools of Indian Philosophy: Hindu philosophy has six major schools, namely, *Vaisesika* of Kanada, *Nyaya* of Gautama, *Samkhya* of Kapila, *Yoga* of Patanjali, *Purva-Mimansa* of Jaimini and *Vedanta* or *Uttara Mimansa* of Vyasa. These are orthodox schools as they follow the authority of the *Vedas*. Jainism and Buddhism are regarded as heterodox schools because they reject the authority of the *Vedas*.

Dharmashastras: The rich Dharmashastra literature espouses the moral, ethical and legal code of conduct for individuals as well as rulers. The literature can be divided into three categories, namely, *Dharmasutras* (600 BCE), *Smritis* (1-800 CE) and *Dharmanibandhas* (1100-1800 CE). Several commentaries have also been written on the subject of *dharma*. The *Dharmasutra* literature is rooted in the *Vedas* but non-Vedic *dharmasutras* are also known. Examples of *dharmasutras* of the latter kind include *sutras* ascribed to Buddha, Brahaspati, Kanuva, etc.

India has a long tradition of innovation in political and economic governance. The *Manusmriti* (1000 BCE) is the oldest such treatise and it lays down the code of conduct to be followed by rulers and individuals in different walks of life. It has influenced social, political and economic thought significantly. Although it has been criticised as being patriarchal, the basic code of behaviour laid down in the *Manusmriti* is logical for the times it was written in. Kautilya's *Arthsastra* and many other subsequent treatises have built upon the *Manusmriti*. India has a long tradition of political institutions. India was divided into several republics. They had their own way of choosing the monarch and establishing various institutions of governance. Some of the terms used those days like *Sabha, Samiti, Parishad*, etc., are current even today. Among the major works of political science, *Shantiparva* of the *Mahabharata, Dandaniti* of Usanas, *Arthasastra* of Kautilya, *Nitisara* of Kamundaki, Vidurniti, *Panchatantra, Hitopdesha*, etc., can be included. The Thirukkural (1st century BCE) in Tamil is often considered the Veda of the Tamils. It relies heavily on the *Vedas* and *Manusmriti*.

K.P. Jayaswal (1881-1937) in his book, *Hindu Polity: A Constitutional History of India in Hindu Times,* carried out an extensive study of the growth and evolution of Hindu law, jurisprudence and political systems over centuries. His masterly early 20th century work, based on the study of Vedic literature as well as inscriptional and numismatic records, covers the study of sovereign assemblies in Vedic times, Indian republics, Hindu monarchies, the *Janapadas* and *Mahajanapadas* or regional assemblies, etc. He describes at length the characteristics of political institutions like the king, the council of ministers and administration of justice, economics and other institutions. Jayaswal mentions several works of antiquity dealing with the principles of governance and politics. He points out that governance was studied much before Kautilya wrote the *Arthasastra* (300 BCE) which mentions the names of at least twenty authors before him.

Vivekananda and Aurobindo

Vivekananda is a major figure who introduced the West towards the essentials of Hindu religion, particularly *Vedanta*. His contribution towards the resurgence of Hinduism in modern times is unmatched. He emphasised the primary of spiritual life, inner strength and the essential unity of all religions. In 1897, he founded the Ramakrishna Math, which reinterpreted Hinduism in contemporary light. Vivekananda introduced the West to the essentials of Hindu thought and helped to generate a new awareness of Hinduism in the world. He believed that Hinduism would give a new spiritual impetus to the world.

Aurobindo's political philosophy could be called spiritual nationalism. He stressed those aspects of Hindu tradition that spoke of spiritual evolution through complete surrender of human consciousness to the Supreme Being.

At the philosophical and psychological level, Hinduism provides a world view in which the universe is a family. The individual is a reflection of the ultimate reality; truth always prevails and the search for truth is paramount. There is non-duality at the level of ultimate reality but multiple ways to reach that reality. The cycle of birth and rebirth continues and the task before the individual is to overcome this cycle. Goals by themselves are unimportant and there is no time frame to arrive at them. The primacy of action is established and the attachment to goals is discouraged. In the Hindu world view, nature is to be respected, feared, worshipped and propitiated.

At the social level, the king and the ruled have duties to each other. The king should rule in accordance with *dharma* and should take care of the wellbeing and welfare of the people. The duties of every individual are defined in accordance with skill and capability. The conduct of the king should be above board and in accordance with *dharma*. Hierarchy is to be respected. But it is not immutable. The Varna system divided society in accordance with professions. This was a division based on the considerations of efficiency. The social rigidities that crept into the caste system, bringing in the issue of birth, etc., happened over a course of time. These were distortions which many social reformers have tried to purge. Casteism is the scourge of Indian society. The efforts to bring social reforms should continue in this direction.

Does India have a Strategic Culture?

It is surprising that with so much of richness and depth in ancient Indian thought, a question is still being asked whether India has a culture of strategic thinking. Tanham (1992), in a study sponsored by RAND Corporation, argued that India had primarily defensive thinking due to its geography and its cultural belief systems, the legacy of British colonialism and India's preference for strategic autonomy. In his opinion, India, unlike China, never had a grand strategy. To be sure, his question was in the context of national security and military power but the debate has expanded to the larger question about the Indians' ability for thinking strategically for their country. Tanham did not say that India does not have a strategic culture, but what he said was that Indians have a defensive mindset. However, many analysts interpreted Tanham's argument as an assertion that Indians cannot think strategically. Tanham's argument got support from many influential strategic thinkers like K. Subramanyam, who were frustrated that Indian foreign policy was all defensive, timid and cautious.

However, there have been opposite views too. In 2006, Rodney Jones published a study for Defence Threat Reduction Agency Advanced Systems and Concepts Office in which he came to the conclusion to the effect that Indians did have strategic culture with distinctive traits. He wrote, "India's strategic culture is not monolithic, rather it is mosaic-like, but as a composite is more distinct and coherent than that of most contemporary nation-states. This is due to its substantial continuity with the symbolism of pre-modern Indian state systems and threads of Hindu or Vedic civilisation dating back several millennia." He identified the following elements of Indian Strategic Culture:

A. **Philosophical and Mythological Foundation**
   - Sacred permeates Indian identity;
   - Goals are timeless, not time bound;
   - India's status is a given, not earned;
   - Knowledge of truth is the key to action and power;
   - World order is hierarchical, not egalitarian.

B. **Instrumental Implications**
   - India's external visage is enigmatic;
   - Self-interest expressed externally is impersonal and absolute;
   - Contradictions in the real world are natural and affirmed;
   - Force has its place, but guile may trump force;
   - Actions have consequences, good intent does not absolve injury;
   - Trust is in right knowledge and action, is impersonal, and hard to build or replenish;
   - Security is sedentary (encompasses a geographic setting and way of life);
   - Strategy is assimilative (appearance changes, reality is constant)."

Jones is not the only one to identify the elements of Indian strategic culture. Many people are revising their ways about Indian culture and thought. Kissinger, in his *World Order* (page 114) devoted several pages to the Hindu conception of the Hindu world order and outlined certain important features of the same. Kissinger notes that Hindu cosmology operates on a vast time scale in which kingdoms would rise and fall and the universe would be destroyed and recreated. Referring to the *Bhagwad Gita*, he further noted, "This central work of Hindu thought embodied both an exhortation to war and the importance not so much of avoiding but of transcending it. Morality was not rejected, but in any given situation the immediate considerations were dominant, while eternity provided a curative perspective." He quoted from the *Arthasastra, Ramayana, Mahabharata* and *Bhagwad Gita* to prove his point. The debate in the literature now seems to indicate that most analysts do think that India has a strategic thinking but Indian thinking is defensive. Many have argued that an old civilisation could not have survived without having a strategic culture.

India is a multicultural society with a rich tapestry of cultures, languages and thinking. The ancient Indian texts, not just of Hinduism but also of Buddhism and Jainism as well as text in several languages, provide a vast storehouse of Indian strategic thinking. It is also argued that the *Arthasastra* is a broad-based treatise on statecraft, some of whose tenets are of universal significance and relevance today. More recently, the works of Vivekananda, Aurobindo and Gandhi also indicate support to the view that Indians can think strategically.

Ancient Indian thought dwelt at length on the nature of warfare. The Hindu concept of war is very different from the concept of war in the West. In Western history, war has been associated with "un-relieved barbarism." In contrast, Kautilya, writing in the 3rd century BC, talked about three kinds of victories in war. The first category was *Dharmavijaya* in which the victor was content with the submission of the defeated and did not eye his territory or wealth. The second category was *Lobhavijaya* in which the victor gained land and money from the defeated king, and the third category of victory was the *Asuravijaya* of the barbaric victor who defeated the king and robbed him of his son, wife or life. According to S. Gurumurthy, the third kind of victory was "abhorred and detested in ancient India." The conquered states were allowed to preserve their political, social and cultural identity. The ancient Hindu texts are replete with emphasis on morality and ethics in warfare.

Even in post-independent India, there is no dearth of examples of Indian strategic thinking. India has fought five wars in the last 70 years. It has been involved in out-of-area contingencies militarily in Sri Lanka and

Maldives in the mid-1980s. It has undertaken numerous humanitarian assistance and disaster relief operations in Iraq, Yemen, Libya, Sri Lanka, Nepal and Maldives, and conducted many counter-insurgency and counter-terrorism operations in difficult areas and has been a part of the UN peacekeeping effort. Non-alignment was a successful strategy adopted to keep India out of the messy Cold War conflicts. Successive Indian prime ministers have displayed a sense of realism to deal with the challenges of security and development. The signing of a nuclear agreement with the USA in 2008 was a piece of strategic thinking. The present government's approach to the Indo-Pacific, the policy of 'Security & Growth for All' or the Act East Policy is also a strategic initiative. Therefore, the criticism that India lacks strategic thinking is untenable.

Prime Minister Modi Promotes Indian Culture

During his travels and interactions abroad, Prime Minister (PM) Modi has been putting forward the ideas of Indian culture for the world. A notable example of this was India's outstanding success in getting the United Nations General Assembly (UNGA) to declare June 22 as International Day of Yoga. This is recognition of Indian culture and its contemporary relevance. Yoga is spreading fast across the world among all sections of the global population. There are many ideas like this which can form an Indian narrative.

The PM has frequently mentioned the idea of *Vasudhaiva Kutumbukam* in his speeches. It means that the world is a family. Underlying the basic unity of mankind, this is a powerful idea at a time when despite globalisation the world is fragmenting. At the World Economic Forum Summit meeting in Davos in 2018, he said: "As a representative of India, Indian-ness and Indian heritage, the subject of this forum for me is as contemporary as it is timeless. Timeless, because in India from time immemorial we continue to believe in uniting the mankind and not in dividing them or creating fissures. In the ancient books written thousands of years ago in Sanskrit, Indian philosophers have propounded the thesis of *Vasudhaiva Kutumbakam*. It means that the whole world is one family. In essence, we all have been joined with each other like a family and our destiny links us with a common thread. Today, this concept of *Vasudhaiva Kutumbakam* is even more relevant in bridging the gaps and distances."

Shri Modi pointed out how the Indian tradition of respecting and preserving nature is relevant today. On the issue of climate change, the Indian Prime Minister went straight to the heart of the problem—greed-based exploitation of Mother Nature has led to a conflict between man and Nature: "On several occasions, you must have heard of deep synergy with Nature in the Indian tradition. In our ancient texts written thousands of years ago, man was described as: "*Mata Bhumi, Putro Aham Prithvya*" i.e., we the humans are children of Mother Earth. Why is there a kind of war between Nature and mankind if we are the children of Mother Earth?" He went on to say, "In the beginning of one of the most important religious texts called the *Upanishad*, a seer has described to his disciples about the changing nature of the world: '*Tena Tyaktena Bhunjitha, Magradha kasya sividdhanam.*' It means that one should enjoy the worldly pleasures with austerity and one should never covet what belongs to others. Around two thousand five hundred years ago, Lord Buddha has given primacy to the concept of *Aparigraha*, which means using things as per necessity, in his teachings. The concept of 'trusteeship' propounded Mahatma Gandhi, the 'Father' of the Indian nation, was also in favour of using and exploiting things as per need; He straightaway opposed the idea of greed-based exploitation."

PM Modi linked the growing wave of protectionism with the philosophy of Gandhi. He said: "And the growth of global supply chains has also stopped. The solution to this worrisome situation against globalisation is not in isolation. Its solution lies in understanding and accepting the change, it lies in making smart and flexible policies with the changing times. India's 'Father of the Nation' Mahatma Gandhi had said, "I do not want that the walls and windows of my house are closed from all sides. I want the breeze of the cultures of all the countries to freely move in my house. But at the same time it will not be acceptable to me that this wind blows away my feet off the ground." Following this philosophy of Mahatma Gandhi and contemplation, today's India is welcoming the life-providing waves of the world with full confidence and boldness." He invoked the ancient Indian wisdom to say that India will always be a force for harmony: "Not only this, a predictable, stable, transparent and progressive India will continue to be the good news in an otherwise state of uncertainty and flux. An India where enormous diversity exists harmoniously will always be a unifying and harmonizing force."

Not only for us and not only for our country, thinkers and sages and monks of India and Indian society since ancient times the Indian society, have dreamt about *Sarve Bhavantu Sukhinaha, Sarve Santu Niramaya, Sarve Bhadrani Pashyantu, Makashchid Dukha Bhag Bhavet*—which means all of them become happy, all of them are healthy, there is welfare of everybody and nobody should suffer. And they have also shown the path to achieve this ideal and to realise this dream. *Sahnavatu, sah nau bhunaktu, sah veeryam karvaa vahe, Tejaswinadhitmastu ma vidvishavahe.* This thousand-year-old Indian prayer means that we all work together, walk together, our talents flourish simultaneously and there is never any hatred between us. The great Indian poet of the last century and Nobel Laureate Gurudev Rabindranath Tagore had imagined such a heaven of freedom, "Where the world has not been broken up into fragments by narrow domestic walls. Let us together create such a heaven of freedom where there is cooperation and co-ordination and not divide and fracture. Let us all get the world rid from its cracks and unnecessary walls."

Credit goes to PM Modi for having articulated the fundamentals of Indian thinking at the global stage, not for pontificating but for analysing the true nature of today's problems and suggesting ways to tackle them. Ancient Indian thinking, suffused with spiritualism and without discarding materials, stresses the need for a balance between the two.

A lot is said and written about the Sustainable Development Goals suggested by the UN. The balance between development and environment is at the core of sustainable development goals. The implementation of the goals is a major task. In the Indian thinking, the king is advised to ensure the *yoga kshema* or the welfare of his subjects. Indeed that is his primary duty. If all states agree with this basic truth, it should be possible to achieve sustainable development of mankind.

Conclusion

The above survey has sought to show that India has a rich tradition of strategic thinking and it is possible to cull the kernel of Indian strategic thinking from ancient Indian texts. Indian culture is rich and encompasses a variety of shades besides Hinduism. This survey has been limited to only Hinduism because that is the oldest culture of the land. But, due to its inclusive nature, many other shades of thinking have also appeared and form composite Indian culture. Buddhism and Jainism are examples. Tamil Sangam literature is also a rich source of Indian thought. Later, the Bhakti movement, Sufi culture, Sikhism and many sects and regional variations have enriched Indian culture. It is necessary to delve deep into the regional varieties and shades of Indian culture to identify the sources of Indian strategic thinking. It is superficial to say that Indians lack a culture of strategic thinking. It is possible to build a strong Indian narrative based on the values of Indian culture from ancient and modern Indian thought. Sri Aurobindo summed it up aptly as follows: *"India can only survive this new, powerful world with fresh divine creations of her own spirit, cast in the mould of her own spiritual ideals. She must meet it by solving its greater problems, through solutions arising out of her own deepest and largest knowledge."*

NOTES

1. *Indian Strategic Thinking*. Keynote Address by Dr. Arvind Gupta, Director VIF, In Seminar *Exploring the Roots on India's Strategic Culture*, October 5, 2017 (New Delhi: IDSA) URL: http://www.vifindia.org/directorremarks/keynote-address-by-dr-arvind-gupta
2. Munshi, K. M. "Foreword." in *Vedic Age*, by R.C. Majumdar. Department of Ancient Indian Culture, Bharatiya Vidya Bhavan. 1951.
3. See "Ananda Coomaraswamy: A Case for Cultural Nationalism" in Anirban Ganguly, *Debating Indian Culture*, New Delhi, DK Printworld, 2013, pp. 33-42.
4. S. Gurumurthy, "Case for India Specific Economic Model." *Culture and Development*, Vivekananda Kendra.
5. S. Gurumurthy, http://www.newindianexpress.com/opinions/columns/s-gurumurthy/2016/nov/19/sri-sri-ravi-shankar-the-soft-power-exponent-of-india-1539708.html
6. Rajiv Malhotra, '*Indra's Net*,' *Harper* Collins Publishers India, pp. 12-13.
7. Quoted in S. Gurumurthy, "Case for India Specific Economic Model," *VIF Perspective: Securing India*, Wisdom Tree, New Delhi 2017.
8. Ibid, p. 41.
9. See *Encyclopedia of Hinduism*, India Heritage Research Foundation, Mandala Publications, New Delhi, 2013.

10. See *Encyclopedia of Hinduism*. Also see P.V. Kane, *History of Dharmashastra*, Bhandarkar Oriental Research Institute, Pune, 1962.
11. K. P. Jayaswal, *Hindu Polity: A Constitutional History of India in Hindu Times,* Chaukhambha Sanskriti Pratishthan, Delhi, Delhi Edition 2005.
12. Tanham, George K, *Indian Strategic Thought: An Interpretive Essay*, Santa Monica, Calif.: RAND Corporation, R-4207-USDP, 1992. As of March 08, 2018, https://www.rand.org/pubs/reports/R4207.htmlGeorge K. Tanham.
13. Rodney W. Jones, *India's Strategic Culture,* Prepared for: Defense Threat Reduction Agency Advanced Systems and Concepts Office, 2006, https://fas.org/irp/agency/dod/dtra/india.pdf
14. Ibid, p. 5.
15. Henry Kissinger, *World Order,* p. 114, URL: https://is.muni.cz/el/1423/podzim2017/MVZ253/um/H_Kissinger_-_World_Order, accessed on April 12, 2018.
16. S. Gurumurthy, "Religious Faith and Modern Civilization" in Joshi et al. (2008), *Transcending Conflicts: Indian and Eastern Way*, New Delhi: Global Foundation for Civilizational Harmony (India), pp. 516-517.
17. Prime Minister's statement on the subject ''Creating a Shared Future in a Fractured Word" in the World Economic Forum (January 23, 2018), URL: http://mea.gov.in/Speeches-Statements.htm?dtl/29378/Prime_Ministers_Keynote_ Speech_at_Plenary_ Session_of_ World_Economic _Forum_Davos_January_23_2018.
18. This phrase originally appears in the *Maha Upanishad* (VI.71-73), a minor *Upanishad* belonging to the so-called group of Visnu Upanishads. I thank Dr. Arpita Mitra of VIF for drawing my attention to this.
19. Ibid.
20. Ibid.
21. *Complete works of Sri Aurobindo*, Vol. 20, p. 43.

(*Dr. Arvind Gupta is the Director of the VIF, and an expert on strategic and international security affairs. He is a former Deputy National Security Adviser and Secretary, National Security Council Secretariat (2014-2017).*

∗

Contemporary: Economic Theory

5

WHERE ECONOMICS AND STRATEGY INTERSECT: A POLITICAL ECONOMY APPROACH TO GLOBAL POWER

Prabhat Prakash Shukla

Introduction

This essay attempts to understand the role of economic power in shaping the world since the Second World War. It focuses on the main strand of economic developments over this period, and it is important to clarify what it does not do. It does not look at subsidiary (or, at best, parallel) processes, important though they also were, processes such as the Cold War or the limited *détente* that began in the early 1970s. It also ignores the quiet struggle between the UK and the USA over economic influence until about the mid-1960s.

This point may require a little elucidation. It is not that the Cold War or *détente* were less important. But their importance lay in the military and strategic arenas—the *détente* of the 1970s in particular was of historic significance, but that was because of the cross-recognition of the two Germanys (thus ending the uncertainty of the early 1960s when Kennedy, Khrushchev, and Erhard led the USA, the Soviet Union and West Germany, respectively) and of the Oder-Neisse frontier; and, of course, the limitation of nuclear arms. But from the economic point of view, these processes were put in the shade by the much bigger magnitudes of capital flows in the West and among the oil producers.

Equally, it ignores the emerging challenges to the US domination of the world economy in recent years. It does not, thus, look at the Chinese Belt and Road Initiative (that has been done separately), or the emergence of crypto currencies, nor does it look at the Russian (and possibly Chinese) drive for a gold-backed alternative to the US dollar. All these are unquestionably important, but now, their success is far from assured. There is time before these need to be the subjects of detailed study.

The First Phase: European Recovery and US External Imbalances

The study begins with the European Recovery Programme, or the Marshall Plan, as it is more commonly known, which ran from 1948 to the end of 1951. By way of a backdrop, the Bretton Woods institutions—the International Monetary Fund (IMF) and the World Bank—had been established and had placed the US dollar at the centre of the international financial system. It was the only currency that was convertible into gold at a fixed price ($35 per ounce) and all other currencies were fixed in relation to the dollar. Devaluations beyond a narrow range could only be done with IMF permission where the USA had veto voting power and were only permitted in cases of "fundamental disequilibrium" which was not defined.

Marshall Aid turned out to be necessary because the European recovery after the war was slow in coming. By 1946-47, there were signs of serious unrest and the fear of Communist advances if the economies of the countries were not to show some quick and substantial improvement. Two features of Marshall Aid are worth highlighting. First, it was large. The total value over the period 1948 to 1952 was approximately $12.5 billion (in current dollars, a bit over $450 billion, using gold prices as the convertor). The US Gross Domestic Product (GDP) in 1952 was a little under $60 billion. What this did was to leave little American assistance for other countries—a point frequently made by US officials in discussions with other countries, including India.

The second feature was that it marked the line of cleavage in the Cold War. The countries that accepted the aid were Austria, Belgium, Denmark, France, Greece, Iceland, Italy, Luxembourg, the Netherlands, Norway,

Portugal, Sweden, Switzerland, Turkey and the United Kingdom as well as the bizone of Germany, later to become the Federal Republic of Germany (FRG). Those that rejected US assistance were the USSR, Albania, Bulgaria, Czechoslovakia, Hungary, Poland, Romania and, of course, the Soviet part of Germany, later to become the German Democratic Republic (GDR). These countries formed the Warsaw Pact and the Soviet-led economic cooperation arrangement under the Council for Mutual Economic Assistance (COMECON). Finland, though a capitalist country, also refused Marshall Aid. It became a byword throughout the Cold War for sensitivity to Soviet concerns, and gave the term 'Finlandisation' to the discourse during those years. Yugoslavia, part of the Communist International (Comintern) in 1948, rejected Marshall Aid, but in 1949 asked to be included. It did receive US assistance, but outside of Marshall Aid.

These European countries also committed to accept the "friendly advice" of the USA to develop economic integration among themselves, including West Germany. This served the dual purpose of tying the FRG with the West economically, which was a major goal, because the country had not yet been taken into the North Atlantic Treaty Organization (NATO)—that was to happen in 1955, after the failure of the European Defence Community. The second major objective was to find a large enough economic area to absorb the investment already made in the oil industry in West Asia including the pipelines that were to transport Saudi and other oil into Europe. The important thing in this connection is to note how the money was used. Over 10 per cent was spent on oil imports, almost entirely from the Middle East, and a slightly smaller amount was spent on transport—also oil fired or undergoing conversion from coal to oil. This marked the beginning of a three-way economic commitment involving the USA, those parts of Europe that accepted Marshall Aid and West Asia, with Saudi Arabia at its centre. A little bit of background to this development may add clarity as regards the drivers of these changes.

As far back as December 1943, while the Second World War was still on—but after the German surrender at Stalingrad had determined the outcome and the Teheran Conference between Roosevelt, Stalin and

Churchill had just ended—the oil company, California Arabian Standard Oil Co (later ARAMCO) requested the US Administration for permission and backing to supply oil from Saudi Arabia to West European markets. In short order, this request was approved and finance amounting to a maximum of $160 million was also provided to be repaid over 25 years. Certain conditions were attached, including building up a reserve, and that ARAMCO (its new name from January 1944 onwards) would not sell oil to any party deemed inimical to US interests by the State Department.

By April 1944, the policy was elaborated in greater detail. The Inter-Divisional Petroleum Committee of the State Department announced its aims with regard to Middle East oil in the following terms: *"Facilitation, by international agreement and otherwise, of substantial and orderly expansion of production in Eastern Hemisphere sources of supply, principally in the Middle East, to meet increasing requirements of post-war markets removal, by international agreement and otherwise, of impediments to the exploitation of Middle Eastern concessions held by United States nationals."*

The phrase "by international agreement and otherwise" catches the eye—diplomat-speak for the use of coercion if persuasion were not to work. And it was used on a regular basis—in Syria in 1949, in Iran in 1953, in the Suez in 1956, to name a few. But the more important purpose of discussing the role of oil is to bring out its importance for the USA, an aspect that will feature in a bigger way in the discussion of developments in the international economy in the late 1960s and early 1970s.

It would be helpful to quantify this emerging triangular relationship. European imports of crude in the period of Marshall Aid were as follows:

Year	Imports of Crude
1947	5 million tons
1948	11 million tons
1949	29 million tons
1950	31 million tons
1951	54 million tons

European refining capacity showed a similar increase. It rose from 24 million tons in 1948 to 40 million tons in 1950, and to 77 million tons by

1952. All the oil came from wells owned by US, British and British-Dutch oil companies. Most of the refining was done in refineries with the same ownership pattern, and the same went for the retail distribution.

For once, the European Recovery Programme (ERP) served its purposes as per design. It integrated Germany, it moved the European economies from coal as the primary fuel to oil, and it drew a line of cleavage between the Soviet and Western blocs. There were problems of course, most notably the dollar shortage caused by the fact that the USA was running persistent surpluses with the Europeans who were unable to make the settlements in their balance of payments. Accordingly, the USA extended regular loans to the countries amounting to another roughly $9 billion over the period from 1952 to 1960.

By this latter date the success of the ERP was well established and the member-states were running surpluses with the rest of the world, so that they could make their currencies convertible on current account. In 1957, six of the leading countries of the ERP—France, West Germany, Italy, Belgium, the Netherlands and Luxembourg—set up the European Economic Community (EEC), and thus began a period of changing trade patterns between the USA and Europe and, by extension, in the global economy.

The reason was that, as the European surpluses grew and, with it, the fear that the US dollar would face devaluation pressures, countries such as France asked to redeem their dollar holdings into gold. This was the period of fixed exchange rates, and dollar convertibility into gold at the fixed parity of $35 per ounce. This faced the USA with a double dilemma—how to preserve the Bretton Woods system, with fixed exchange rates and convertibility into gold, and yet fix the persistent and growing trade deficits. At the same time, they also wanted to provide for the growing liquidity needed to finance the rapidly growing global trade—growing faster by a factor of two to three than the global output. The table below illustrates the scale of the US deficits between 1959 and 1973.

Table 1: The US Balance of Payments, 1959–1973 (in $ billion)

Year	Trade Balance	Current Balance	Basic Balance
1959	0.91	−2.14	−2.00
1960	4.89	1.80	−3.20
1961	5.57	3.07	−3.11
1962	4.52	2.46	−3.69
1963	5.22	3.20	−5.04
1964	6.80	5.79	−6.19
1965	4.95	4.29	−6.19
1966	3.82	1.94	−4.12
1967	3.80	1.54	−5.36
1968	0.64	0.96	−1.08
1969	0.61	−1.63	−2.27
1970	2.16	−0.32	−3.02
1971	−2.72	−3.91	−6.27
1972	−6.99	−9.81	−1.67
1973	0.62	0.67	−2.52

Source: US Department of Commerce, *Survey of Current Business.*

The Second Phase: The Oil-Finance Cycle and Financialization

In actual fact, as the US archives show, the problem between Europe (and, increasingly, Japan) on the one hand and the USA on the other was more acute than these figures suggest, for the deficits of the USA with those countries were larger. Several ideas were at this stage floating in the Nixon Administration by 1969, but the dominant theme was that a devaluation of the dollar was the way to fix the persistent trade deficit. After an initial minor adjustment, which did not yield the desired result, Nixon took the step in August 1971 of taking the dollar off gold, and imposed domestic price controls as well as import tariffs of 10 per cent across the board.

The availability of monetary gold was the obvious constraint on the issuance of dollars in the period when the dollar was linked to gold, for that was the second problem in using the dollar as the international currency for financing trade. It is revealing therefore that the South Africans were running their mines at full capacity, and, in 1970, produced the highest output in their history, as the chart below shows. This amount, 1,000 tons in 1970, represented two-thirds of the world output. But even this amount was not sufficient to meet the requirement and it tapered off once the gold window closed.

Figure 1: South African Gold Production 1940–2012

In the event, this did not help the external balance except for a short while, and the downward pressure on the dollar continued. Nor was the USA the only major economy facing difficulties. The UK, which had already once devalued the Pound in 1967, continued to face balance of payments difficulties, and decided to let its currency float in 1972. The Japanese and the Swiss followed a few months later, and by 1973 most of the major currencies were floating, including the US dollar, though the Europeans maintained a band within which their currencies could float against one another.

In parallel with this process, a few others were also in train, and would collectively transform the global economy, and the US role in its management. Three processes are discussed next. None of them would have been possible but for the freedom given to the dollar by the abandonment of the gold standard, and the floating of exchange rates. The three processes were:

(i) Increase in oil prices driven by Organisation of Petroleum Exporting Countries (OPEC);

(ii) Loosening of US monetary policy, with the dollar freed from the constraints of maintaining any parity with either gold or other currencies; and

(iii) Rise in the role of the banks to deal with the flow of petrodollars into the European money markets, overwhelmingly into London.

The rise in oil prices began in the late 1960s, when Libya began its hard bargaining with Occidental Petroleum Corporation. As an independent company, it enjoyed little official support, and was heavily dependent on Libyan oil as its only major source of crude. Its leverage was further increased by the difficulties created by Nasser over the Suez Canal in 1967, leaving Libya and Algeria as the only countries that could supply oil to Europe without needing to transit the Suez Canal.

Colonel Gaddafi, who had taken over in a coup in September 1969, finally succeeded in raising the tax payments charged to Occidental on its oil. One after another, the other oil companies agreed to the higher taxes, which then fed back into arrangements with the Persian Gulf producers. This started a chain of increasing demands, which culminated in the Teheran Agreement of 1971 that saw an increase of some 50 per cent (from 80 cents a barrel to $1.25 per barrel) in the amount of tax paid by the oil companies to the producer countries. This was accompanied by a programme of annual increases all the way up to 1975.

This is what led the US State Department oil expert, James Akins, to remark: *"With the possible exception of Croesus, the world will never have seen anything quite like the wealth which is flowing and will continue to flow into the Persian Gulf."*

The Akins article is remarkably prescient on a subject notoriously hard to predict, and is recommended to the inquisitive reader—not only for the information it provides on oil politics, but equally for the way it leads to the other two aspects mentioned above. For he goes on to examine how the massive surpluses that OPEC was going to earn could be utilised.

And that brings in the US financial and monetary response to these developments. It would be useful to pause, though, and stress that all this was happening before the October 1973 Yom Kippur War upset even these arrangements, and led to a partial embargo and hence still higher prices for oil. This, in turn, provided even higher surpluses for the OPEC, especially Arab, countries.

Why this becomes important to note is that, after the US abandoned the gold standard in August 1971, Paul Volcker—then the Under Secretary for International Affairs at the Treasury—remarked at one of the meetings of a working group that the developing countries would have to bear the burden of adjustment, given the policies the West was following. The exact quote is in the third person in a report from a staffer from the office of the Presidential Assistant for International Economic Affairs: *"Paul noted that both the OECD and the US ideas of equilibrium call for the LDC's to bear a significant part of the adjustment burden!"*

And so indeed it turned out; the table below, shows the nature and magnitude of the current account deficits the least developed countries had to face throughout the 1970s and beyond.

Table 2: Global Current Account Balances 1973 to 1980

	1973	1974	1975	1976	1977	1978	1979	1980
Industrial Countries	11.3	–9.6	19.4	–0.5	–4.6	–30.8	–7.8	–44.1
OPEC	6.2	66.7	35.0	40.0	31.1	3.3	68.4	112.2
LDCs	–8.7	–42.9	–51.3	–32.9	–28.6	–37.5	–57.6	–82.1

Source: IMF Annual Reports, various issues.

The loose monetary policy that marked the 1970s has been well documented. Nixon was facing re-election in 1972 and needed positive economic results after the upheavals described above. He, therefore, appointed a new Federal Reserve Chairman, Arthur Burns, who loosened M1 from $228 billion to $249 billion between December 1971 and December 1972. The previous 12-month period under the long-serving Chairman, William McChesney Martin saw a move from $198 billion to $203 billion.

The essence of the loose monetary policy became clear towards the end of the decade, as inflation rose to 14 per cent by 1979, but allowed two large oil price hikes to be absorbed by the global economy—with the developing countries being the exception, which indeed had to bear the burden of the changing economic strategies. How they coped with the burden is the third part of the changes that followed the abandonment of the Bretton Woods arrangements in the early 1970s.

This was the role of the private commercial banks in the handling of the unprecedented funds that accrued to the oil exporters. Since the end of the war, the job of transferring capital was left to governments, as Marshall Aid itself showed, or to the World Bank and the IMF. At this stage, an informal consensus emerged among the financial managers of the world—the IMF, Organization for Economic Cooperation and Development (OECD), and the main central banks—that the handling of these large funds would be left to the private banks, as they, the governments or the international financial institutions, could not do the same job adequately. The traditional lenders, particularly the IMF, were constrained by quota limits and conditionalities. In point of fact, even the banks were uncertain about their ability to handle and recycle such large amounts of capital. The geographic location of the recycling centre was to be the City of London, because both continental Europe and the USA had fairly tight banking regulations, which would not permit the free-wheeling practices that made such recycling possible. Thus, the Eurodollar market was unleashed—though it had existed on a small scale since at least the late 1950s.

A recent book by Carlo Edoardo Altamura titled *'European Banks and the Rise of International Finance'* provides useful insights into the process. The main driver was the British financial establishment, led by the Bank of England, which recognised that the City was singularly well-placed to provide the banking services needed to undertake the task of recycling. The interesting insight the book provides is that even the banks were not quite sure they could cope with the challenge of recycling. The following quote from one of the British members of the Trilateral Commission, Sir Philip de Zulueta, to the Governor of the Bank of England is illustrative: *"At the Brussels meeting we had among other things a discussion about the recycling of Arab oil money. The bankers present, of whom the most important were David Rockefeller himself and Alan Hockin (Executive Vice President of the Toronto Dominion Bank) but included some Europeans, expressed considerable worry about the capacity of the private banking system to re-cycle the extra Arab oil money into medium term credits..."*

Among other issues, the bankers were concerned about the maturity mismatch, since the deposits were short-term, the loans medium- to long-term, and the straight fact that many of the countries to which loans were advanced were poor credit risks. But in a pattern that was to repeat itself in the early 2000s, there was no better option, as the surpluses kept pouring in. The only safeguard adopted was syndication—loans to developing countries were divided among a number of banks and these syndicated loans parcelled out the credit risks among the participant banks.

To sum up, the situation that the USA and the developed world faced in the early 1970s involved some tough choices. The dollar was in an unsustainable position, being both a national currency and an international one. The demands of the latter meant that the USA had to run persistent deficits on its balance of payments; in addition, because trade was rising several times faster than global GDP, the issuance of dollars had to be faster than the national growth would warrant. Inflation, and hence, depreciation, was built into this system. Moreover, the USA was running consistent deficits on its balance of payments, and so there was always a downward pressure on the currency.

The only way to control the situation was to go the way Nixon chose, or to curtail the money supply and induce a recession, which is how the issue was faced by Federal Reserve Chairman Volcker in the late 1970s, which is discussed below.

For once, the decision was to accommodate the rise of the petrodollar and its recycling through the Eurocurrency markets. This, in turn, meant the financialization of the US economy, and the empowerment of the commercial banks in a way that has not been seen since the Great Depression.

It also meant empowering Europe in a way not seen since the war. Those with long memories will recall the public and sharp airing of differences in the 1970s between the Europeans, particularly the French, on the one side and the Americans on the other. Authors like Mary Kaldor wrote 'The Disintegrating West,' as a harbinger of things to come, with Europe emerging as an independent force, co-equal of the USA, in international affairs. And a young economist, Fred Hirsch, spoke of the need for a "controlled disintegration" of the global economy as a legitimate aim for the 1980s.

The Third Phase: Controlled Integration of the Global Economy

The riposte was not long coming, and it was Volcker again who set the stage. Fittingly or not, he delivered the first Fred Hirsch memorial lecture in 1978, Hirsch having died in January the same year aged 47. Instead of controlled disintegration, Volcker spoke of the need for a "managed integration" of the global economy. He was then the President of the New York Federal Reserve Bank, and was shortly to be appointed Chairman of the Federal Reserve Board. In arguing for managed integration, he conceded that the USA was no longer the dominant economic presence, but argued that a coordinated approach with Japan and Europe would best serve the interests of the three, also making the point that such an approach would avoid currency volatility and at the same time prevent unhealthy competition between the three for advantageous positions in the developing countries. Also noteworthy is the following passage: *"For one thing we have learned that even large exchange rate changes have not been nearly as effective as hoped in achieving adjustment of long-standing imbalances in current account positions. Where clear improvements have been made, they can be traced to changes in relative demand pressures, or to structural changes such as North Sea oil."*

This relative demand management was the tool he was to employ to good effect upon taking over at the Fed, for that was the result of his shift towards money supply targeting, causing interest rates to rise to 20 per cent by the end of 1980. The stated aim was to end the high inflation (14 per cent at its peak in the late 1970s). It also had the effect of breaking the oil-finance recycling as many of the developing countries in Latin America and East European countries (to whom smaller amounts were extended) were unable to service the loans. The graph below, which shows what the result of this monetary tightening was, is taken from an IMF study.

The implications of this for Europe were spelt out by an ex-President of France well-versed in the ways of high finance, Giscard d'Estaing, in an

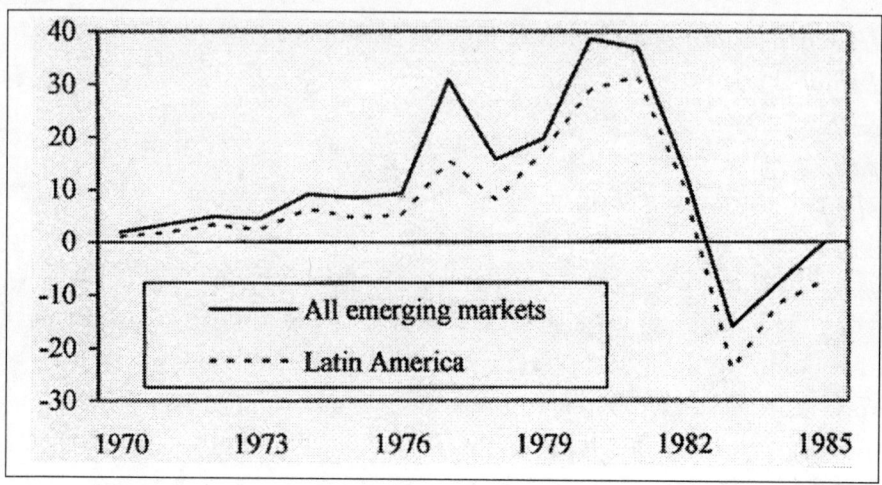

Figure 2: Bank Flows to Emerging Markets 1970–1985 (in US$ billions)

Source: World Bank, Global Development Finance. Bank flows include short-term financing.

article in *Foreign Affairs,* written in 1983, at a time when the US recovery was well under way: *"Traditionally a US recovery has fuelled exports of developing countries, increasing their orders of equipment goods from countries such as Japan, Germany and France, and the interdependence between European countries has led to diffusion in Europe of these expansionary forces, thereby sustaining the world recovery. This time, and due to the international debt crisis, developing countries will not be in a position to benefit fully from the US recovery."*

This passage also provides some insight into the active diplomacy then under way on the North-South Dialogue. Evidently, the European economies were at risk of an economic "decoupling" because of the policies adopted in the USA. Of course, these policies also affected the USA itself in a long-term way, and it would be well to spell out some of features of the new economy that was slowly taking shape. The most important feature was the decline of the traditional manufacturing industries and rise of international finance as the new driver of the economies of many of the developed countries. Here is how Altamura, already quoted above, puts it: *"After the end of the gilded age of Fordist capitalism, a new compact for growth had to be found. The compact that started to take place in the Western world*

(Europe for the purpose of our work) in the early 1970s, after the crumbling of Bretton Woods and, particularly, after the first oil shock, was a compact based on less and less regulation on financial movements and institutions. It was based on the centrality of the banking and financial sector as opposed to the public hand and industrial sector as the engines of growth, and, finally, was based on the collusion between controllers and controlled, which increased the moral hazard."

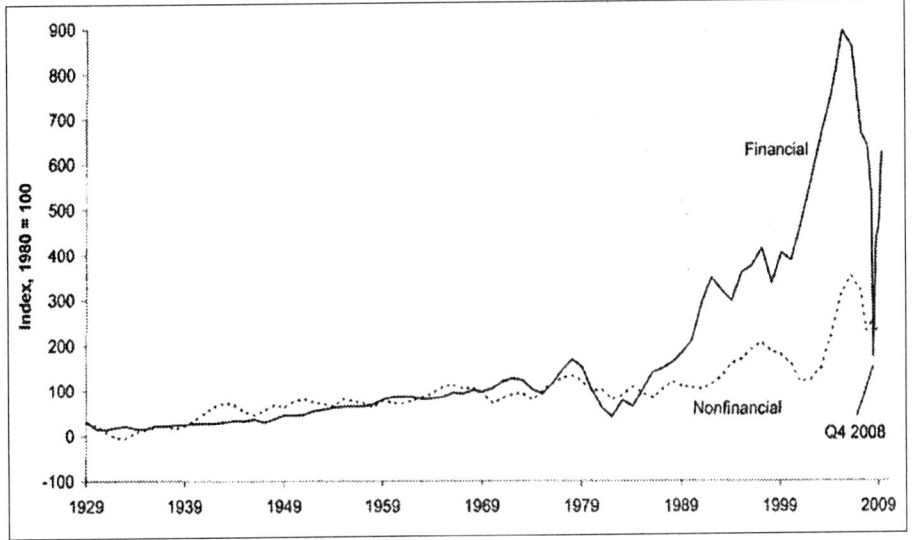

Figure 3: Real Corporate Profits, Financial vs Non-Financial Sectors

Source: Bureau of Economic Analysis, *National Income and Product Accounts*, Tables 1.1.4, 6.16; calculation by the author. Financial sector excludes Federal Reserve Bank. Annual through 2007, quarterly Q1 2008-Q3 2009.

The result of this empowerment of the banks was that the commercial banking sector in the USA grew by orders of magnitude over the period 1978 to 2007. The commercial banking sector held assets of $1.2 trillion in 1978, equivalent to 53 per cent of GDP. They rose to $11.8 trillion in 2007 or 84 per cent of GDP. Over the same period, investment banks grew even faster, going from $33 billion or 1.4 per cent of GDP to $3.1 trillion, or 22 per cent of GDP. Profitability in the sector grew significantly more rapidly than in other corporate sectors combined, as the chart below shows.

Two additional features stand out, and are worth spelling out, for they were to be repeated in aggravated form by 2008. The first was the emergence of large-scale global surpluses, which could not be productively employed in the country, or countries, originating them. These were the OPEC member-states at this time. Having no place to deposit these surpluses, such as the IMF or even the Bank for International Settlements (BIS), all the countries concerned agreed that it was best for the private banks to take in these funds and employ them where possible. In the 1970s, the focus of these deposits was the offshore commercial banks. But by the 2000s, the US financial services industry had been liberalised to an extent where they could handle the funds onshore.

The second feature was the recycling of these funds to countries, some of which were questionable credit risks. As the amount of surpluses grew, the banks were perforce looking at riskier investments. The same was to happen in the 2000s, of course, and that is what gave rise to the subprime loans. The difference was that in 1979, Volcker could apply the brakes on the oil-finance cycle by curtailing money supply, and the US economy could take the shock because its own exposure was limited to offshore commercial banks and the debtors were also foreign countries. Three decades later, it was a different story.

But all that was still to come. In the 1980s, the Mexican default in the summer of 1982 forced the hand of the US financial establishment to ease up on money supply, and that began a financial bull run that has continued—with occasional hiccups—to this day. For comparison, the Dow Jones Industrial Average (DJIA) ranged between 600 and 1000 from 1965 to 1982. It was a little above 700 in August 1982, when the Fed announced that it was abandoning monetary targeting. Twenty years later, it was above 10,000. (See Figure 4).

This twenty-year period also saw a few significant changes in the global economy. The most important, without question, was the relative decline of Europe, and the rise of Asia, as it also became the most important trade partner of the USA. And within that process, the world saw the rise of Japan in the 1980s, and its stagnation from the mid-1990s.

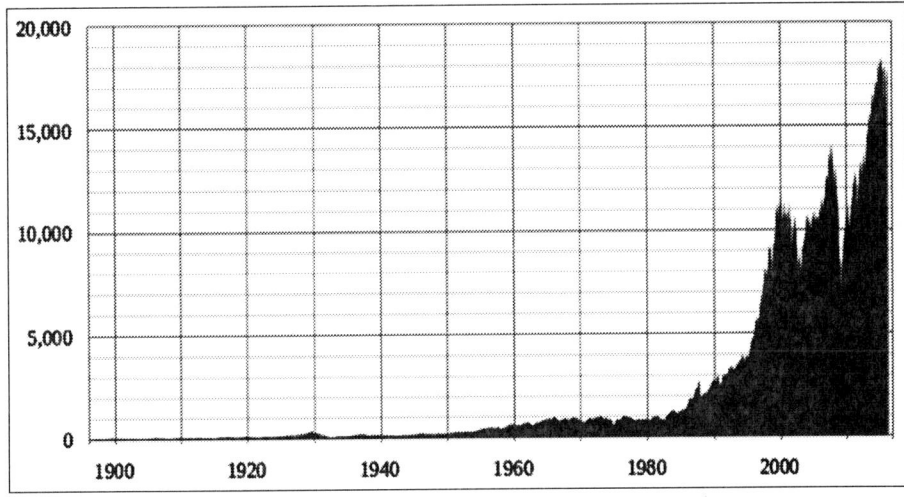

Figure 4: Dow Jones Industrial Average 1900–2014

A second feature was the liberalisation of the US financial sector. The improbable reality of the US economy up to the 1970s was that it was heavily controlled and regulated—the result of the post-1929 experience and the New Deal regulation. Banks were divided into commercial and investment functions under the Glass-Steagall Act of 1933. Regulation Q set limits on the interest they could pay on deposits, and they could not cross state borders. Others such as the Bank Holding Act and the Interest Equalisation Tax were further constraints. The process of removing these began in the 1980s, which gradually eroded, and finally repealed Glass-Steagall and also, along the way, permitted the growth of moral hazard. The Savings & Loans bailout in the late 1980s cost the taxpayer some $125 billion. Later, in 1998, saving Long-Term Capital Management (LTCM) was similarly helped out by the New York Federal Reserve Bank, though no public funds were used. Nonetheless, several analysts noted that the New York Fed had brokered a better deal for the LTCM shareholders than would have been possible without such intervention. And there was, of course, the bailout of Bear Stearns by the New York Federal Reserve Bank, whose role was described by Volcker as "actions that extend to the very edge of its lawful and implied powers."

The Fourth Phase: Growth Shifts to Asia

Meanwhile, the real economy was also undergoing shifts of an unprecedented magnitude. With Europe struggling after the Latin American debt crisis—several commentators described the situation as "Eurosclerosis" while Asia was gaining economic heft. In the 1980s, Japan was the fast-rising economy, and the usual spate of writing ensued describing Japan as the coming economic leader of the world.

As is well-known, that did not happen. And the reasons for that not happening are well-documented, and deserve treatment in some detail. The first point to note is that the Japanese economy did not stagnate from the late 1980s though it is frequently believed that the crash of the stock market at the end of December 1989, when the Nikkei was close to 40,000, marked the downturn. In actual fact, Japan's GDP continued to grow until 1995. It was $3.0 trillion in 1989, and reached $5.3 trillion in 1995.

The cause of the stalling may be found in the rise of China, and this came about in three stages—the devaluation of the Yuan and the simultaneous rise in the yen; the Asian Financial Crisis; and the entry of China in the World Trade Organization at the end of 2001.

The devaluation of the Yuan by nearly 50 per cent (from Y5.8 to the $ to Y8.7 to the $) on 1 January 1994 had the effect of making asset prices and labour costs significantly cheaper for foreign investors. The table below, taken from ADB *Key Indicators of Developing Asian and Pacific Countries* for various years, provides an indication of how Foreign Direct Investment (FDI) behaved over the period just before and just after the devaluation, and how the Asian Financial Crisis affected the region in terms of FDI flows. It suggests a clear movement of FDI into China in ever growing amounts, and either stagnant, or diminishing investment into other South-East Asian countries. The partial exceptions are Singapore and, to a lesser extent, Thailand.

Table 3: Total Net Foreign Direct Investment (in US$ million)

Countries	1990	1995	1997	1998	2007
East Asia					
China, People's Rep. of	2657.0	33849.0	41673.7	41118.1	121418.3
Hong Kong, China	...	...	...	-2220.0	6712.0
Korea, Rep. of	-263.1	-1776.2	-1605.2	672.8	-13696.7
South Asia					
India		96.0	2143.0	3562.0	2480.0	15545.0
Sri Lanka	41.6	53.1	429.8	193.0	548.0
Southeast Asia					
Indonesia	1093.0	3742.0	4677.0	-241.0	1164.2
Malaysia	2332.0	6642.0	6787.7	2708.0	-2561.7
Philippines	528.0	1361.0	1113.0	1592.0	-514.0
Singapore	3541.0	4748.0	2849.1	5148.9	11837.0
Thailand	2402.0	1183.0	3298.0	7360.0	7819.4
Vietnam	120.0	1780.0	2220.0	1671.0	6550.0
Developed Member Countries					
Australia	4272.4	2792.5	3819.2	1889.0	1624.7
Japan	-48968.9	-22591.0	-22767.8	-20960.2	-50999.5
New Zealand	...	4984.3	2120.1	-131.7	821.3

The next table shows the effects of this large-scale FDI into China. It shows the growing importance of FDI in China's export performance. Enterprises with foreign funding contributed 31 per cent to China's exports in 1995, just as the boom was starting. By 2005, when the boom was in its peak years, their contribution was 58 per cent.

Table 4: China's Inward FDI and Exports by Foreign Funded Enterprises (Nominal), 1995-2005

Year	FDI (in $ bn)	Total Exports (in $ bn)	Exports by FFEs (in $ bn)	Share of FFE Exports (in %)
1995	37.52	148.78	46.88	31.51
1996	41.73	151.05	61.51	40.72
1997	45.26	182.79	74.90	40.98
1998	45.46	183.71	80.96	44.07
1999	40.32	194.93	88.63	45.47
2000	40.72	249.20	119.44	47.93
2001	46.88	266.10	133.24	50.07
2002	52.74	325.60	169.99	52.21
2003	53.51	438.23	240.31	54.84
2004	60.63	593.33	338.59	57.07
2005	60.33	761.95	444.18	58.30

But there is an even more striking pattern when the direction of trade flows is also taken into account. Table 3, taken again from ADB (*op. cit.*), reveals the shift between 1990 and 2007. On the export side, it shows a major shift in Chinese exports towards the USA and Europe, with both doubling (or better) in percentage terms—which would also be obviously in absolute terms, given the huge increase in China's export quantities. For almost all the other countries, the opposite process is under way. Exports to both the above destinations decline, while exports within Asia go up significantly, which for most countries, means to China. Only India and Indonesia provide partial exceptions, and then too, not very significant in quantitative terms. In plain language, China became the funnel through which raw materials and intermediate goods were finished and exported to the USA and Europe.

Table 4 showing the changing pattern of imports is equally revealing. The imports of all countries, except China, go up from Asia, and down from the USA and Europe. China's imports from all three regions decline, which indicates that it was importing ever larger amounts from other sources—mostly oil and other raw materials not covered in the three jurisdictions included in these tables. Here, then, we have the new pattern that emerged over the period from the mid-1990s to the mid-2000s, and this brings out the nature and source of China's huge current account surpluses. To go further, the bulk of the surpluses arose from exports to two destinations, the USA and the EU. The USA alone accounted for over 25 per cent of total exports in 2005, and for 18 per cent as late as 2016.

Table 5: Direction of Trade: Merchandise Exports (per cent of total merchandise exports)

Country of Origin	To Asia		To Europe		To North and Central America	
	1990	2007	1990	2007	1990	2007
China, People's Rep. of	67.7	40.8	14.7	23.5	10.0	22.9
Korea, Rep. of	34.0	51.4	15.5	16.1	33.4	17.5
India	21.0	32.6	47.2	23.4	16.3	17.6
Indonesia	64.3	60.8	12.8	13.3	13.9	12.5
Malaysia	58.0	57.1	16.6	13.5	18.1	17.3
Singapore	47.1	64.7	17.2	11.3	23.0	11.6
Thailand	37.8	54.1	25.3	15.5	25.3	14.5
Vietnam	39.1	36.8	48.1	23.1	0.6	25.0
Australia	50.4	60.5	17.1	12.5	12.9	7.6
Japan	26.1	42.8	23.0	16.8	36.3	24.9
New Zealand	30.4	32.4	21.7	15.3	16.9	15.7

Table 6: Direction of Trade: Merchandise Imports (per cent of total merchandise imports)

Country of Origin	To Asia		To Europe		To North and Central America	
	1990	2007	1990	2007	1990	2007
China, People's Rep. of	48.4	40.4	24.1	14.5	15.8	9.4
Korea, Rep. of	33.5	46.7	13.1	12.6	25.3	12.0
India	17.3	29.9	41.3	21.6	12.9	9.2
Indonesia	43.4	70.7	22.5	8.4	13.7	5.1
Malaysia	50.6	60.3	17.9	13.2	18.1	11.6
Singapore	48.2	54.4	15.9	14.1	16.9	13.5
Thailand	53.3	56.4	19.7	11.0	12.1	7.6
Vietnam	34.1	69.1	21.3	10.4	0.4	3.9
Australia	32.4	49.0	27.5	23.8	26.4	14.8
Japan	25.1	40.8	19.8	13.4	27.2	14.0
New Zealand	24.0	42.0	25.0	17.7	20.0	11.5

The Fifth Phase: Unsustainable Surpluses Again

Thus, in the real economy, China was running up surpluses of a magnitude that even the Japanese—in their halcyon days—did not enjoy, leading to unprecedented surplus accumulation by China. At the same time, the OPEC countries were also enjoying a sustained rise in oil prices, which were to peak at over $140 per barrel (Brent) in 2008. Croesus was left far behind. A revealing datum is the figure for money supply in the USA. M3 is the broadest measure commonly used, and it captures the newer forms of money market funds, as well as external sources. In the US Fed data, they are also used to show the figures for non-M2 M3, and this figure, which captured these new sources, rose from 1 per cent in 1959 to 35 per cent in 2006.

Once again, the global economy was faced with excessive surpluses with nowhere to use them. This time, the bulk of the monies was deposited in the US banks, particularly in the Wall Street banks, now freed from all constraints. They had also developed new and unregulated instruments with which to recycle these colossal amounts. Inevitably, this required dropping diligence standards for evaluating loan recipients. And this time, instead of syndicating loans, the safeguard employed was securitisation in the form of Mortgage-Backed Securities and other derivatives. Despite some efforts at regulating these activities, nothing was done to control them. It was in essence a repeat, with some change of technique and major actors, of the oil-finance recycling of the 1970s.

At least one person in a position of authority seemed to sense the dangers in the situation. When Fed Chair Greenspan began raising interest rates in 2004, he testified before the Senate, where he said, *inter alia*, *"We cannot be certain that this benign environment will persist and that there are not more deep-seated forces emerging as a consequence of prolonged monetary accommodation."* (emphasis added).

Given the elliptical way central bankers use language, it is hard to be certain as to the meaning of this sentence. His book, *'The Age of Turbulence,'* also does not clear the meaning. But it would be a reasonable assumption that this was on his mind, in the same way that the excess liquidity in the global system was in the late 1970s. In fact, in later years, Greenspan has squarely blamed the global savings glut for the financial crisis.

And Greenspan did not confine himself to statements. In the subsequent meetings of the Fed Open Market Committee, interest rates were raised 17 times on the trot, in a sequence that seems unimaginable today. What is even more striking in comparison, when the cycle of upward moves began in 2004, was that unemployment was at 5.6 per cent, and core inflation between 1.5 and 2 per cent—that is significantly worse in terms of unemployment, and not much different in terms of inflation as compared to the present situation. And yet, he raised rates, whereas today there is a marked concern to hasten slowly and then too with every mark of extreme reluctance.

Of course, there was in between the searing experience of the financial crisis, or the Great Recession, as it is coming to be called. Enough has been written about it, and this essay does not intend to go over the ground here. Some of the major post-crisis features of the global economy are worth highlighting. Arguably the most important change has been the effect on global trade. This has led global growth since the late 1940s, and has registered a growth rate of 6.8 per cent annually between 1985 and 2007. Post-crisis, it has slowed down and has barely kept pace with global GDP growth, even falling below in some years, and going negative in years such as 2015—both in terms of value and volume.

In turn, this behaviour of global trade has meant that export-dependent economies have been adversely affected. As the world's leading exporter, China has faced serious challenges in maintaining its growth rate. And that brings in the major feature, the rapid growth in Chinese debt. The open indebtedness in China is now 250 per cent of GDP, and there is more from the shadow system. The Chinese are themselves more open about their economic problems than much of the Western conventional media. Thus, for instance, the Chair of the People's Bank of China described the latent risks in the financial system as "hidden, complex, sudden, contagious and hazardous." This came after warnings from the IMF and the BIS, as well as downgrades by some rating agencies regarding the very same issue—Chinese debt levels. This level of debt accumulation in so short a period of time is without precedent in post-War history. In graphic form:

All of the above demonstrates not just the downside risks facing the Chinese economy in the post-crisis period; it also indicates the dependence of China on benign US policies, especially with regard to interest rates and trade. On the first count, higher interest rates will cause China also to tighten its debt issuance or risk a depreciation of the Yuan—and there are several well-known China bears who are shorting the currency. But it will also affect China's external debt, which is of the order of $1.5 trillion. This is why Fed Chair Janet Yellen finally broke her silence on the relevance of China in decision-making on interest rates in September 2015, when she decided against raising them and invoked China 16 times in her press conference. This was in stark contrast to the Fed, which had barely talked about global worries earlier.

On the second count, China is even more dependent on the USA for continued growth. In 2016, for instance, China's export surplus with the USA was of the order of $350 billion. Its overall surplus was $510 billion, so the USA contributed just under 70 per cent of China's trade surplus. This is in conformity with the long-term pattern of US-China trade.

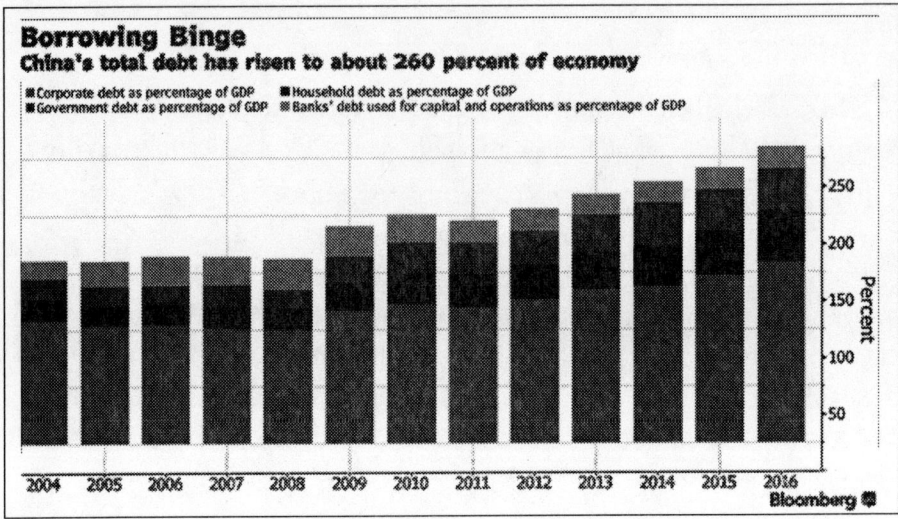

Figure 5: China's Total Internal Debt 2004-2016

Source: Bloomberg Intelligence.

There is the counter-argument that "China owns US debt," or that the "US is addicted to Chinese debt"—suggesting that there is mutual dependence so that China also has leverage over the USA. In fact, China owns a little less than 6 per cent of US Government debt, which is about the same as Japan. Adding corporate debt to the numbers puts Japan well ahead of China. Plus which the various Quantitative Easings have shown that in the final analysis, the USA does not need any outsider to buy its bonds. At its peak, the Fed was buying (and "twisting," that is, swapping maturities) a trillion dollars annually on its own. To prove the point, it may be recalled that China sold $188 billion of US Treasury bonds in 2016—with little effect on yields.

To offer some final thoughts: the narrative above has been aimed at showing that the USA has ensured its economic domination of the global economy essentially through financial control, after the industrial domination was irretrievably lost in the late 1960s. The financial flows, and the management of currencies, enabled the USA to direct its support through the process of "managed integration" described above. In turn, this brought the blessings of the US effective demand to the EEC, then Japan, and finally, China. This last is being played out now, and there are vested interests in keeping it going, just as there are—especially in the new Trump Administration—forces that seek an altogether new system and pattern of international engagement.

It is early yet to discern the contours of this new pattern. But some tentative conclusions are possible. Firstly, the heavy reliance on trade-led global growth is under strain. It was breaking down anyway even before 2017, but is now part of the strategy of the new Administration. This would have far-reaching implications for both the global value chains that emerged over the last two decades or so, and for the financialization of the US (and Western more generally) economy that took shape under the oil-finance cycle.

The role of Brexit is also worth noting. The Eurocurrency markets depended on the City in order to function, and that was among the main drivers of the British entry into the EEC, as it was then called. Now, the pull-out of the UK from the EU could very well be the harbinger of a new financial system to displace the current one.

These are huge changes, and are calling forth huge opposition. The outcome of this struggle will determine the kind of world that emerges.

Conclusion

Some winding up remarks would be in order now. Perhaps a good starting point would be to state what should be obvious from the foregoing—the USA is not in decline. Since the late 1960s, the US GDP share in the global output has been fluctuating between 22 and 24 per cent. In 2016, it was 25 per cent. One could argue about the nature and quality of the growth, but the basic fact cannot be controverted. The notion of decline has been linked to the undoubted rise of China. But China has filled the space vacated by the USSR, Europe, and Japanese stagnation. China's growth, as has been argued in this essay, is itself dependent on the US policies of loose money and open trade, especially its imports. This is changing, if the Trump Administration follows through on its new economic approach. And so far, it gives every indication of being serious about this.

Equally, the dollar is not under threat. Its role in international reserves remains unchanged, even enhanced. It accounted for 62 per cent of international reserve holdings in 1996, and that has gone up slightly to 63 per cent currently, as of end-2016. The Euro has increased slightly over the same period. The combined value of the D-mark, the French Franc, and the ECU was a little shy of 18 per cent in 1996; it is 20 per cent now. There is also the Greek debt issue, which has not yet been finally resolved. The IMF has not joined in yet, pending a review of the repayment programme of the government for sustainability. After satisfying itself on that score, it will join the assistance package in 2018.

The Chinese Yuan is in the 1 per cent handle at present, but it entered the SDR basket only last year, so its future will need to be tracked. So far, though, China has maintained strict—and tightening—capital controls, so it is unlikely that its share will rise significantly until capital controls are eased. Gold-backed movements are also worth monitoring, especially since China is now the largest gold producer in the world, and Russia and Uzbekistan are also among the top ten.

The foregoing analysis has also attempted to show the nature of the functioning of the global economy since the late 1940s. It has been an economy led and controlled by US power, which has been sustained by increasing financialization and dollar dominance, especially since the end of the Bretton Woods arrangements in the early 1970s. It has also been a system where trade has acquired a leading role in fostering economic growth. And once again, as the export destination of first resort, the USA has had the power to direct the speed of that economic growth. It has also used its pulling power to shift growth from one jurisdiction to another—Europe initially, Japan and finally China.

All this has not been without external challenges, and internal doubt. As early as in 1952, the incoming Eisenhower team posed the problem inherent in international trade, that of persistent surpluses and deficits. The point was made in the following words: *"How is it expected that a world system of trade and payments, free of quantitative restrictions and exchange controls and with convertible currencies, would be kept in balance? In other words, what equilibrating forces are expected to operate so as to prevent persistent surpluses and deficits (not accounted for by normal capital flow)? Under the gold standard the notion was that an inflow of payments produced by an export surplus would tend automatically to increase prices in the surplus country and reduce prices in the deficit country, thus stimulating imports into the surplus country and deterring imports into the deficit country. Whatever may have been the validity of this notion in the past it is clear that under present and foreseeable circumstances there is no direct or automatic connection between the inflow and outflow of payments and internal price levels."*

This was written at a time when the USA was running surpluses with the rest of the world, and so is all the more prescient. But once the tide turned and the USA was facing the prospect of persistent deficits, the same problem was seen differently. Kissinger noted in a memo to President Nixon that "the present monetary system puts very little real pressure on surplus countries to act short of intense political pressure from the rest of the world."

This indeed gets to the heart of the problem of international trade and finance. Surpluses are deemed good but deficits bad—and yet, you cannot have one without the other. And when the surpluses become as large as they did in the 1970s and in the early 2000s, the global economy faces the problem of how to utilise them. Both times, financial institutions found a way to put these surpluses to some use, and inevitably, they were economically unsustainable.

It appears possible that the new US Administration has understood that these are structural problems in the global economy and its management since the 1940s. The structure of the US economy itself has had perforce to change to accommodate these patterns of capital and trade flows, but this has come at a cost—frequent financial crises, poor job growth, and persistent deficits in the external balance, with corresponding volatility of the dollar. Not only has the new economic team openly rejected the long-standing commitment to free trade, it has also supported external policies—like the full-throated support of candidate Trump for Brexit, when the incumbent President voiced open discouragement for it. It would be wise to prepare for a radical shake-up of the global economy.

One of the consequences that appears to be happening already, and even before the current Administration took office, is a slowdown in international trade. The period after 2012 saw stagnation, and even negative growth, especially in 2015, both in value and by volume. The situation has improved a little in recent years, but even now, the growth in trade is no faster than overall global growth. This is slow by historical standards, when trade has outstripped global growth by a factor of two or three.

This implies that domestic demand will grow in importance as a driver of growth. The Chinese leaders recognise this, and have been talking since the last ten years about the need to boost domestic demand. The results so far have fallen short. But India is in the happy situation of having one of the most buoyant domestic consumption economies in the world. The changes described in this essay suggest that India needs to nurture this and the best way is to reduce the burden of direct taxes—on income, on corporate profits, and on property-related transactions—and to reduce the burdens of regulations and inspection. Not only will this play to our strengths, it will also provide a true free-market approach to managing the economy, something that has long been promised, but not really delivered so far. The experience of several countries is that reducing taxes does indeed raise revenues after an initial dip, through better compliance, and through higher economic growth. The times are propitious for such an approach.

There is another insight that the history of the last seven decades has to offer—depreciating one's currency is no help in fixing an external imbalance. The US example also bears this out. In terms of gold prices, the dollar has fallen from $35 per ounce, to close to $1300 per ounce today – and the USA continues to run persistent deficits. And the dollar has not weakened just in terms of gold. It has been all over the place against the currencies of its main trading partners, including periods of extended weakness to no avail.

India itself offers a compelling example. A dollar bought Rs. 3.21 in 1947, whereas today it is in the range of Rs. 65. That is a 20-fold decline, and there has been a similar decline vis-à-vis other currencies as well. Yet, we have run deficits in our balance of trade every year, except two in the 1970s. Indian policy-makers would be well-advised not to work to weaken the rupee since it will not help our external balance. The current US Administration has, to boot, placed India on the watch list for policies that deliberately weaken the rupee. We have been buying over a billion dollars per month for the past few years, whether intending to weaken the currency or not. But that has been the effect. And it has not helped our trade balance.

Finally, the inquisitive mind will be struck by the close linkages between the economic and political. If Marshall Aid divided Europe along the line of cleavage of East and West, the Yom Kippur War served to raise oil prices and the launch of the oil-finance cycle. Similarly, there is fertile ground for inquiry into the gold production and its link to the dollar, to the US Interest Equalisation Tax, and perhaps even to apartheid. Similarly, the breaking of the oil-finance cycle in the early 1980s led to major pro-democracy movements in South America. The distinction almost universally drawn between the economic and the strategic is probably a misleading one—and that is what this essay has tried to demonstrate.

REFERENCES

1. David S. Painter, 'Oil and the Marshall Plan,' *The Business History Review*, 58 (3) Autumn, 1984, pp. 359-383.
2. Foreign Relations of the United States: Diplomatic Papers 1944, 'The Near East, South Asia, and Africa', *The Far East Volume V*, Doc 890F.6363/91, 27 December 1943; and Doc 800.6363/1515a, 3 March 1944.
3. Foreign Petroleum Policy of the United States: Memorandum by the Inter-Divisional Petroleum Committee of the Department of State, 1944811.6363/4-1144, April 11, 1944.
4. All figures are taken from Jon Kimche, 'Seven Fallen Pillars,' Secker & Warburg, London 1953, p. 21.
5. Keith Pilbeam, 'International Finance', Macmillan 1998.
6. South Africa Gold Production, https://commons.wikimedia.org/w/index.php?curid=30203661.
7. James Akins, 'The Oil Crisis: This Time the Wolf is Here,' *Foreign Affairs*, April 1973.
8. Foreign Relations of the United States: Foreign Economic Policy: 1969-76, Volume III, 'International Monetary Policy, 1969-72', Document 173 of 1 September 1971.
9. Pilbeam, No. 5, p. 291.
10. Carlo Edoardo Altamura, 'European Banks and the Rise of International Finance: The post-Bretton Woods era' (*Kindle Locations 3258-3262*), Routledge Explorations in Economic History, Taylor and Francis, Kindle Edition.
11. Paul Volcker, 'The Political Economy of the Foreign Affairs', November 1978, p. 9, https://www.newyorkfed.org/medialibrary/media/research/quarterly_review/1978v3/v3n4article1.pdf
12. Johannes Wiegand, 'Bank Recycling of Petro Dollars to Emerging Market Economies during the Current Oil Price Boom', *IMF Working Papers*, 08/180, https://www.imf.org/external/pubs/ft/wp/2008/wp08180.pdf

13. Valery Giscard d'Estaing, 'New Opportunities and New Challenges,' *Foreign Affairs*, Fall 1983.
14. Altamura, No. 10.
15. Johnson & Kwak, 13 Bankers, Vintage Books, New York 2011, pp. 59–61.
16. China Statistical Yearbook (1996-2006): National Bureau of Statistics of China; quoted in WeishiGu, Titus O Awokuse, Yan Yuan, 'The Contribution of Foreign Direct Investment to China's Export Performance', paper prepared for presentation at the American Agricultural Economics Association Annual Meeting, Orlando, FL, July, 2008, p. 28.
17. *New York Times*, 21 July 2004.
18. China's Central Bank Chief Warns of 'Sudden, Contagious and Hazardous' Financial Risks, *Bloomberg News*, November 4, 2017, https://www.bloomberg.com/news/articles/2017-11-04/china-s-zhou-warns-on-mounting-financial-risk-in-rare-commentary
19. Patrick Gillespie and Heather Long, @CNN Money, 'Janet Yellen invokes China 16 times in 1 hour,' September 18, 2015,http://money.cnn.com/2015/09/18/news/economy/china-yellen-global-economy-worry/index.html
20. Foreign Relations of the United States: 1952-54, Volume I, Part 1, Economic and Political Matters, Document 16, dated 11 December 1952.
21. Foreign Relations of the United States: 1969-76, Volume III, Foreign Economic Policy; International Monetary Policy, 1969-72, Document 124, dated 7 May 1969.

(Prabhat Prakash Shukla is a former Indian Foreign Service Officer. During a career spanning 37 years, he served in Moscow, Brussels, London and Kathmandu, among other places. He served in Delhi twice, including as the Diplomatic Adviser to the Prime Minister from 1996 to 2000. He is currently a Distinguished Fellow at the VIF)

*

Contemporary: Foreign Policy

6

REBOOTING INDIA-RUSSIA TIES

Kanwal Sibal

The international environment is changing, with new opportunities and challenges. India is not where it was since the early 1990s. Our economic growth, even if it has been less spectacular than that of China, has changed international perceptions about India as a trade and investment partner. Our developmental needs remain formidable and governments have to satisfy rising public expectations. On many global issues, whether related to climate change, clean energy, trade and investment issues, India's role has become more prominent. Our foreign policy has to be aligned to these new realities, and a new balance in external relations has to be forged in a way that our interests are optimally advanced.

Consequently, our relations with the West, especially the USA have acquired a new salience. This has given rise to a perception that under Prime Minister Modi we have neglected our relations with Russia. This would not be an objective view. Modi has launched a host of development campaigns such as Make in India, Digital India, Skill India, Smart Cities, Start-Up India, Clean India and the like. For implementing them, his government has to reach out to the advanced industrialised countries for partnership, as the technological, management and even financial inputs can best be obtained from them. In the fields of health, renewable energy, clean coal technologies and solar power, we are again being pulled towards the West, as is the case with innovation as a whole. Education and people-to-people contacts also drive us towards the English-speaking West, rather than to Russia.

Russia has, however, its own place in our foreign policy, underpinned by elements that our other relationships, even as they grow stronger for pragmatic reasons, lack to the same degree. Our ties with Russia are based on trust, strong bonds of friendship that have stood the test of time, geo-political understanding, a sense of reliability, shared views on the conduct of international relations based on respect for sovereignty, non-interference in the internal affairs of countries, multilateralism and the like. These are elements to be valued. The Modi government, as the governments before, understands the importance of our ties with Russia, irrespective of minor irritants that crop up occasionally because of Russia's hard-headed pursuit of its own interests that emphasise commercial advantage over any nostalgia of the past. We have also to maintain stability and trust in our ties with Russia at a time when its relations with the West have sharply deteriorated and have pushed it towards China.

The belief that contacts with Russia have slowed down with the Modi government would be misplaced. Modi has had occasion to meet Putin on a few occasions, at the BRICS, G-20 and Shanghai Cooperation Organisation (SCO) Summits (the last on Russian soil). During the year, our President participated in the Moscow celebrations to mark the 70th anniversary of Russia's Victory in World War II. The Russian Speaker led a parliamentary delegation to India this year. Other important visits have been those of Russian Deputy Prime Minister Rogozin, who is in charge of relations with India, and the Russian Defence and Interior Ministers. On our side, our External Affairs and Defence Ministers have visited Russia this year.

Modi visited Russia for the 16th India-Russia summit. The regularity with which these summits have been held ever since Putin acceded to power testifies to the value the two countries attach to them as occasions to take stock of the relationship, assess ongoing programmes, address issues, explore new areas of cooperation, all in a bid to keep cementing the relationship as well as building on it in all feasible areas.

Defence remains the most important pillar of our relationship with

Russia. On the one hand, it provides an enduring base to our special and privileged strategic partnership while, on the other, it overloads the relationship in one area where any setback is seen as a blow to the structure of the entire relationship. Our developing defence ties with the USA, for instance, which have a logic of their own, are seen by Russia through the prism of its defence ties with us. We are also put in a position where we have to keep nurturing our ties with Russia with additional defence deals, even when problems relating to earlier ones are not fully resolved.

In his press comments in Moscow, Modi mentioned that we have made progress on a number of defence proposals that would boost defence manufacturing in India and our defence readiness with next generation equipment. He did not specify them, except the Inter-Governmental Agreement on manufacture of the Kamov 226 helicopter in India as the first project for a major defence platform under the Make in India mission. Actually, this project was taken out of the tendering process and allotted to Russia during the 2014 summit in New Delhi as one to be implemented with the private sector. It would appear that the effort to identify a suitable Indian private sector partner has failed, with the result that Hindustan Aeronautics Limited (HAL), which was to be excluded, will now participate in the implementation of the project and will be given the responsibility to identify the right private sector partner.

The Joint Statement issued on the occasion of Modi's visit has a generally worded, bland paragraph on defence cooperation. Interestingly, Defence and Military-Technical Cooperation figures in it after Trade and Investment, Energy, Education and Science and Technology, Culture and People-to-People Contacts and Space Cooperation. In actual fact, defence cooperation remains robust. Before Modi's visit, we announced that the purchase of the potent S-400 Air Defence System from Russia had been approved by the Defence Acquisition Committee. It was obviously premature to identify it as a summit deliverable as a lot of negotiating work lies ahead. On the fifth generation aircraft, the existing confusion about India's interest and role in the project remains, though those in the know maintain that India is participating in the project and that reports about Russia going ahead with the project without India are not quite correct. Russia has built prototypes of the PAK-FA which is not yet a fifth generation fighter. Each prototype built contains new stealth features; it is a work in progress. India is therefore not out of the game. The contract for four additional frigates is also on track, but it could not be announced during the visit because all the contractual details have not been fully tied up yet. There is a component of Make in India in it.

Nuclear power cooperation is the second strategic pillar of our relationship. Modi said in Moscow that the pace of our cooperation in nuclear energy is increasing, with progress on our plans for 12 Russian nuclear reactors at two sites. The joint statement "welcomed progress in identifying the second site in India for additional six nuclear reactor units." It was expected that the second site for which Russia has been pressing would actually be specifically announced, as it is not content with repeated reiterations at the political level that a second site would be identified. It appears that the decision for a second site in Andhra Pradesh has been taken by us, but we could not, and did not, want to announce the decision formally in Moscow as some prior administrative procedures have to be completed on our side and the desire to guard against public agitation of the kind that we saw at Kudankulam influenced the decision. India is keen that as Russia proceeds to construct 12 nuclear reactors, there should be progressive transfer of technology, with the 12th reactor giving us full domestic production capability. This might be too aspirational on our part, but we are insisting on localisation, the parameters of which will, however, be determined on a practical basis. Our goal is to embed localisation in the whole process of acquiring Russian nuclear reactors. The joint statement contains an agreement to actively work towards localization of manufacturing in India under the aegis of Make in India and in tandem with the serial construction of nuclear power plants. In this context, the finalization of the Programme of Action for localization between RosAtom of Russia and the DAE has been welcomed by the two sides. With units 3 and 4 at Kudankulam already approved, it was expected that the General Framework Agreement on KK 5 and 6 would be announced. Both sides were negotiating intensively until the last minute to reach an agreement but could not do so. However, it is understood that the remaining ends will be tied up in the next few months.

India has long pressed for greater access to Russia's abundant oil and gas resources, with limited success. It is only in recent years that Russia has been more forthcoming. Western economic sanctions and the need for cash resources for developing Russia's vast reservoir of oil and gas account for greater readiness on Russia's part to have Indian companies invest. We have an opportunity now that we should not miss. Modi noted in Moscow that India is enlarging its investments in the Russian hydrocarbon sector. Russia will expand LNG supplies to India by the Gazprom Group from the Arctic fields through joint projects in which our side is interested. ONGC Videsh Limited has acquired 15 per cent stake in Vankorneft, an oil field that we have long coveted, and may get another 10 per cent. Rosneft is also in negotiations with Oil India on investments, having earlier "concluded some details of a deal" under which it will pick up 10 million tonnes of crude from Rosneft. In turn, Rosneft will pick up 49 per cent stake in India's second largest oil refinery in Vadinar in Gujarat. Indian Oil Corporation Limited and Oil India Limited have signed a memorandum with Rosneft which paves the way for acquisition of 10 per cent stakes in the Taas-Yuriakh oil assets in East Siberia.

The poor trade levels between India and Russia constitute a glaring weakness in our bilateral ties. At $ 10 billion, trade between India and Russia is unconscionably low. This means that large sectors of our economy and entrepreneurs, especially in the modern sectors of our economy, are not sufficiently connected with Russia. Efforts in the past to expand trade through setting up several joint business groups have not borne fruit. The target of raising the trade turnover to $ 30 billion by 2025 fixed in the earlier summit and reiterated this time is decidedly ambitious. During the summit, Modi and Putin addressed CEOs of Indian and Russian companies about which Modi spoke positively. Putin has listed high technology, innovation, energy, aircraft building, pharmaceuticals and diamonds as promising areas for India-Russian cooperation. Of the 16 agreements and MoUs signed during the summit, the MoU for cooperation between Heavy Engineering Corporation (HEC) & CNIITMASH for upgradation and modernization of HEC's manufacturing facilities, and the MoU in the field of investment cooperation in the Russian Far East between Tata Power

Company Limited and the local Ministry for Development, have considerable potential. A Free Trade Agreement between India and the Eurasian Economic Union has been under discussion. At the summit, the sides expressed support for early finalization of a draft Joint Study Group report to consider the feasibility of such an agreement.

With the breakdown of Russia-Turkey relations after the downing of the Russian bomber over Syria, on which Modi expressed the full sympathy of the Indian people, the positive outcome of discussions between the phytosanitary and veterinary authorities of both the countries to finalize mutual market access for agricultural and processed food products, including dairy products, was welcomed. Russia is very keen to source from India products it was importing from Turkey, and the summit document recognised this as a new and promising area for development and diversification of bilateral trade.

During the discussions in the UN General Assembly earlier this year, India was disappointed by the position Russia took on the start of text-based negotiations on UN Security Council (UNSC) expansion. The summit's joint statement removes the ambiguity on Russia's position on UNSC reform and India's permanent membership, with Russia regarding India as a deserving and strong candidate that can bring an independent and responsible approach within the UNSC and reaffirming its strong support to India's candidature for a permanent seat in a reformed UNSC. In our summits with Obama and Abe we had signed on to bold formulations on the Asia-Pacific and South China Sea, disregarding Chinese sensitivities. Russia shows understanding of China's position in this area. In Moscow, we have used formulations that skirt concerns about freedom of navigation and overflights and have opted for more bland and non-controversial ones. The importance of the Russia-India-China (RIC) format finds mention in the joint statement.

India and Russia are threatened by terrorism and religious extremism. Our agencies may be working together closely to monitor the threat, but in joint statements that we draft with the Russian foreign ministry, the Russian side tries to avoid formulations that could be seen to be pointedly directed at Pakistan. The joint statement condemns terrorism in all its forms and manifestations, with a call for the elimination, once and for all, of all 'safe havens' of terrorists. This is an all-embracing formulation that covers the wider region and is not Pakistan-specific. Modi himself has been pushing for the early completion of negotiations on the Comprehensive Convention on International Terrorism, which the joint statement endorses. However, there is no reference to the early trial of those accused of the 2008 Mumbai terrorist attacks. On other global issues, Russia has supported India's early accession to MTCR and NSG as well as the Wassenaar Arrangement.

The joint statement expresses concern about the aggravation of the security situation in Afghanistan, including along its borders. Both sides recognise that terrorism and extremism pose the main threat to the security and stability of Afghanistan, the region and beyond. In this regard, the need for joint and concerted efforts and cooperation among countries in the region to address the challenge of terrorism in all its forms and manifestations, including the dismantling of terrorist sanctuaries and safe havens, and disrupting all financial and other support for terrorism, was emphasised. There are extensive references to Syria, Iraq and East Ukraine in the joint statement, essentially along the lines that Russia would have wanted. This could have been balanced by more supportive formulations by Russia on our Pakistan problem, without necessarily naming the country, but this did not happen.

Modi was right in saying in his joint press conference with Putin that he sees Russia as a significant partner in shaping a balanced, stable, inclusive and multi-polar world. He stated that his conviction had deepened that this relationship truly meets the test of a special and privileged strategic partnership. He noted that Putin and he had a high degree of convergence in our positions on global issues. According to Putin, Modi's visit was very timely and would make it possible to 'synchronise watches' on the main areas of cooperation between the two countries. It is understood that the Russian side was very satisfied with the summit. In which case, doubts that India had neglected its relations with Russia at some cost should be set at rest.

(Amb. Sibal has been India's Foreign Secretary (2002-03). Earlier, he has been India's Ambassador to Turkey, Egypt and France. Presently, he is a Distinguished Fellow at the VIF)

*

7

Information and Communication Technologies: Key to Transform India

Davinder Kumar

Role of Information and Communication Technology

India lives concurrently in three ages, namely, agricultural, industrial and Information with varying instances of overlap and constant transition from one to another. Indian society, therefore, is transforming continuously. The challenge is to manage this transformation. India has long been bedevilled by various divides: between rich and poor, city and village, literate and illiterate, besides larger socio-cultural ones. Much has been written about the digital divide: a new societal schism between those who possess digital devices and have the capability of using them and, on the other hand, those who do not.

It is believed that Information and Communication Technology (ICT) can be mechanisms that enable developing countries to not only close the gap but 'leapfrog' stages of development. One can use ICT to serve as a digital bridge, an enabler that not only obviates any digital divide, but helps to reduce many of the other disparities in society. The Digital Era ushered in by the ICTs and Media has opened up exciting possibilities for India. India realized the potential of ICT for all-round development and started building the infrastructure and capacities in the mid-Nineties. It is now poised to make a big transformation that will alter the very fabric of society.

While the past few decades of ICT progress has shown significant promise, it has only laid the foundation for what is about to come. We are now at a position where the next wave of innovation in the form of mobile, broadband and Cloud will be the catalyst for an entirely new socio-economic model. This new age will deliver growth and prosperity based on greater social cohesion and environmental sustainability. The resulting networked society holds the potential to truly shape the future and leave a positive legacy for generations to come. ICT has not only empowered individuals, it is an instrument of governance and central to human life and development. It is a tool for expeditious narrowing of the divide in society and meeting the aspirations of common man. Establishing a correlation between internet, mobile and growth of a country, a report by the Indian Council for Research on International Economic Relations (ICRIER) said that a 10 per cent increase in internet penetration in India can increase the gross domestic product (GDP) by 1.08 per cent while a 10 per cent increase in mobile penetration can increase the GDP by 1.5 per cent.

India has made reasonable progress in the last decade or so towards:
- Establishment of ICT infrastructure,
- Enhancing the reach of the electronic media, and
- Extension of e-services in the finance, health, public distribution and education sectors to ensure better governance.

The development has been differential. The situation, however, is changing rapidly with the mobile telephone revolution that is under way and greater penetration of the internet.

Let us take stock of some of India's major achievements in the field of ICT thus far:
- India, with nearly a billion mobile telephones, has the second largest mobile subscriber base in the world,
- Thirty per cent of these are Smartphone users,
- India, at 462 million users (April 2016), again has the second largest number of internet users in the world with more than 30 per cent in the rural areas,
- India has the second largest terrestrial optical fibre network by route kilometres in the world,

- India has the largest undersea optical network in the world,
- India downloaded 9 billion applications in 2015 alone,
- More than 90 per cent of its population has access to TV which is transforming rapidly into a fully digital service. Indian TV has about 800 channels broadcasting in 14 languages,
- The Passenger Reservation System (PRS) of Indian Railways provides reservation services to nearly 1.5 to 2.2 million passengers a day on over 2,500 trains running throughout the country,
- The PRS Application CONCERT (Country-wide Network of Computerized Enhanced Reservation and Ticketing) is the world's largest online reservation application,
- Freight Operation Information System of Indian Railways earns a revenue of 40 million dollars a day and operates through 5 data centres,
- India announced its National Policy on Electronics in 2012 to boost electronic manufacturing,
- India promulgated the IT ACT 2000 and subsequent amendment in 2008.

The Government approved the National e-Governance Plan (NeGP), comprising 27 Mission Mode Projects and 8 components, on May 18, 2006. In 2011, four projects—Health, Education, PDS and Posts—were introduced to make the list of 27 MMPs to 31 Mission Mode Projects (MMPs).

Mission Mode Projects (MMPs)

Central MMPs	State MMPs	Integrated MMPs
• Banking	• Agriculture	• CSC
• Central Excise & Customs	• Commercial Taxes	• e-Biz
• Income Tax (IT)	• e-District	• e-Courts
• Insurance	• Employment Exchange	• e-Procurement
• MCA21	• Land Records (NLRMP)	• EDI For e-Trade
• Passport	• Municipalities	• National e-governance Service Delivery Gateway
• Immigration, Visa and Foreigners Registration & Tracking	• e-Panchayats	• India Portal
	• Police (CCTNS)	
• Pension	• Road Transport	
• e-Office	• Treasuries Computerization	
	• PDS	
• Posts	• Education	
• UID	• Health	

Vision

It is to "Make all Government services accessible to the common man in his locality, through common service delivery outlets and ensure efficiency, transparency and reliability of such services at affordable cost to realise the basic needs of the common man." In order to promote e-Governance in a holistic manner, various policy initiatives and projects have been undertaken to develop core and support infrastructure. The major core infrastructure components are:

- State Data Centres (SDCs),
- State Wide Area Networks (SWAN),
- Common Services Centres (CSCs),
- National e-Governance Service Delivery Gateway (NSDG),
- State e-Governance Service Delivery Gateway (SSDG), and
- Mobile e-Governance Service Delivery Gateway (MSDG).

The important support components include:

- Core policies and guidelines on Security, HR, Citizen Engagement, Social Media,
- Standards related to Metadata, Interoperability, Enterprise Architecture, Information Security, etc.,
- New initiatives include a framework for authentication, viz., e-Pramaan and G-I Cloud, an initiative which will ensure benefits of Cloud computing for e-Governance projects.

Despite the successful implementation of many e-Governance projects across the country, e-Governance as a whole has not been able to make the desired impact and fulfil all its objectives. The main reasons for this are the inadequacy of essential pre-requisites. Some of these are:

- Political will resulting in lack of thrust in implementation,
- Comprehensive Policy Framework and consequent lack of synergy,
- Absence of an empowered and dedicated organisation,
- Non-availability of indigenous technology (HW, SW, Networking, Process re-engineering, change management, etc.),
- ICT infrastructure,
- Qualified Human Resource particularly for System/Large system integration,

- An electronic eco system and manufacturing base,
- Inclusive growth that covers electronic services, products, devices and job opportunities,
- Standards, Audit and Availability,
- Training and awareness of users,
- Legal framework, and
- Security.

India has taken steps to overcome these inadequacies. In order to transform the entire ecosystem of public services through the use of Information and Communication Technology, the Government of India has launched a number of flagship schemes and projects to transform India into a digitally empowered society and knowledge economy. Projects like Digital India, National Broadband Network (Bharat Net), Make in India, 100 Smart Cities and Aadhaar would change the digital landscape substantially with direct impact on security, governance, transparency and accountability.

Digital India

The Digital India programme is a flagship programme of the Government of India to transform India into a digitally empowered society and knowledge economy. The initial estimate for the Project is 16 billion US dollars over the next four years. The Digital India programme is centred on three key vision areas:

- Digital Infrastructure as a Core Utility to Every Citizen,
- Governance and Services on Demand,
- Digital Empowerment of Citizens.

Digital Infrastructure as a Utility to Every Citizen:

- Availability of high-speed internet as a core utility for delivery of services to citizens,
- Cradle to grave digital identity that is unique, lifelong, online and authenticable to every citizen,
- Mobile phone and bank account enabling citizen participation in digital & financial space,

- Easy access to a Common Service Centre,
- Shareable private space on a public Cloud,
- Safe and secure cyberspace.

Governance and Services on Demand
- Seamlessly integrated services across departments or jurisdictions,
- Availability of services in real time from online and mobile platforms,
- All citizen entitlements to be portable and available on the Cloud,
- Digitally transformed services for improving ease of doing business,
- Making financial transactions electronic and cashless,
- Leveraging Geospatial Information Systems (GIS) for decision support systems & development.

Digital Empowerment of Citizens
- Universal digital literacy,
- Universally accessible digital resources,
- Availability of digital resources/services in Indian languages,
- Collaborative digital platforms for participative governance,
- Citizens not required to physically submit government documents/certificates.

Programme Management Structure
(a) Cabinet Committee on Economic Affairs (CCEA) for programme-level policy decisions.
(b) A Monitoring Committee on Digital India under the chairpersonship of the Prime Minister.
(c) A Digital India Advisory Group headed by the Minister of Communications and IT.

Pillars of Digital India
The Government of India hopes to achieve growth on multiple fronts with the Digital India Programme. Specifically, the government aims to target nine 'Pillars of Digital India' that they identify as being:

1. Broadband Highways,
2. Universal Access to Mobile Connectivity,

3. Public Internet Access Programme,
4. e-Governance—Reforming Government through Technology,
5. e-Kranti—Electronic delivery of services,
6. Information for All,
7. Electronics Manufacturing,
8. IT for Jobs,
9. Early Harvest Programmes.

Services

Some of the facilities that are being provided through this initiative are Digital Locker, e-education, e-health, e-sign and national scholarship portal and many more as listed below.

Botnet Cleaning Centres. As the part of Digital India, the Indian Government planned to launch Botnet cleaning centres.

DigiLocker. Digital Locker facility will help citizens to:

- Digitally store their important documents like PAN card, passport, mark sheets and degree certificates,
- Provide secure access to Government issued documents,
- Provide authenticity services through Aadhaar,
- It is aimed at eliminating the use of physical documents and enables sharing of verified electronic documents across government agencies.

Digital Life Certificates. The 'Jeevan Pramaan' scheme launched by Prime Minister Narendra Modi has given a sigh of relief to millions of retired government employees. With this, the pensioner will do away with the requirement of submitting a physical life certificate in November each year and can now digitally provide proof of their existence to authorities for continuity of pension.

Attendance.gov.in. Attendance.gov.in is a website to keep a record of the attendance of Government employees on a real-time basis. This initiative started with implementation of a common Biometric Attendance System (BAS) in the central government offices located in Delhi.

Digital Boost to MGNREGA. Another commendable initiative is the digital boost to the flagship rural job scheme MNREGA. A total of 35,000 gram panchayats are covered to ensure better implementation through a mobile monitoring system. This initiative will help the implementation agencies with live data from the worksites, an online and real-time updating of database, real-time visibility of the data for complete transparency and location of assets with geo-tagging for easy verification.

MyGov.in. MyGov.in is a platform to share inputs and ideas on matters of policy and governance. It is a platform for citizen engagement in governance, through a "Discuss," "Do" and "Disseminate" approach.

Twitter Samvad. Amongst the most popular initiatives is the Twitter Samvad which will enable citizens to be the first to know about new government initiatives and actions. It is a service that lets leaders and government agencies communicate with the people through tweets and SMS.

SBM Mobile App. Swachh Bharat Mission (SBM) Mobile app is being used by people and Government organisations for achieving the goals of Swachh Bharat Mission.

Madad (Help). Launched by the External Affairs Minister, the portal 'Madad' will enable Indian citizens living abroad to file consular grievances online to address them promptly. The initiative will speed up forwarding and handling of complaints, improve tracking and redressal and escalate unresolved cases.

e-Sign framework. E-Sign framework allows citizens to digitally sign a document online using Aadhaar authentication.

SMS-Based Cyclone Warning System. As part of the Digital India initiative, this program is to create an SMS-based weather information and disaster alert system. Information on warnings will be disseminated to officials involved in administration, district magistrates/collectors besides fishermen, farmers, and the general public.

Online Registration System (ORS). The e-Hospital application provides important services such as online registration, payment of fees and appointment, online diagnostic reports, enquiring availability of blood online, etc. Example AIMS have started OPD services through e-health.

National Scholarships Portal. National Scholarship Portal is a one-stop solution for end-to-end scholarship process right from submission of student application, verification, sanction and disbursal to end beneficiary for all the scholarships provided by the Government of India.

e-Money. The Department of Posts (DoP) has planned to provide electronic money order service to 70 per cent of its total post offices by December. According to officials, this service will enable India Post to remit money next day to the doorstep that earlier took about a week. Also, it will make the whole process secure and fast. People can send a maximum of Rs. 5,000 through e-money order. With this, the department has seen a tremendous growth in commission from money order service to about Rs. 600 crore in 2014-15, up from Rs. 481.6 crore in 2011-12.

Online Facility for Firms to File Single Return. In an effort to ease the complexities of doing business and reduce cost, the Labour Ministry launched an online facility for firms to file a common return on its portal to comply with as many as eight labour laws at one go. With this, companies can now file a single unified return which will reduce the cost of business transactions.

Online Facility to Issue PAN Card in 48 hours. An online facility under which a PAN card will be issued within 48 hours of applying. Under this initiative, special camps will be organized throughout the country including rural areas to help people get PAN cards.

PRAGATI (Pro-active Government and Timely Implementation). It is an interactive platform launched by Prime Minister Narendra Modi for public grievances redressal. It is aimed at monitoring and reviewing programs and projects of the Government of India as well as state government initiatives and also addressing the common man's grievances. This step is expected to make governance in India more efficient and responsive.

Projected Impact of Digital India
- By 2019 Broadband in 250,000 villages,
- Universal phone connectivity,

- Net Zero Imports by 2020,
- 400,000 Public Internet Access Points,
- Wi-Fi in 250,000 schools, all universities,
- Public Wi-Fi hotspots for citizens Digital Inclusion,
- 17 million youth trained for IT, Telecom and Electronics jobs,
- Job creation: Direct 17 million, and indirect at least 850 million,
- E-Governance and e-Services. India to be leader in providing e-Services across Government, Agriculture, Industry, Health, Education, Transportation, etc.,
- Create 28,000 Business Process Outsourcing (BPO) seats in various States,
- Set up at least one Common Service Centre in each of the gram panchayats in the state,
- Digital Literacy Mission will cover sixty million rural households,
- Connect 550 farmer markets in the country through the use of technology.

National Optical Fibre Network—NOFN (Bharat Net)

The NOFN will provide nationwide broadband connectivity in the form of "Information Highways" which will help move ideas, information, services, economic transactions and social interactions and have become the carriers and catalysts of development. Broadband connectivity will carry vital content —education, health services, market intelligence, agricultural information, etc.—that can transform communities.

NOFN proposes seven lakh kilometres (700,000) of optical fibre to be laid to connect 250,000 gram panchayats in three years. It will connect to one million kilometres of optical fibre laid under the State Wide Area Networks (SWAN). Public Wi-Fi spots will be provided around the clusters after that and all villages will be provided with internet connectivity. The NOFN project is estimated to cost about Rs. 20,000 crore (3.5 billion US dollars).

Smart Cities Mission

- The Smart Cities Mission is an urban renewal and retro-fitting program by the Government of India to develop 100 cities all over

the country making them citizen-friendly and sustainable.
- The Union Ministry of Urban Development is responsible for implementing the mission in collaboration with the state governments of the respective cities.
- The Government of India has a vision of developing 100 smart cities as satellite towns of larger cities and by modernizing the existing mid-sized cities.

While each city will have its own plan, large-scale application of ICT would be an essential and common feature. This would be in the areas of security, water, energy, garbage, infrastructure and environment management; extension of citizen-based services like education, banking, health, entertainment, transportation; practically everything. Twenty cities have been selected for the current year through a very transparent and detailed selection criterion. In the next two years, 40 cities would be taken up each year. Thirteen more cities were added a few days ago due to pressing demand from States.

The financial outlay is Rs. 48,000 crore (8 billion US dollars) over the next three years from the central budget and a similar amount from the states. To start with, each selected city will get Rs. 200 crore in the first year and Rs. 100 crore for the next three years.

AADHAAR Project

Aadhaar is a 12-digit individual identification number issued by the Unique Identification Authority of India (UIDAI) on behalf of the Government of India. This number will serve as proof of identity and address anywhere in India. Any individual, irrespective of age and gender, who is a resident in India and satisfies the verification process laid down by the UIDAI can enrol for Aadhaar. Each individual needs to enrol only once, which is free of cost. Each Aadhaar number will be unique to an individual and will remain valid for life. The Aadhaar number will help provide access to services like banking, mobile phone connections and other government and non-government services in due course.

Aadhaar is:

- Easily verifiable in an online, cost-effective way,
- Unique and robust enough to eliminate the large number of duplicate and fake identities in government and private databases,
- A random number generated, devoid of any classification based on caste, creed, religion and geography.

As of 30 April 2016, 100.9 crore (1,009 million) Aadhaar numbers have been issued in the project. It is the biggest such project in the world. Expenditure was one billion dollars up to January 2016. Aadhaar numbers are linked for:

- Direct bank transfer of subsidies,
- Opening of bank accounts and other Government schemes for uplifting the poor,
- SIM cards,
- Enrolment of all prisoners,
- With matrimonial advertisement for profiling of men,
- With voter identification system.

In LPG distribution alone, the Government detected 3.73 crore (37.3 million) bogus connections and thus saved Rs. 21,000 crore (3.5 billion US dollars) in subsidies in the last two years. Another Rs. 15,000 crore (2.5 billion US dollars) have been saved due to the discovery of 1.5 crore bogus ration cards due to digitization and link up with Aadhaar.

Prime Minister's Jan Dhan Yojana (PMJDY)

Another massive and the biggest scheme in the world (Guinness Book of World Records) to empower the citizens provides for Direct Transfer of Subsidies and cuts out corruption by middle men and provide life insurance:

- Accounts opened till 4 May 2016—217 million,
- Debit cards issued—180 million,
- Cards linked with Aadhaar—98 million,
- Balance in accounts—6.5 billion US dollars.

SAY and ASMITA

The Human Resources Development (HRD) Ministry is set to launch a programme next month that would probably be the world's largest student tracking system. The Shala Asmita Yojana (SAY) aims to track the educational journey of close to 25 crore (250 million) school students from Class I to Class XII across 15 lakh schools in the country. In other words, this online database will carry information about student attendance and enrolment, mid-day meal service, learning outcomes and infrastructure facilities, among other things, on one platform for both private and government schools. 'Asmita' stands for All School Monitoring Individual Tracing Analysis.

The Government will track students through their Aadhaar numbers. According to official estimates, almost 65 per cent of school students in the age group of 5 to 18 years have Aadhaar numbers. Those who do not will be given a unique identity number for tracking.

Some Other Major ICT Projects

- Crime and Criminal Tracking Network and System (CCTNS),
- National Land Record Modernisation Programme (NLRMP),
- MCA 21; e-Governance initiative of Ministry of Company Affairs for easy and secure access to services,
- National Intelligence Grid (NATGRID).

This article gives a glimpse of India's ongoing transformation through deployment and exploitation of ICTs, ICT infrastructure and introduced some of the major ICT projects under way for national development and empowerment of citizens. India is in the process of creating a world class information infrastructure and provide citizen-centric services at the door step. There are many more projects under implementation at the national, state and ministry/department levels. The Railways alone has 61 major ICT projects under implementation.

India is thus sitting at the cusp of a big digital revolution and hopes to become a very powerful digitally connected nation by 2020.

(Lt. Gen Davinder Kumar is a former Signals Officer-in-Chief of the Indian Army. Later, he served as the CEO & Managing Director of Tata Advanced Systems Ltd. He is a Distinguished Fellow at the VIF)

*

Contemporary: China

8

CONSECRATION OF CHINA'S 'NEW PERIOD' PEOPLE'S LIBERATION ARMY

Gautam Banerjee

> "The structure of troops will be optimised to improve the quality and efficiency of the army. A 'revolution' of the management of the military will be rolled out with modern management techniques so that the army is managed professionally. Decision-making, enforcement and supervision powers should be separated and distributed in a manner that ensures they serve as checks and balances on each other but also run in parallel."
>
> —*Xi Jinping, November, 2015.*

A Home Run of Military Modernisation

At the dawn of 2016, the People's Republic of China (PRC) officially promulgated the commencement of the final phase of restructuring of its apex setup for management of national defence as well as its highest organisation for the exercise of military command and control over its 2.3 million-strong People's Liberation Army (PLA). Thus commenced the 'home run' of military modernisation—a landmark endeavour that had commenced in the early 1980s at the instance of Deng Xiaoping.

Wisely listed at the final ladder of the 'Four Modernisations' and commenced after the modernisation of the other three foundations of national power had made some headway, the process of modernisation of the PLA, as expected in any such super-venture, had to negotiate through much resistance, disputes and debates over the past three decades or so before finding principle acceptance in 2011. It was finally brought to the concluding phase by the end of 2015 with typical Chinese strategic foresight and professional perseverance, the entire progression having been much reported and discussed over time. Even then, the purpose of comprehensive understanding of the recent promulgation of defence reforms and apex level restructuring of the PLA's command and control may be better served by delving deeper into the determinants which shaped it.

Tradition of Political Initiatives

Right from imperialist times, military restructuring, always done at political behest, has been a regular process in China, as exemplified by its evolutionary forms of 'Banner', 'Green Standard', 'Beiyang', 'Peasant', 'Route', 'National' and 'Peoples' armies. In modern times of Western military dominance, the Qing modernisation of the 1860s, which oriented China's military establishment towards modern technology, was a noteworthy event indeed. Thereafter, such operational upgrades and force restructures have invariably followed all major changes in China's governing system—for example, in 1906, 1917, 1936 and after the Communist takeover in 1949. In 1970, Lin Biao had proposed a comprehensive range of organisational upgrades and rationalisation of manpower to rid the PLA of the ills effects of the 'Cultural Revolution'; this led to differences with Mao Zedong and his eventual assassination. By the mid-1970s, the modernist ideologue, Deng Xiaoping, had been sent to the doghouse and Zhou Enlai, the most balanced leader, had died. These setbacks put paid to the idea of military modernisation, much to the relief of the old crop of Communist Party of China (CPC) honchos and PLA Generals whose grip over power-and-pelf was better maintained by the continuation of the status quo.

PLA's First Phase Modernisation

In 1979, having had to stretch to its limits to finally get the better of Vietnamese resistance, the PLA was shaken enough to revive the call for modernisation; Mao's absence from the scene and re-emergence of Deng helped. The cause, however, could not make much headway against the entrenched Party-PLA cabal, opposed as they were to the restructuring of the PLA through manpower reduction, professional military training and induction of latest weapons and equipment as these could only be at the cost of rhetorical communist education, vested avenues of patronage and benefits accruing out of commercial ventures. These ventures had come up during the 'Great Leap Forward' (it actually turned out to be a bloody 'leap into disaster') when it was expected to raise its own resources through farming and other trades, and went on to form the PLA's own 'empire'. Subsequently, that empire got further strengthened when the PLA, being the only organisation capable of doing so, had to be called upon to undertake construction, engineering and social development schemes in remote and backward areas. Thus, over the years, the PLA's traditional clout helped it build up its industrial and business assets, and with it, vast cadres of non-military and quasi-military ranks and file, the numbers of which nearly equalled the combat troops. With passage of time, the extraordinary authority that the PLA wielded over societal affairs gradually turned this empire, much contrary to the pristine military ethos, into a refuge for bloated manpower, obsolete technology, inefficiency, nepotism, financial losses and corrupt practices. Having tasted that authority, the old guard was loathe to be denied that in the name of turning the romanticised 'people's army' into some unknown, compact, high-technology force.

Thus, while the tug-of-war on such contentious issues continued amongst the modernist and orthodox factions, schemes directed at modernisation of unit level capabilities in terms of weapons, equipment and communications could still proceed. In the same vein, modern battle procedures in 'battalion group' configurations could be evolved, which, in the mid-2000s, eventually led to the realisation of the 'modular' structure for integrated all-arm operations. In so adapting, the PLA's professionally focused hierarchy, while remaining stoic against larger resistance, proceeded to prepare grounds for future modernisation of the higher echelons of its war machine.

Towards Conceptual and Structural Modernisation

The resistance to more substantial changes at higher levels was finally overcome when witnessing the revolutionary military capabilities of the

American-led coalition forces during Gulf War-I, a chastised Chinese leadership could no more overlook the obsolescence of the PLA's theories and structures in terms of modern warfare. Besides, the situation had now undergone a change. The PRC was economically and institutionally strong as never before, and by relieving the PLA of the non-military burdens of a 'people's army', it was now quite capable of restructuring it according to the tenets of the 'Revolution in Military Affairs' (RMA)—with 'Chinese Characteristics', of course. The proviso was that, firstly, the excessive manpower, non-military ventures and corrupt practices had to be cut out to consolidate into a combat force that was capable of being modernised, and secondly, the heaviest stumbling block against modernisation, the CPC-PLA cabal, had to be reined in. The PLA hierarchy also realised that to bring about a RMA, it was imperative to invest in modern air and naval forces which could not only cover the trimming of manpower of the dated and sluggish ground forces, but could go further to elevate PLA's overall combat capability.

The stage was thus set to wean the PLA away from its ineffective military and non-military burdens. But this had to be done in a graduated manner so as to protect the stakeholders' interests. Vast cadres of redundant quasi and non-combatant employees could thus be gradually re-assigned to civil sectors, and finally, the stagnant military organisations converted into 'People's Armed Police Force' (PAPF) and various other construction and industrial agencies. Time was also required to build up a modern military industry by various overt and covert means, and equip the forces with modern military wherewithal.

The period of the late-1990s and mid-2000s therefore saw the PLA, while continuing with unit-level modernisation, elevating itself to the next stage to restructure its field formations. Assimilation of the concept of *'Integrated Joint Warfare'* (IJW) under *'Conditions of Informationisation with Chinese Characteristics'* to prosecute *'Localised War'* in what is termed as the *'New Period'* was the thrust area during this period. The concept of *'Integrated Logistic System'* was also developed and applied at the 'Unified' tri-service level, thus bringing much efficiency in sustenance of remote military deployments.

Finally, under the third stage of modernisation, the PLA's role, charter, structure and geographical areas of responsibilities at the theatre level were redefined. The notable features of this initiative were the consolidation of 11 Military Regions (MR) into seven Military Area Commands (MAC), conversion of army-intensive formations and theatre command headquarters into joint tri-service composition, and creation of distinct air force and naval hierarchies. Lack of experienced joint warfare commanders and staff was answered at this stage by the creation of a 'War Zone Command' which would be implanted, when needed, on the warring MAC to take over the conduct of IJW. Simultaneously, larger numbers of selected officers trained hard to imbibe the expertise of joint warfare. This was also the period when the upgrade of field formations from regimental to brigade configurations and integration of single-service 'Group Armies' into joint-services 'Combined Corps' found fruition. Meanwhile, as many as four lakh of the bloated manpower had been reassigned and transfer of most of the unnecessary industrial ventures affected.

Communism versus Generalship

But just as 'RMA with Chinese Characteristics' was being applied to the PLA's modernisation, there was much debate, even acrimony, over the supremacy or otherwise of communist ideology over professional excellence. While the traditional school argued that the fervour of communism drove the soldiery to greater achievements, the modernist school pointed out that rather than the robotic hoards, modern war needed highly trained and fully skilled soldiers, and therefore, communist education and party work could not supersede full time military training and skill development. In the interest of effective modernisation, the CPC endorsed the latter point of view and thus emerged a crop of highly professional military leaders who did not have to display their communist affiliations. Much to the chagrin of the hard core communist generals and the PLA's Political Commissariat, these officers concentrated on building a *'New Period'* PLA in which the PLA Army (PLAA), PLA Air Force (PLAAF) and PLA Navy (PLAN) integrated into the IJW mode to prosecute *'Active Defence'* under, as mentioned earlier, *'Conditions of Informationisation with Chinese Characteristics'* in any of the *'Localised'* theatres of war.

By 2008 or so, necessitated by the arrogation of controlling leverage into the grip of professional military brass, there had to be one more correction to the power equation in the CPC. The supremacy of the CPC over the PLA had to be reiterated by, firstly, making it obligatory for the pure professionals to commit to party loyalty if not pure communist ideology, and secondly, rewarding their professional positions with due weightage as compared to that of the communist ideologues. Party loyalty, implicit obedience of the Chairman of the CPC and the Central Military Commission (CMC), and probity in conduct were thus reinstated as the prime qualities of higher military leadership.

By 2011, modernisation at unit, formation and theatre levels was well underway. Nearly 20 per cent of the forces had been modernised and brisk progress was being made to cover the entire 'teeth' elements of the PLA. It was time to prepare for the final stage, that of subsuming the PLA's apex military decision-making body into the CMC and so customising it to conform to the unequivocal supremacy of the CPC. This indeed was the purpose as enunciated in the PLA's declaration of 'Grand Mobilisation, Liberation and Thorough Clean Up of Military Ideology'.

PLA's Apex Controlling Body

To understand the underlying principles of the restructure of China's apex military decision-making body, a brief look at its structure and function so far would be in order.

This is a system wherein the CPC controls the entire gamut of national endeavours, leaving the Government of the PRC to implement the principles and policies enunciated by it. This arrangement is rendered workable by having both the bodies replicating, more or less, a common hierarchical structure as well as the membership. More importantly, the military establishment is but an intrinsic, subordinate organ of the CPC and its personnel are its committed members, formally or otherwise. This system therefore keeps the military leadership beholden to the Party's control while participating in the entire system of the PRC's governance. As usual, there are agreements and differences between the two in which opinions and alignments are regularly forged across the lines.

From the time the thrust on modernisation commenced in the early 1980s, the apex controlling body of the PLA, that is above the seven MACs, consisted of two tiers. At the top tier was the 10-member CMC, two of them Vice-Chairmen and all of them Party-PLA leaders, with the General Secretary of the CPC and the President of the PRC being concurrently appointed as its Chairman. This is a trend mostly followed in the Chinese system as it helps establish a singular head to lead China under the guidance and assistance from a select group of all-powerful Party loyalists. The CMC exercised political control over the PLA, and to that purpose, maintained the Party's grip over the military establishment by preserving to itself the matters related to law, discipline, inspection, military diplomacy and audit.

So far, at the second tier, the PLA General Headquarters (GHQ) controlled the purely military matters through its four 'Departments', namely, the General Staff, General Political, General Logistic and General Armament Departments. The General Staff Department, which controlled all operational matters, was more or less a PLAA-centric headquarters with PLAAF, PLAN, Second Artillery and People's Armed Police Force (PAPF) hierarchies embedded in it. Tasking of the Second Artillery, the nuclear and missile force, was however controlled directly by the CMC while the PAPF's budget as well as its peacetime employment was controlled by the Ministry of Public Security. The General Political Department handled, through its Political Commissariat embedded in all echelons, the political aspect of the military establishment such as communist education, motivation and welfare of personnel and maintenance of Party influence over what is principally a Party's armed organ. The General Logistic Department attended to the Integrated Logistic System and the General Armament Department was in control of research, development, production and procurement of military hardware including that for the nuclear and missile forces. Of course, there had been many need-based modifications incorporated into the Department from time to time.

CPC Politburo

Obviously, the first was the preserve of hard-core military professionals, the second was a set up of Party dedicated military officials, the third was the domain of military and civil logisticians and the last department was the preserve of scientists, military and civilian technocrats and military industrial establishments. A similar structure existed at the MAC level too. Since the 1990s, the pursuit of comprehensive military modernisation had ratcheted up the clout of the General Staff Department which had come to dominate the entire set up, somewhat to the discomfiture of the Political Commissariat.

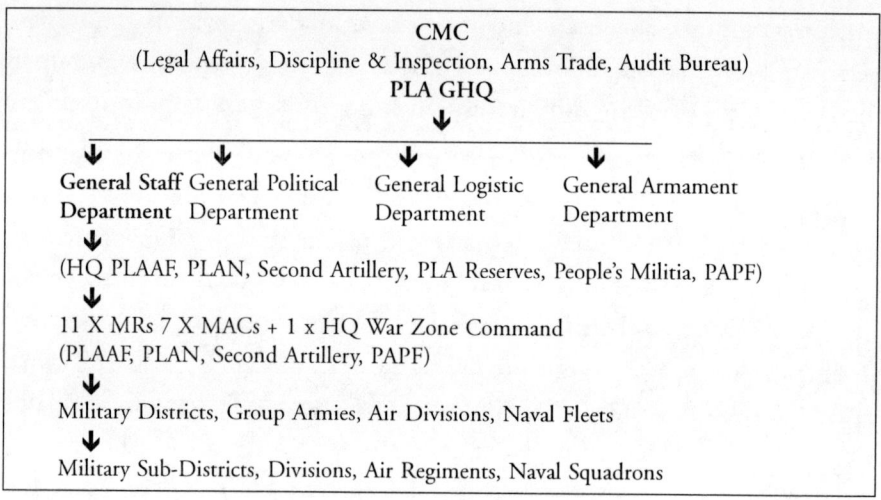

Figure 1: PLA's Apex Hierarchy Till 2015

In short, the CMC as well as the PLA GHQ had been PLAA-centric in composition and control while the other Services functioned as its branches. However, as discussed above, gradually over the past decade or so, the PLAAF and PLAN hierarchies have been upgraded and inducted into the CMC membership and all lower echelons of the PLA's chain of command. Similarly, over the years, many new 'offices' had been added to the PLA GHQ to cater to the staff work associated with the modern features of warfare, such as nuclear, information, cyber, space and media warfare. In the overall context, the effort had so far been directed at fostering a higher level of service-specific professionalism at the one end, and upgrade of the other Services to equal partnership in tri-service joint-ness at the other.

Final Phase of Modernisation

Having made satisfactory headway through incremental additions and modifications in a manner that operational equilibrium is not upset during the transition period, in 2011, the PLA's two-tier apex command and control structure was ready for formal switchover to a designated Joint-Services model with Chinese characteristics, so to say. As mentioned earlier, the ball was set rolling through the formal enunciation of a policy statement titled 'Grand Mobilisation, Liberation and Thorough Clean Up of Military Ideology.' Thus commenced, over the next four years, a series of systematic assimilation of the new 'Offices' that had been added to the PLA GHQ and conditioning the higher commanders and staff to the operationalisation of a 'New Period' PLA.

In 2014, according to the final agenda of the China's military modernisation, a 'Leading Group for Reforms' was constituted to implement the intended restructure of the two-tier command and control system. Hundreds of serving and retired professionals were drafted to organise hundreds of debates, brainstorming and experimentation in military bases across the country before the restructure was certified for implementation. Finally, through the issuance of a formal executive order from the office of the President of the PRC-General Secretary of the CPC-Chairman of the CMC in December 2015 in the form of 'Guidelines on National Defence and Military Reforms', the PLA GHQ was subsumed into the CMC, and the apex command and control structure of the PLA, which was under experimentation and training since 2011, finally inaugurated. Even then, to prevent loss of organisational control and balance, 'transitional work offices' have been given time till 2020 to settle the systemic changeover. Five years have thus been earmarked for the officials to gain more executive experience, formalise the rules of business and office procedures, make necessary adjustments and finally settle down to a *'seamless system in which the CMC takes charge of the overall administration of the PLA, the PAPF and the People's Militia and Reserve Forces, Battle Zone Commands focus on combat preparedness, and various military services pursue development'*.

The reformed structure of PLA's apex level management is now a one-tier configuration that encompasses all aspects of military expertise, Party control, science and technology, defence industry, military diplomacy and military as well as Party discipline—all to be directly controlled by the CMC. The four Departments of the erstwhile PLA GHQ are now subsumed into the CMC which is made up of seven 'Departments', three 'Commissions' and five 'Offices' as shown below.

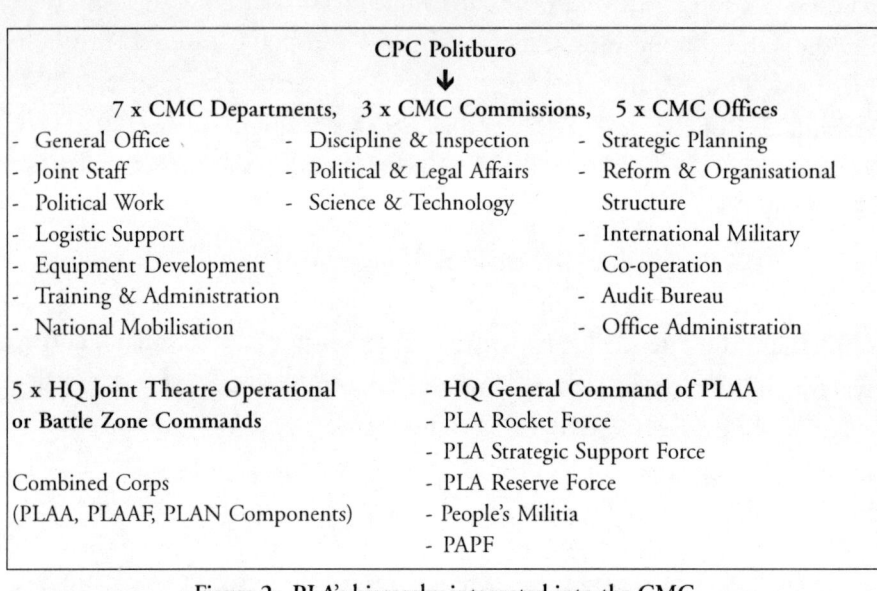

Figure 2: PLA's hierarchy integrated into the CMC

Organisational Control of the Reconstructed CMC

Drawing inferences from the PLA's organisational culture, published reports of Chinese origin and the fundamentals of military principles and practices, the notable features of the reconstructed CMC may be summarised as follows:

(a) As stated earlier, in an astute display of deep military insight, the CMC had already introduced, in quantums over the past five years or so, most of the changes either in full or in skeleton form, to be functionally operative on an experimental basis and for training. In fact, over these years, the CMC had been gradually integrating the functions of the PLA GHQ and its four departments into its fold.

(b) The all-powerful and PLAA-predominant General Staff Department of the PLA GHQ has been converted into a 'CMC Joint Staff Department' dedicated to joint, tri-service operational policy-making and control. Its diverse functions like military training, trials, administration and mobilisation have been separated into full-fledged and specifically chartered CMC departments, all in tri-service mode.

(c) The General Political Department of the PLA GHQ has been reconstructed into the 'CMC Political Work Department'. The change possibly conforms to the policy of making command and commissariat appointments somewhat interchangeable and so assuage the ever-contentious relationship between military commanders and their *bête noire*, the political commissars. Generally in the past, the latter used to be Party fundamentalists in uniform who arrogated higher authority, but with the commencement of the process of modernisation, these had been upstaged by the professional military officer corps. The change is expected to balance the equation, with a tilt towards military professionals with Party affiliation.

(d) The 'CMC Logistic Support' and 'CMC Equipment Development' departments are respectively restructured versions of the General Logistic and General Armament Departments of the erstwhile PLA GHQ. Civil-military integration in both the Departments is expected to improve management of military land, infrastructure and supply chain in the first named and brisk upgrade of military hardware in the second.

(e) The three 'CMC Commissions' are Party-predominant oversight mechanisms to nurture the PLA's Party-dedication and moral as well as legal probity among the military fraternity. Together, the 'CMC Discipline & Inspection Commission' and 'CMC Political & Legal Affairs Commission' are also charged with bringing about reforms in military wages, housing, insurance, military justice, inspection, discipline and post-retirement welfare of the soldiery. Most significantly, in line with the PLA's thrust area, it also provides for an unencumbered preserve for the development of the PLA's scientific temper.

(f) The five 'CMC Offices' are the military-diplomatic think-tanks charged with strategic innovations, monitoring the implementation of reforms and modernisation schemes and military diplomacy. Creation of these 'Offices' indicates the seriousness that the Chinese accord to political articulation of military power. Besides, of course, there are the Offices to audit and administer the house.

Indeed, catering to a major concern in the CPC hierarchy, the restructure brings about an intimate degree of integration among military professionals, Party loyalists and civilian experts. Notably, even if subscribing to the exercise of command and control through joint headquarters, the executive organs are retained in single service, single branch configuration, as it must be in the interest of nurturing domain skill and experience. The reform also aims at manpower right-sizing from 2.3 million to 2 million that would facilitate the PLA's recuse from non-military functions and orient its focus on force-modernisation.

Command Functions of the Restructured CMC

Having combined the 10-member CMC and four Departments of the PLA GHQ, the top two tiers of PLA's operational control and administration are now merged into just one reconstituted CMC made up of a total of 15 Departments, Commissions and Offices. Apart from exercising apex-level control over all operational and administrative aspects of the PLA, in its new form the CMC also exercises direct command over certain organisations, as described below:

(a) Notwithstanding the switch to tri-service joint-ness, a dedicated headquarters to administer the PLAA is still needed because of its huge combat and non-combat establishments, vast scope for manpower reassignment, smooth transfer of its industrial ventures and the need to oversee the extensive range of modernisation schemes. To this purpose, a 'HQ General Command of PLAA' has been created out of the erstwhile PLA GHQ to function under the direct command of the CMC.

(b) The PLA Second Artillery, China's nuclear and conventional missile force, earlier had only its action switch in the CMC's control. Presently, under a new nomenclature of 'PLA Rocket Force' (PLARF), it has been fully brought under the direct control of the CMC. The implications are, one, there is no intermediate headquarters to go through in seeking its employment, and two, freed from generalist obtrusions, the specialist force would find autonomy in its evolution.

(c) Between the General Staff and Armament Departments of the erstwhile PLA GHQ and many of the civilian-faced science and technology organisations, development of China's nuclear and conventional missile forces had so far been a multiple-department effort. Besides, elements dedicated to information, space, cyber, psychology and media warfare had been added to the PLA GHQ from time to time. The experience gained thus has permitted the consolidation of the entire set up into one 'PLA Strategic Support Force' (PLASSF) which, functioning under the direct command of the CMC, is mandated to undertake conjoined operationalisation of all aspects of the information age war at strategic as well as tactical levels. Under a shorter and direct command, control and administrative hierarchy, the PLASSF is expected to synergise all the above-mentioned kinetic and non-kinetic modes of warfare in support of the PLA's overall strategy.

(d) The restructure has also brought the 'PLA Reserve Force' and the 'People's Militia' under the direct command of the CMC. Under the reforms, the loosely structured Reserve Force is to be streamlined into designated units, while ridding the Militia of non-effective camp followers and trimming its number down to half a million. These steps are aimed at better preparation and response of the Reserve Forces, regulation of the control of local Party offices over the Militia, and significantly improving welfare measures for ex-servicemen.

(e) Due to rising challenges against preservation of internal security, the PRC has had to strengthen its armed police organisation. The

PAPF is thus revamped from being an appendage to the sectoral PLA formations into a distinct force with its dedicated hierarchy, largely ex-military manpower and light hardware transferred to it from PLA surpluses. Presently, in its armed, anti-rebellion functions, the PAPF has been brought under the direct control of the CMC, while its peacetime administration and control remains in the hands of the Ministry of Public Security. At the field level, however, the PAPF is under the functional control of the PLA.

HQ Joint Theatre Operational or Battle Zone Commands

As for the PRC's combat forces, the seven MACs are restructured into five 'Battle Zone Commands' (BZC) without any change in the location or tasking of subordinate formations like the Combined Corps, the Group Armies and the corresponding PLAAF and PLAN elements. Thus while the areas of responsibilities for prosecuting theatre or localised war have somewhat expanded, the overall force levels and operational tasking of the field formations may not undergo any major revision.

Map 1: The PLA's New BZCs

The advantages of this restructure accrues from: one, conversion of all five theatre command headquarters into an integrated joint operational composition in place of just one centrally controlled War Zone Command; two, flexibility in intra-theatre build up and force-application; and three, thinning the establishment—most of it being reassigned into the expanded CMC, some to build up new units for the PLAAF, PLAN, PLASSF and some to the PAPF. Notably, due to expansion of the CMC, PLARF, PLASSF, etc., the overall number of top appointments remain more or less the same, and that serves the purpose of career protection.

Congruence of Strategic Orientation and Restructure

Analysis of the final phase of China's military modernisation and reforms would not be complete without a brief mention of the conceptual revolution that the PLA has adopted to turn itself into a super-power military. The thinking process had gained a quantum boost in the early-2000s but its revelations came under wider external scrutiny only after 2011 or so, when China's aggressive behaviour in the region escalated to start hurting the interests of the so far by-standing powers.

The connection between China's military concepts and practices is clear from the themes propagated through China's 'Defence White Paper' of April 2013, and the 'White Paper on Military Strategy' of May 2015. Highlights of the enunciations of these policy documents are as follows; verbatim quotes are used selectively to convey the right intent:

(a) Enunciating the concept of 'Diversified Employment of China's Armed Forces' in its Defence White Paper of 2013, the PRC tasked the PLA to secure its core objectives of sustaining 'national strength, national unification and territorial integrity.' Moreover, the PLA was also mandated to bring about 'peaceful development through integrated civilian-military effort' and to facilitate 'contribution to world peace and regional stability.' Implicit in all that was the charge of safeguarding the CPC's 'ruling position.'

(b) To that end, build-up of powerful armed forces 'in conformity to China's status' is considered imperative. The aim is to build a new type of 'lean, joint, multi-functional and informationised' military force with 'Chinese Characteristics.' The stated purpose is to 'safeguard border, contain separatist forces, ensure security of coastal and air territories, protect national maritime, outer space and cyberspace rights and interests, and prevent aggression.' The strategy adopted is to 'win local wars' by recourse to 'active defence'—a form of pre-emptive aggression to be described as 'counter-attack in self-defence'—the option of 'resolute nuclear counter-attack if China comes under nuclear threat' being in order.

Based on the parameters enunciated in the White Paper on Military Strategy of May 2015, the military objectives are sought to be achieved by the following measures:

(a) Building a 'smaller, adaptable PLAA' that is structured in 'small, multi-functional and modular units.' The objective is to 'reorient from theatre defence to trans-theatre mobility to execute precise, multi-dimensional, trans-theatre, multi-functional and sustainable operations'.

(b) Building a 'blue water' PLAN as a 'combined, multi-functional and efficient marine combat force' with capabilities for 'strategic deterrence and counterattack, maritime manoeuvres, joint operations at sea, comprehensive defence and comprehensive support', the last role apparently referring to PRC's expanding maritime initiatives. The objective is for PLAN to shift focus from the strategy of 'territorial waters defence' to that of 'joint offshore waters defence' and open seas protection.'

(c) The focus of the PLAAF from 'territorial air defence to both defence and offence', and creation of an 'air-space defence force structure' that can meet the requirements of 'informationised operations.. This objective is to be met by having a 'fully-functional air force' with 'boosted capabilities for strategic early warning, air strike, air and missile defence, information countermeasures, airborne operations, strategic projection and comprehensive support'.

(d) Commitment to the maintenance of an 'effective Missile Force' is reiterated.

(e) Lastly, enhancing the quality of national defence through 'mobilisation' and 'reserve force building' is also a part of the agenda. These steps are necessary to retain the ability to reinforce a leaner standing PLA should such a need arises. Inter alia, these steps permit rightsizing the PLA from being a manpower intensive peoples' force to an informationised one, and so make it practical to achieve military modernisation.

The above-mentioned strategies are promulgated only after the military objectives are formally crystallised through discussions, training and trials and then followed with assured progression in translating these into the PLA's modernisation. The recent restructure of the PLA's apex command and control set up is the culminating stage of that endeavour.

Concluding Observations

The modernisation of the PLA is well underway; it is estimated that about 20 per cent of it has been fully modernised to the scale of advanced capabilities, 20 per cent is under various stages of modernisation, 40 per cent maintain their still useful 1980s composition and the rest are to be gradually thinned out. Meanwhile, in July 2015, the PRC's National People's Congress passed a comprehensive 'National Security Law' covering, besides the areas of domestic interests, even the technological, military and environmental aspects related to outer space, polar regions and cyber security. This Law accords constitutional authority for the state power to deal with resistance against the CPC's policies including those related to national defence. It was therefore an appropriate juncture to implement the final and key phase of that long process of defence reforms, that is, restructuring the PLA's apex level command and control organisation.

Assimilation of the PLA GHQ into the CMC does not *per se* change the PLA's regional or territorial force-posture. That however may not comfort the hapless subjects of the PRC's military high-handedness because a modernised PLA now stands further empowered for synergised prosecution of war by a joint, Party-integrated strategic command and control mechanism.

Sustained progress over the past quarter of a century of military modernisation in due consonance with the development of new strategies illustrates the traditional Chinese wisdom of nurturing her military institution, and so deriving political dividends in good measure. Further, promulgation of strategic policies and translation of such policies through comprehensive modernisation of the PLA's force-structure as well as the restructure of its apex level command and control mechanism is a quantum lead in effective empowerment of the PLA.

To wit, China's official stance enunciated that, *"China must have a strong military...China doesn't need to worry about military aggression. But there is more about national security.... With a strong army, China can be more politically appealing, influential and persuasive, and will make it easier to network....As we gain more trust from other countries, many of them will no longer be dependent on the US for security and on China for economic benefits.... our military strength has to be demonstrated to the world.... The army needs to be able to fight battles and provide real deterrence.... The supreme art of war is to subdue the enemy without fighting."*

China's neighbours may take due cognisance.

(Lieutenant General (Retd) Gautam Banerjee, PVSM, AVSM, YSM, is a former Chief of Staff, Central Command and a former Commandant of the Officers' Training Academy, Chennai. He is now the Editor and Senior Fellow at the VIF)

*

Contemporary: Pakistan

9

MISSING FACTORS IN INDIA'S POLICY TOWARDS PAKISTAN

Tilak Devasher

Many in India often wonder why we do not have better relations with Pakistan and how long will we keep on bickering and fighting. Many also point to the perils of a miscalculation given that the two countries are nuclear weapon states. The most famous articulation has, of course, been that the bilateral dialogue should be 'uninterrupted and uninterruptible.'

For the last 70 years, every political government in India has tried to engage with Pakistan to develop a policy that would enable us to live as normal neighbours; some of our finest diplomats have spent their careers in implementing such policies; there have been hundreds of back-channel discussions—Track 1.5, Track 2, Track 3 and so on. All such efforts have mostly come to naught. Today, 70 years after India was partitioned, we are still where we were with Pakistan even as the world around us has changed fundamentally. This must compel us to ask a basic question—what is the missing element in our policy formulation and practice that has resulted repeatedly in a one-step forward-two-steps-backward relationship with Pakistan.

We have possibly ignored one key element on a long-term basis in our approach towards Pakistan. That is whether a positive relationship with India fits into Pakistan's ideological and security narrative based on its perception of India. Pakistan's perception of India has four components:

(i) Issue of Identity—How Pakistan uses anti-India sentiments to cement its national identity.
(ii) Claim for Parity—Why and how Pakistan seeks parity with India.
(iii) The Kashmir Fixation—How and why the quest for a solution on Kashmir is so inflexible.
(iv) The Pakistani Mindset—How the peculiar mindset developed towards India adversely impacts Indo-Pak relations.

Issue of Identity

Identity was and remains a critical issue in Pakistan for at least two reasons. First, the geographical areas that came to constitute Pakistan in the east and the west had never existed earlier as a single country. Second, as the newspaper *Dawn* stated as late as in 2000: 'Since its inception Pakistan has faced the monumental task to spell out an identity different from the Indian identity. Born from the division of the old civilization of India, Pakistan has struggled for constructing its own, a culture which will not only be different from the Indian culture but that the whole world would acknowledge.' Thus creating a Pakistani identity required erasing any 'Indian-ness' within Pakistan. As Aparna Pande notes, 'Denying the Indian-ness of Pakistan's identity meant emphasizing the 'Hindu-ness of India and reinforcing the 'Islamic' nature of Pakistan'. However, into the seventh decade of its creation, Pakistan has yet not been able to establish an overarching 'Pakistani identity'. Created in the name of Islam, its leaders were to find that Islam was not an effective glue in either defining a common Pakistani identity or in keeping the country together as it was in creating one. As a result, the alienation of different ethnic groups, despite being Muslims, continues to be a persistent phenomenon in Pakistan.

At its creation, Pakistan inherited four provinces in the west (Balochistan, North West Frontier Province or NWFP, Punjab and Sindh), and one in the east. East Pakistan was the most homogeneous province, ethnically and linguistically. In the west, however, there was considerable ethnic and linguistic diversity. The conundrum that faced Jinnah and all his successors was that these geographical areas that came to constitute Pakistan shared only a common religion and little else. There was no common history, culture, language or ethnicity. The challenge for the new state was to weld these disparate ethno-linguistic identities into one Pakistani identity. Jinnah's two-nation theory that was the basis for Pakistan claimed that the Muslims of the Indian subcontinent constituted a separate 'nation' which bore a distinct and potentially sovereign political identity and that religion could bind diverse ethno-linguistic identities. The shaping of a Pakistani identity thus became hinged on Islam. Maulana Azad, incidentally, had pointed out the fallacy of such an argument saying that Jinnah's thesis of religion forming the basis of a state had no sanction in the Koran.

Prof. Waheeduz-Zaman graphically enumerated Pakistan's identity dilemma in these words: "...If we let go the ideology of Islam, we cannot hold together as a nation by any other means. If the Arabs, the Turks, or the Iranians give up Islam, the Arabs yet remain Arabs, the Turks remain Turks, the Iranians remain Iranians, but what do we remain if we give up Islam?" A rhetorical answer was given in 1980: 'If we are not Muslims, what are we? Second rate Indians?' Wali Khan perhaps best exemplified the identity dilemma when he said, "I have been a Pakhtun for thousands of years, a Muslim for 1300 and a Pakistani for just over 40."

The moot question is why, despite the passage of almost seven decades, Pakistan has not been able to develop an overarching national identity. There is no easy answer. In my view, leaving aside the theological argument that was put forward by Maulana Azad, the forging of a unique religion-based Pakistani identity was problematic because it had to be forged in a geographical area that had historical states with significant linguistic, cultural and ethnic diversities. Here people instinctively thought of themselves as Bengalis, Sindhis, Baloch, Pakhtuns or Seraikis rather than as Pakistanis. These areas were pre-dominantly Muslim so Islam or an Islamic way of life was never in danger there. It was not Islam that kept them united but their linguistic, cultural and historic bonds. Islam could not supplant these bonds in the same manner that it could in the Muslim-minority provinces of British India. In these provinces, especially in north India, the fear was that under representative government, where numbers mattered, the Hindu majority would swamp them. Thus, due to their minority status, the Islamic identity in the Muslim minority provinces of British India was very salient.

Unlike India that accepted the principle of 'unity in diversity,' Pakistan, by largely ignoring the diversity of its people, tried to superimpose a common Islam-based Pakistani identity on the dominant ethno-linguistic identity. This led to the breakaway of East Pakistan to become Bangladesh and bruising insurgencies in Balochistan, the fight for which is continuing today. The situation in Khyber Pakhtunkhwa (KP), Sindh and in Punjab itself is festering and could explode for differing reasons. Failure to acknowledge ethnic diversity in the elusive quest of a national identity was a challenge in 1947. It remains a challenge even after seventy years.

Given the failure to create a national identity by any other means, Pakistan has resorted to the tactic of raising the threat from India—that India would undo partition—as the cement to bind the multiple identities of Pakistan. While this can hardly be the basis of a sustainable national identity, it has implications for Indo-Pak relations. In fact, as soon as India became the negative reference point for defining Pakistani nationalism, there was no way Pakistan could develop a new and positive identity for itself, or develop normal relations with India. It meant that Pakistan would need a 'Hindu' India constantly as an essential reference point for its *raison d'être* and its national identity would continue to be a negative, anti-India narrative.

India, therefore, needs to factor in this element in its approach towards Pakistan that for the Pakistani leadership, especially military, the projection of a hostile India is the *sine qua non* of their own tenuous identity. Without such negative projection of India, there is danger of losing their identity. Thus, normalization of relations with India, let alone friendship, would demolish the carefully crafted and nurtured nationalist narrative since 1947 and erode their sense of self.

Claim for Parity

Identity apart, a crucial element of Pakistan's attitude and policy towards India hinges on one factor: the desire for parity—military, political and regional parity. It is this obsessive and fixated yet elusive search for parity with India that accounts for the trajectory of its defence, security and foreign policies. It also explains the various stratagems that Pakistan has adopted over the decades and continues to adopt unmindful of the consequences for its own survival. The various strands of this strategy consist of: the use of terrorists or non-state actors to inflict 'a thousand cuts' in order to 'soften' India for talks; development of nuclear weapons; use of borrowed power; and relatively large expenditure on defence, both conventional and nuclear. This compulsive need for parity harks back to the history of the subcontinent and to the Pakistan movement itself. Believing itself to be the inheritors of a millennia of Islamic rule over the Indian subcontinent, especially of the Mughals, Pakistan feels that its inheritance demands that it be treated as at least equal, if not superior, to India. The core of the Muslim League's demand for a separate Muslim homeland, i.e., Pakistan was the quest for parity with the Congress and parity between Hindus and Muslims, despite the Muslims being in a minority. This quest for parity, rather than being buried with the creation of Pakistan, was carried over into the new state and parity with India has become a fixation with its leaders and especially with the Pakistan Army. It is this quest that makes and defines them as Pakistanis. Without assertion of such parity, they would be seen to have acquiesced to 'Hindu' subjugation.

Two examples will illustrate the point. First, in the run-up to the May 1950 visit of Prime Minister Liaquat Ali Khan to the USA, Finance Minister Ghulam Mohammad met George McGhee, Assistant Secretary of State for Near Eastern, South Asian and African affairs. During the meeting, Ghulam Mohammad told McGhee that the USA had to appear to treat Pakistan on par with India; it was 'of utmost importance'. McGhee related later that Liaquat was accorded a reception equal to what Jawaharlal Nehru received. Second, in 1954, the then prime minister of Pakistan, Mohammad Ali Bogra, reflected the Pakistani view on Kashmir when he said that, "When there is more equality of military strength, then I am sure that there will be a greater chance of settlement." Six decades later, the tune of parity has not changed. Following US President Obama's visit to India in January 2015, the Pakistan Foreign Office lamented that an India-USA partnership would alter South Asia's 'balance of power' and create a 'regional imbalance'. This argument was taken forward during the US–Pakistan talks on security, strategic stability and non-proliferation in Washington in June 2015. Prior to the talks, the Pakistan foreign secretary stated that the US nuclear deal with India had affected the strategic stability that existed in South Asia before the deal.

India will have to factor in this Pakistan obsession for parity in its own approach to Pakistan. The implication is that Pakistan will always act as a spoiler to ensure that India does not get something that it does not get—for example, a seat at the UN Security Council or membership of the Nuclear Suppliers Group.

The Kashmir Fixation

Complicating matters for Pakistan is not merely the self-imposed quest for parity with India but the fact that since 1947 it has been a revanchist state. For Pakistan, Kashmir was and is the 'unfinished agenda' of Partition. It was the 'K' in the acronym Pakistan. Kashmir acquired greater salience after Bangladesh broke away from Pakistan. Issues of revenge against India apart, the creation of Bangladesh effectively buried the two-nation theory and the use of Islam to weld a national identity. Even though rationalizations were made about Islam not being effectively used by a secularized elite, the fact was that Pakistan needed another crutch as an ideological nationalist narrative. This crutch became the 'Ideology of Pakistan' of which Kashmir was an integral part. Kashmir thus became a 'rallying ground'...and 'No Pakistani leader, present or future, was allowed to ignore the significance of the Himalayan territory, and especially its connection to Pakistan.... All of Pakistan was made hostage to the Kashmir conundrum.' As a result, Pakistan's position on Kashmir is frozen in time without an alternative strategy. Its military strategy to wrest Kashmir by force as in 1947, 1965 and 1999 has repeatedly failed. Its semi-military strategy of using terrorists since 1989 to force India to come to the negotiating table in a weakened position has not been successful either. It has failed to develop any coherent political strategy except to intermittently raise the issue of human rights violations. This has not worked either.

But despite repeated failure, Pakistan will not relent on Kashmir. Let us see 'Why'.

Z.A. Bhutto, in 1969, perhaps gave the best explanation in his book, 'The Myth of Independence'. He wrote, "Why does India want Jammu and Kashmir?... she retains the state against all norms of morality because she wants to negate the two-nation theory, the basis of Pakistan. If a Muslim majority area can remain a part of India, the *raison d'être* of Pakistan collapses.... For the same reasons, Pakistan must continue unremittingly her struggle for the right of self-determination of this subject people. Pakistan is incomplete without Jammu and Kashmir both territorially and ideologically. Recovering them, she would recover her head and be made whole, stronger, and more viable. It would be fatal if, in sheer exhaustion or out of intimidation, Pakistan were to abandon the struggle, and a bad compromise would be tantamount to abandonment; which might, in turn lead to the collapse of Pakistan. If, however, we settle for tranquil relations with India, without an equitable resolution of disputes, it would be the first major step in establishing Indian leadership in our parts, with Pakistan and other neighbouring states becoming Indian satellites."

Though Bhutto was hanged by the Pakistan army, his articulation of Pakistan's relentless quest for Kashmir has been followed assiduously by all subsequent rulers—civil and military. The elements he identified, especially the impact of a Muslim majority province in India on Pakistan's *raison d'être*, are the bedrock of Pakistan's Kashmir policy. This is despite the fact that the USA had realized the futility of such a policy being pursued by Pakistan as early as on 13 October 1965, when it informed its ambassadors in New Delhi, Karachi, London and in the UN of the fact that the Pakistan government had refused to admit, even after the stalemate of the 1965 round, that 'Pakistan's policy of attempting to force a Kashmir settlement has failed. Its only hope of getting one lies in reversing its present course and seeking a reconciliation with India, which will simultaneously assure Pakistan's long run security vis-à-vis India. It is a simple fact that no Kashmir settlement is possible when both sides are becoming more antagonistic and more frozen in their positions than the reverse.' This assessment remains as valid today as it did in 1965. Thus, when elements in India prescribe talking to Pakistan as a means of coming to grips with the situation in J&K, they are playing into the hands of Pakistan. First, they give Pakistan the veto power over what is essentially an Indian issue. Second, they present to Pakistan on a platter what it has been seeking to achieve for decades through military and semi-military means—to make India come to the negotiating table for talks on Kashmir.

India would have to inevitably factor in this element in its policy of Pakistan's quest for Kashmir, a quest described again by Bhutto as, "Let it be known beyond doubt that Kashmir is to Pakistan what Berlin is to the West, and that without a fair and proper settlement of this issue, the people of Pakistan will not consider the crusade for Pakistan complete". In fact, it was Bhutto who had always argued that only by sustaining the tempo and degree of tension could the situation be qualitatively altered. "Confrontation, confrontation, confrontation," he claimed, "is the key to the India-Pakistan dispute'. What we see happening on the Line of Control (LoC), for example, is an illustration of such a prescription.

The Pakistani Mindset

The issues of identity, parity and Kashmir have crystallized into the Pakistani mindset towards India. At various times, Pakistan has viewed India (seen synonymous to Hindu) as a cowardly 'pushover' adversary because the 'Hindu (i.e., Indian) has no 'stomach for a fight'. As Ayub Khan was to put it so graphically, "As a general rule, Hindu morale would not stand more than a couple of blows delivered at the right time and place. Such opportunities should, therefore, be sought and exploited." Forceful and successful Indian reaction has invariably refuted such assumptions and surprised the Pakistanis. For example, led to believe that one Pakistani Muslim soldier was equal to ten Hindu Indian soldiers, the inability to take all of Kashmir in 1965 was a rude awakening for the Pakistani public. Notes British Brigadier Bidwell: "...the repulse of the Pakistanis by the Indians in 1965 was the first reversal of [the unbroken trend of Muslim victories in the subcontinent going back eight centuries] and a truly historic occasion."

Such an attitude towards Hindus has been reinforced in the school curriculum. According to a Pakistani study, "Hatred against India and the Hindus has been an essential component of the 'Ideology of Pakistan' because for its proponents, the existence of Pakistan was defined only in relation to Hindus, and hence the Hindus had to be painted as negatively as possible..." It also needs to be noted that the concept of terror has crept into Pakistani thinking and strategy. Based on their perception of the Muslim rule of the sub-continent, Pakistan has held that the Hindu, i.e., Indian, was submissive. Consequently, through terror alone could a decision be imposed on him. According to Brig Malik's 'Quranic Concept of War', a compulsory reading in army establishments since Zia's time, once a condition of terror into the opponent's heart is obtained, hardly anything is left to be achieved. In fact, terror is not a means of imposing a decision upon the enemy; it is 'the' decision that is to be imposed upon him. It is this belief of 'terror as a means of warfare' that has been used to justify covert Pakistani support for terrorist groups operating in Kashmir and other parts of India, a part of which rules that to strike 'terror into the hearts of the enemy' his faith must be weakened. Furthermore, this standard of terror is equally applicable to 'nuclear as well as conventional wars', thus making terror an adjunct to Pakistan's nuclear strategy.

The various elements of the Pakistani mindset towards India has been distilled in a publication titled 'India: A Study in Profile' by then Lt Col Javed Hassan for the Command and Staff College, Quetta. It is widely read and is prescribed reading in various Army institutions. After an analysis of 2,000 years of Indian history, the study concludes: (i) India has a poor track record of projection of power beyond its frontiers; (ii) It has a hopeless record in protecting its own freedom and sovereignty despite having larger armies; (iii) Dismal performance of the military is matched by the near-total absence of any popular resistance against foreign domination; (iv) The key traits of the Hindu are presumptuousness, persistence and deviousness; (v) India has been unable to exist as a single unified state; (vi) India was unviable, and Pakistan only needed to give it a push and this artificial "Hindu" state would implode.

Given his views on Hindus and thus on India, it is hardly surprising that Javed Hassan, who by 1999 was a Force Commander Northern Areas (FCNA), was one of the 'infamous four' who, along with Musharraf, Chief of General Staff Lt Gen. Mohammad Aziz, and X Corps Commander

Lt Gen. Mahmud Ahmad, planned a scheme like Kargil. The whole scheme was based on the assumption, underlined by Hassan, on how the 'Hindu' would cave in before a superior power. Such a massive miscalculation, based on half-baked knowledge and *a priori* assumptions, can have disastrous consequences in the future, given that both countries are nuclear-weapon powers. Such attitudes reflect the Pakistan Army's cultural hostility towards India. This is unlikely to change in the near or medium future.

Indo-Pak Dialogue

How do these various strands of Pakistan's perception of India impact on Indo-Pak relations? The inability to develop a positive national identity and hence dependence on a negative anti-India identity, the elusive quest for parity with India that dominates Pakistani thinking, the obsession about Kashmir in order to deny India a Muslim majority province and finally the negative mindset developed about India have combined to freeze to the grooves any talks between India and Pakistan. Hence, anything that India proposes, any initiative that India takes (like the invitation to the Pakistan Prime Minister together with other SAARC leaders to attend PM Modi's swearing-in ceremony or PM Modi's December 2015 visit to Lahore), have ground to dust precisely because they adversely impact Pakistan's ideological and security narrative. By themselves, these one-way initiatives taken by India will not unfreeze these grooves.

It is hardly surprising, therefore, that the Indo-Pak dialogue since 1947 has been characterized by a roller coaster of expectations and disappointments. Whether it was the Nehru–Liaquat talks post-Partition, or the Swaran Singh–Bhutto talks of 1962–63, or the composite dialogue process of the 1990s and the next decade, the results have been the same barring some positive movement on issues like connectivity (road and rail), trade, and visas and so on. A major achievement was the Indus Waters Treaty of 1960 that has withstood the test of time and war, and the ceasefire on the LoC in the first decade of the new century. But on issues like Kashmir and terror attacks against India, there has been no forward movement. Of late, a noticeable feature of the dialogue has been that whenever they are to begin, or have proceeded for a while, a terrorist incident takes place in

India or on Indian interests in Afghanistan that vitiates the atmosphere for the continuation of the talks. Invariably, the footprints of the perpetrators can be traced back to Pakistan.

In reality, there has been no forward movement on contentious issues between the two countries. For Pakistan, Kashmir has to be on top of the agenda on any discussion. However, what do India and Pakistan talk on Kashmir? Ignoring the legitimacy of Kashmir's accession to India, all Pakistan wants is to acquire, at the minimum, the Kashmir Valley on the basis of the two-nation theory. For India, whose nationalism is territorial and not religious, this is just not going to happen. Pakistan's entire foreign and defence policies are geared towards the objective of seizing control of the Valley. That is why it keeps harping on the UN resolutions on the one hand and uses non-state actors on the other to promote violence to force India to the negotiating table. Of course, for Pakistan, an unresolved Kashmir issue also serves the useful purpose of whipping up anti-India public opinion to divert attention from any divisive domestic issue and to cement its identity. And keeping Kashmir on the boil also serves the Pakistan Army well, assuring it the pre-eminent place in Pakistan with the first claim on its resources.

For India, the only thing to talk about is the part of Jammu and Kashmir illegally occupied by Pakistan—the so-called 'Azad' Kashmir and Gilgit–Baltistan (GB) both of which jointly constitute Pakistan Occupied Jammu and Kashmir (POJK). Pakistan's hold on both these regions is tenuous—GB's status is opaque and 'Azad Kashmir' is hardly 'Azad' or independent. There is a point of view that realistically speaking the only plausible solution is that the LoC becomes the international boundary. However, this would be realistic only on paper. Apart from the constitutional and parliamentary hurdles, the only thing that such an arrangement would do is to allow Pakistan to take GB and so-called 'Azad' Kashmir off the table. Pakistan would continue its meddling in Indian Kashmir and its objective of seizing control of the Valley would remain intact. It would be India that would suffer by losing its claim on POJK without ensuring that Pakistan stops its proxy war in Indian Kashmir.

For India, Pakistan-fomented terrorism since the 1980s is the number one item on the agenda of talks. By dragging its feet on the investigation and trial of the Lashkar-e-Taiba (LeT) terrorists who planned the 2008 Mumbai attacks and, more recently, the Pathankot, Gurdaspur and Uri attacks, Pakistan has clearly signalled its unwillingness to move ahead on these issues. Claiming to be a victim of terrorism, Pakistan is extremely reluctant to discuss the terrorism that it directs against India. For the past few years, Pakistan has been trying desperately to find some evidence of Indian interference in Pakistan, especially in Balochistan and Karachi. By this, it could claim equivalence with Indian assertions of Pakistan fomenting terrorism on its territory. It could then come to the negotiating table on terrorism as an equal, and not on the back foot.

As part of this strategy, Pakistan has claimed to have presented 'proof' of Indian involvement in Balochistan, which it presented to the USA during the visit of Prime Minister Nawaz Sharif in October 2015. While details are not known, Pakistan kidnapped a former Indian naval officer from Iran, showed him as being arrested in Balochistan and attributed a host of crimes to him without any evidence. A clumsily put together 'confession' of the officer was also circulated. Subsequently, the officer was supposedly tried and sentenced to death. India moving the International Court of Justice (ICJ) has stalled the execution of the officer. The directions of the ICJ to Pakistan not to execute him shows what the international community thinks of the case. Thus Pakistan has failed to find any equivalence on the issue of terrorism. Even otherwise, it was highly optimistic of Pakistan to think that an alleged Indian spy could be equated with decades of Pak sponsorship of terrorism in India.

The question that arises then is whether Pakistan's hostility towards India is eternal? Three elements are noteworthy here:

(i) The reality is that Pakistan has chosen to define its identity as being anti-Indian and this relentless, almost immutable, 'anti-Indianism' has become a part of the very DNA of Pakistan.

(ii) Pakistan has convinced itself that it can maintain its vital interests only by confronting India until all disputes are 'resolved' to its satisfaction. Till that time, confrontation, that has been defined as 'neither peace not war', has to continue. Abandoning the struggle or accepting peaceful relations without the settlement of outstanding disputes on its terms would mean capitulation by instalments and eventual liquidation.

(iii) Kashmir is the pivot of the mindset since Pakistan has internalized that to keep alive and rejuvenate the two-nation theory, a Muslim majority state—Kashmir—cannot be allowed to remain with India since it demolishes the *raison d'être* of Pakistan. Thus, Pakistan has to continue its unremitting struggle for Kashmir.

Under such circumstances, it would indeed be optimistic to imagine that there can be a sustained positive relationship with India. Only when Pakistan re-examines its roots, stops seeking its identity in 'anti-Indian-ness', stops its futile pursuit of parity with India, in a word, drastically changes its psychology and mindset towards India, would there be a possibility of any real progress in bilateral relations. Of course, as neighbours, India and Pakistan cannot help but talk to each other on a host of issues ranging from captured fishermen, people straying across borders, visas, trade, etc. This has to continue. However, to imagine a sustained breakthrough on fundamental issues so long as Pakistan's mindset does not evolve from its anti-Indian-ness would be much too optimistic.

While formulating a long-term cohesive strategy towards Pakistan, India would need to factor in all these various strands of how Pakistan views us and how a positive relationship with India adversely impacts Pakistan's ideological and security narrative. Given such a scenario, what could be the contours of such an approach towards Pakistan in the interim and mid-term? For starters, such an approach would have to factor in the harsh reality that for the past seventy years we have not been able to develop a policy that would allow us to live with Pakistan in peace and as neighbours. If we do not craft new approaches today, in all probability, we will still be in the same position seventy years from now. One such different approach could be as under.

First of all, we should temporarily freeze our attempts to officially talk with Pakistan on Kashmir and even on terrorism and stall any effort on their part to do so. As soon as the Kashmir issue or terrorism emanating from Pakistan is raised at any official forum or level, the talks get derailed very quickly. More often than not, such derailment is the result of violence perpetrated against Indians. Moreover, by talking to Pakistan on Kashmir we create the impression that Pakistan has the veto power on resolving our domestic problem in Kashmir. The temporary moratorium on such official talks would be without prejudice to our position on the issues. The moratorium will also be without prejudice to any action—both kinetic and non-kinetic—that we may take in response to a terrorist attack emanating from Pakistan. Such a step is bound to be controversial and contentious and would take a great deal of political courage. However, criticism can be kept within bounds if no policy announcements are made about such a move. Instead, an atmosphere should be built up in the media that for seventy years talks, both official and back channel, on Kashmir have resulted in no forward movement. Must we, therefore, persist on a path that is leading nowhere?

Second, it would need to be explained, again subtly, that freezing talks on Kashmir and terrorism does not mean that the two countries will not be talking to each other. On the contrary, these official talks should be replaced with intensive engagement on issues that can remove Pakistan's misgivings about India. The Pakistani mindset has been elaborated in this paper. Quite possibly, there would be a view in Pakistan about the Indian mindset towards it. That needs to be articulated and we should be open to discuss it. Thereafter, think-tankers, academics, commentators, journalists, politicians, etc., need to actively engage with their counterparts in Pakistan. This should be done in an open environment and not in secluded back channels that most people do not hear about. This will ensure that discussions have an impact on official and public opinion. Like official talks, back channel talks too do not seem to have progressed to a stage where they can influence policy. The agenda for such engagements should by design not include contentious issues like Kashmir. The focus should be only to address the mindset of Pakistan about issues of identity, parity, the negative mindset and so on.

For example, think-tankers and academics should be able to explain why Pakistan needs to develop a positive identity for itself rather than persist with a negative anti-Indian-ness to cement its various ethnic groups into a Pakistani identity. Likewise, the futility of Pakistan pursuing parity, that too military parity, with India is self-defeating because resources needed in critical areas like water and education are being frittered away on military security. Any illusions that they have about the weakness of the 'Hindus' or the non-viability of India too needs to be dispelled.

All this and more would take time and a lot of effort. It will also have to contend with the entrenched thinking of the 'Establishment' in Pakistan that represents such a mindset. Any sort of impact will not happen overnight and it would take persistence, dedicated effort and political will to stay the course. However, by staying such the course we will, in effect, be chipping away at the biggest hurdle in the bilateral relationship, that of Pakistan seeing a positive relationship with India as adversely impacting its ideological and security narrative. Such an approach has far greater chance of success in the medium-long term than the track that we have pursued for the past seventy years. Once misgivings are chipped away and the negative perception about India is reduced, it would be possible to make a fresh start on really contentious issues.

NOTES

1. Mubarak Ali, 'In Search of Identity', *Dawn*, 7 May 2000, cited in Christophe Jaffrelot (ed.), *Nationalism Without A Nation: Pakistan Searching For Its Identity*, New Delhi: Manohar Publishers, 2002, p. 7.
2. Aparna Pande, *Explaining Pakistan's Foreign Policy: Escaping India*, London: Routledge, 2011, Indian Reprint 2014, p. 44
3. Cited in M. J. Akbar, *Tinderbox: The Past and Future of Pakistan*, New Delhi: HarperCollins India, 2011, pp. 251-52.
4. Michael T. Kaufman, 'Pakistan's Islamic Revival Affects All Aspects of Life', *The New York Times*, 13 October 1980, cited in Husain Haqqani, in *Pakistan: Between Mosque and Military*, Lahore: Vanguard Books, 2005, p. 136.
5. Akbar S. Ahmed, 'Tribes, Regional Pressures and Nationhood', in Victoria Schofield (ed.), *Old Roads and New Highways: Fifty Years of Pakistan*, Karachi: OUP, 1997, p. 14. Wali Khan has also been quoted as saying that he had been a Pakhtun for 6,000 years, a Muslim for 1,300 years, and a Pakistani for twenty five. See Sabel Hilton, 'The Pashtun Code', *The New Yorker*, 3 December 2001, p. 59.
6. George McGhee, Envoy to the Middle East: 'Adventures in Diplomacy,' cited in Husain

Haqqani, *Magnificent Delusions: Pakistan, the United States and an Epic History of Misunderstanding*, New York: Public Affairs, 2013, p. 45.
7. US News and World Reports, 15 January 1954, cited in Aparna Pande, 'Explaining Pakistan's Foreign Policy—Escaping India, London and New York: Routledge, 2011, Indian reprint 2014, p. 48.
8. Anwar Iqbal, 'US-India N-deal affected strategic stability, says Pakistan', *Dawn*, 2 June 2015.
9. Ziring, *Pakistan at the Crosscurrent of History*, Lahore: Vanguard Books, 2004, p. 131.
10. Z.A. Bhutto, *The Myth of Independence*, London: OUP, 1969, p. 180.
11. F.S. Aijazuddin (ed.), *The White House and Pakistan: Secret Declassified Documents*, 1969–74, Oxford: OUP, 2002, pp. 42–43.
12. Statement at Lahore—14 July 1963, cited in Salman Taseer , *Bhutto: A Political Biography*, Vikas Publishing House, New Delhi 1980, pp. 58-59.
13. Speech in Lahore—20 December 1970, cited in Salman Taseer , *Bhutto: A Political Biography*, Vikas Publishing House, New Delhi 1980, p. 65
14. Directive from President Muhammad Ayub Khan to Gen Muhammad Musa, C-in-C, Pakistan Army, cited in Brian Cloughley, *A History of the Pakistan Army, Wars and Insurrections*, Karachi: OUP, 1999, p. 71.
15. Brig, Shelford Bidwell, *Modern Warfare: A Study of Men, Weapons and Theories*, Allen Lane, 1973, cited in Ahmed Faruqui, *Rethinking the National Security of Pakistan: The Price of Strategic Myopia* Ashgate Publishing Ltd, England 2003, p. 6.
16. A.H. Nayyar and Ahmad Salim (eds.), *The Subtle Subversion: The State of Curricula and Textbooks in Pakistan*, Lahore: Sustainable Development.
17. Husain Haqqani, *Pakistan: Between Mosque and Military*, Lahore: Vanguard Books, 2005 pp. 268–69; C. Christine Fair, *Fighting to the End: The Pakistan Army's Way of War*, Delhi: OUP, Indian reprint, 2014, pp. 161–62.

(*Tilak Devasher is a former Special Secretary, Cabinet Secretariat, Government of India. An expert on Pakistan, he is a Consultant to the VIF*)

*

Foreign Policy: Afghanistan
(The analysis predates USA's fall into Taliban's negotiation trap; relevant nevertheless – Ed)

10

AFGHANISTAN IN TRANSITION: INCREASING ROLE OF INDIA

Gautam Mukhopadhaya and Lt Gen Ravi Sawhney

ABSTRACT

Afghanistan is one of India's most important relationships historically, politically, culturally and strategically, from at least the time of Alexander, through the Mughals and the British, until today. Since the 'shocks' imparted by the Soviet intervention, Pakistani grip on the Mujahideen, the end of the Cold War, and the Taliban, India has proactively rebuilt its relationship with, and regained its standing in, Afghanistan as a whole through the smart use of hard and soft power. Nevertheless, it remains a largely Pakistan-centric, security driven, development and trade relationship.

Deteriorating political and security conditions, emergent regional and geo-political developments, improvements in regional connectivity, and fresh political stirrings and elections in 2018-19, demand that India lift its game in Afghanistan with its geographic location and untapped economic potential as its strategic core through a greater commitment to Afghanistan's unity and security, an outward oriented, public-private, resource and people-centred investment partnership, and invigorated regional diplomacy. This paper outlines some ideas in this direction.

Strategic Importance

Few countries can be more important for India from a historical and strategic point of view, as Afghanistan. It has been the staging ground or corridor for virtually every military campaign into India from Alexander to Babur until the advent of the Europeans by the sea route, and has effectively defined India in its own imagination as a continental power at the expense of the maritime. It has been at the crossroads of trade, culture and religion between Europe, West, Central and South Asia, and the Arabian Sea, and a theatre in the 'Great Game' involving not just Imperial Russia and Britain, that has left a lasting legacy in the region in the form of the still contentious Durand Line between Pakistan and Afghanistan, but also virtually every aspiring power in the region and world including lately, China.

Afghanistan has been described as a "graveyard of empires". It became the last battlefield of the Cold War that brought about the collapse and dissolution of the Soviet Union; then, under the Taliban, a laboratory for religious extremism and fundamentalist Islam midwifed by Pakistan, the staging ground for 9/11; and more recently, the first, and still the major frontier in the global war on terrorism. It was a witness to the demise of communism, the birth of radical Islam and is now a testing ground for liberal democracy in the face of Pakistan-sponsored terrorism using faith and religion. In addition, it is still a playground for Pakistan's obsessive search for strategic depth against India through the political use of Islam.

India-Afghanistan Relations

No other country, except Imperial Britain, has had a larger impact on India or at least northern India than Afghanistan. Separated since 1947 by Pakistan, it is easy these days to forget Afghanistan's intimate ties with India through history, trade and culture, as epitomised by the 'Kabuliwala' connection with the 'Pathans' or Pashtun moneylender and trader of dry fruits that is etched in the popular mind and films, and dominates the Indian image of Afghanistan. Fortunately, these images eclipse those of Nadir Shah and Ahmad Shah Durrani and the long line of Central Asian Turks that came from Afghanistan and ruled much of India. The huge Persian influence on almost every aspect of the culture of northern India—statecraft, warfare, courts, language, architecture, music, painting, dress and faith—came to India from historic Khorasan that includes Afghanistan. There is also the geographical and cultural continuity between the Hazaras of central Afghanistan and Kashmir and Ladakh.

This deep historical relationship in which India was not only frequently raided for plunder or conquest, but was also a seminal partner in trade and civilisational exchanges, has now been transformed into a strategic partnership that enjoys national consensus in both countries. The relationship has expanded to include sensitive areas like defence and intelligence sharing. Indeed, paradoxically, for a country that has been in almost continuous turmoil for the last 40 years, and one in the vortex of regional and great power politics since the Soviet military intervention in Afghanistan in 1979, the India-Afghanistan relationship has, in welcome contrast to trends in India's relationship with many of its other neighbours, grown steadily over the last 16 years of democratic post-Taliban rule to become one of its strongest relationships in the region.

Today, this relationship stands cemented at all levels throughout Afghanistan by India's extraordinarily successful development partnership, scholarships for Afghan students in Indian universities, medical treatment and recreation in India, participation of Afghanistan's increasingly successful cricketers in the Indian Premier League, the popularity of Bollywood in Afghanistan, and strategic breakthroughs in connectivity through the Iranian port of Chabahar and an air corridor for Afghan products in the Indian market. A Partnership Council set up under a Strategic Partnership Agreement signed in 2011 held its second meeting in Delhi in September last year.

In addition, from a country that was once viewed somewhat warily in the West as providing the rationale for Pakistan's obsessive interference and sponsorship of terrorism, the new US policy for Afghanistan and South Asia unveiled by US President Trump in August 2017 publicly acknowledged India as a force for peace and development in Afghanistan while bluntly identifying Pakistan as the source of terrorism and instability.

Development Projects

India's development projects in Afghanistan valued at US$ 2 bn at Indian costs have played a key part in this. Few countries, including larger donors like the USA, EU or Japan, can boast of as well distributed development portfolio spanning crucial infrastructure (like the Pul-e-Khumri-Kabul power transmission line in the north, the 218-km Zaranj-Delaram road to the Iran border and eventually Chabahar Port in the southwest, and the Salma Dam in the west), institution-building (the new Afghan Parliament and capacity building through the Indian Technical and Economic Cooperation, or ITEC), education and training (the Afghanistan Agricultural Science and Technology University in Kandahar, over 2,000 seats per year under the Indian Council for Cultural Relations (ICCR), ITEC and Indian Council of Agricultural Research (ICAR) scholarships, and military training in Indian defence training institutions), and small development projects benefiting local communities in far-flung border areas especially Eastern Afghanistan. These have yielded good political dividends. Afghan leaders have frequently described Indian assistance to Afghanistan as far greater than the figures in terms of value for money, both financially and emotionally. For the Afghan people, they are symbols of India's goodwill and friendship that contrast starkly with Pakistan's destructive role in Afghanistan.

These achievements are now being extended through a new generation of projects under an additional US$ 1 bn outlay announced by Prime Minister Modi covering drinking water and other projects crucial to Afghans, and trade infrastructure and promotion initiatives (like Chabahar Port and an air corridor) that will give Afghanistan greater access to the Indian market partially overcoming Pakistan's barriers to transit trade through its territory.

Future Perspectives

Nevertheless, as we look to the future from the perspective of mid-2018, Afghanistan stands at the proverbial crossroads. The first to strike the eye are the dangers and challenges.

Security Situation

From the security point of view, the previous year has been a particularly difficult year for Afghanistan with several high-profile attacks by the Taliban, the Haqqani Network and the Islamic State (IS-K, or Daesh) against the government, security, civilian, religious and public targets throughout the year, including the National Assembly, Supreme Court, police, Shia mosques, embassies, hotels, and even hospitals. Except for a brief period after the placing of Pakistan in the 'grey-list' of the Financial Action Task Force (FATF) of the UN Security Council when there was a brief let-up in high-profile terrorist attacks, not even the more aggressive anti-Taliban Trump strategy has made any difference to the levels of violence in Afghanistan.

This year alone, there has been a spate of major attacks in Kabul and other places against public targets and events including Nowroz festivities, an ambulance, a humanitarian NGO, a voter registration centre, and two back-to-back suicide attacks on April 30 that killed 11 journalists. Together, they have, among them, already caused hundreds of civilian casualties and intense pain. Sectarian attacks attributed to the Daesh had increased. More and more, the Taliban and Daesh appear to be two sides of the same coin minted in Pakistan.

The Taliban continue to put pressure on prominent strategic district headquarters and towns in both the north and south of Afghanistan. According to the US Special Inspector General for Reconstruction of Afghanistan (SIGAR) and other estimates, the Taliban and other insurgents control approximately 57 per cent of the country. The Taliban have also announced their new annual Spring Offensive codenamed 'Al Khandaq' (Al Omari and Al Mansouri were named after the now deceased Mullah Omar and Mullah Mansour in 2016 and 2017) on April 25 targeting US forces and their "agents" (but not explicitly Afghan security forces and legislative elections scheduled for October this year) in response to the Trump strategy, though as the attacks on voter registration centres in Kabul and elsewhere show, elections and civilians remain part of their operations.

The Afghan people have borne 10 years of war against the Soviets, seven years of internecine war during the Najibullah and Mujahiddeen interregnums, six years of oppressive rule of the Taliban, and 16-plus years of unrelenting suicide terrorism from *madarsas*, safe havens and sanctuaries across the Durand Line, and US aerial bombardment and mistakes of the war on terror. Though they have coped with all these unbelievably heroically, they are now fed up with the violence. Terrorism fatigue is setting in. Unless it is addressed, it is difficult to predict which way it will lead, as when Mujahideen infighting in the 1990s paved the way for the Taliban.

Political Challenges

Yet, more challenging than the security situation where the security forces have at least been able to hold their own where it has really counted, beating back attacks on cities and most district headquarters, it is the political challenges that the Ghani-Abdullah government is facing that should be a cause of concern. While President Ghani has brought in a much-needed focus on governance, development and reforms that are supported by India and the West and those seeking a change from past ways of doing politics, they have also taken Afghanistan into dangerous political territory where politics is increasingly divided along tribal lines.

Powerful ethnic leaders like Vice President Dostum and the Governor of Balkh Province, Atta Mohammed Noor have been humiliated in open revolt for months, with Dostum chafing in exile in Turkey defying criminal charges, Governor Noor's refusal to step down after his 'dismissal' by President Ghani late last year, and public outburst against Abdullah exposing internal fissures within the Jamiat. Political behaviour and discourse have taken an ugly turn raising the spectre of a return to the political violence of the early 1990s. President Hamid Karzai too is at odds with the government, challenging the government on critical issues including the Trump strategy. Moreover, democratic institutions have been undermined by lack of elections to the national Parliament (for three years) and district councils. They have finally been announced for October this year along with the commencement of the voter registration process on April 14.

The return of Hizb-e-Islami leader Gulbuddin Hekmatyar from Pakistan has altered and fractured the political balance and space in Afghanistan based on a tacit Bonn compact between a Pashtun President and the mainly Tajik-based Jamiat. With the Hizb-e-Islami back and on his side, President Ghani seems emboldened to pursue his reform agenda at the expense of ethnic and tribal leaders who still command vast loyalties. His efforts to nurture a new generation of progressive ethnic leaders to replace the generation of wartime leaders are still too early to take root in a highly traditional and patriarchal society. While admirable, these developments have the potential to put the post-Taliban compact and consensus under severe stress. In addition, on February 28, President Ghani made an unprecedented, fresh offer of reconciliation talks with the Taliban without preconditions along with political recognition, travel permits, release of prisoners, and relocation of their families. Had the offer been accepted, it could conceivably have led to a peace process, but it could also have upset the ethnic balance in the government even more with as yet unpredictable consequences. Its effective rejection with the spring offensive leaves it in a limbo.

Hopeful Signs

Though negative developments over the past 40 years have been adding up, there have also been a number of hopeful signs and developments.

Governance

First, the headline stories and figures of casualties mask the considerable progress that Afghanistan has made over the last 15 years in terms of GDP growth, life expectancy, poverty reduction, education, health, especially maternal and child mortality, infrastructure and media freedom. Sixteen years of democracy and international assistance have enabled a coming of age of a bright new generation aspiring to build a new Afghanistan free from terror and warlordism.

Anti-war Sentiment

Second, two new developments in Pashtun areas of Pakistan and Afghanistan emanating from the grassroots, have injected fresh hope in an otherwise gloomy environment (*'Going Nationwide: The Helmand Peace March Initiative'*, Ali Mohammad Sabawoon, Afghan Analysts Network, April 23, 2018). Sit-ins and spontaneous civil society protests (that included women), initially in Helmand, calling for a ceasefire and talks between the Taliban and the government under the slogan, 'Enough of War, We Want Peace' (in response to a suicide car bomb attack at the provincial capital on March 23 that left dozens of civilians injured or dead), have entered their second month and spread to other Pashtun and non-Pashtun majority provinces covering some 16 (or half) of Afghanistan's provinces (from the north to south, and from the eastern provinces and Kandahar, to Bamyan, Herat, Jawzjan, Balkh, Kunduz and Badakshan), and are acquiring the character of a country-wide and 'national' movement. A major civil society sit-in planned in Kabul, has been delayed citing security concerns.

While the local Taliban commanders were open to their demands, the leadership's response was negative and the government's reaction slow and confused. However, both the Meshrano Jirgah and Wolesi Jirgah have expressed support for the Helmand demonstrations. A large gathering in Lashkargah planned to mark the first month of the movement had to postpone its resolve to march to Musa Qala, the district centre that serves as the unofficial 'capital' of the Taliban since 2015, pending a clear response from the government. It is to be seen how they react to the new Taliban offensive. Meanwhile, the USA and the Afghanistan National Defence & Security Forces (ANDSF) military operations against the Taliban and Daesh continue.

The sit-ins have been inspired in part by another people's movement across the Durand Line, the Pashtun Tahafuz (Protection) Movement (PTM) launched in Islamabad on February 1 against torture and extra-judicial killings by the Pakistan Army following the suspicious killing of a young Pashtun shopkeeper by the police in Sindh that has electrified Pashtuns across the country. Though called off on February 10 after government assurances that they would fulfil their demands, the hugely impressive peaceful protests led by the charismatic young Manzoor Pashteen have resumed, most recently in Swat. The movement has also had resonance in Afghanistan. A demonstration in support of the PTM (that also voiced support for the Helmand peace sit-ins) was held in Kabul but called off after nine days when a magnetic bomb that no one claimed responsibility for, killed one protestor and injured 14. Notably, there are signs of the movement being emulated by Shias in Baluchistan who have also been victims of large-scale sectarian killings.

So far, news about both of these spontaneous peaceful people's movements have been sustained mainly by social media but downplayed or blacked out by mass media, and therefore perhaps not attracted much wider international attention that they deserve, including disappointingly, in India. There is a risk that they will be derailed by outside agencies attempting to exploit, interfere or seek to make political capital of it.

Political

Third, it is to be seen if and how these promising stirrings of peace and resistance to violence emanating from the Pashtun grassroots can bear fruit in the coming months. Here too the conjunction of parliamentary and district council elections announced for October 2018 and Presidential elections in mid-2019 offer opportunities to channelize these civil society impulses in a peaceful political direction and a new political order though it must be admitted that the chances of these being overpowered or sabotaged far outstrip the hopes of success.

Such a process will also have to deal with the issue of reconciliation with the Taliban. The Helmand and PTM initiatives have opened the possibility of an authentic Afghan-owned, Afghan-led peace process rooted in the people and free from the clutches of Pakistan and other outside players with little understanding of Afghan realities. This should be allowed to flower, and the temptation *of outsiders* to step into it resisted, except insofar as to help create a more propitious environment for the government and local Taliban to talk.

It also offers the possibility of breaking out of a binary argument that since a military solution is not working, reconciliation with the Taliban (with all its implications) is the only other solution. This is a false dichotomy. Stronger efforts to politically defeat the Taliban have not been fully tested. Key to it is addressing local grievances and separating local Taliban commanders from their chain of command, finances and advisers outside the country who are preventing reconciliation at the ground level. Afghanistan does not have to accept an either/or choice between war and a retrograde order held up by criminal, terrorist and covert networks outside Afghanistan's borders—what the generation of Afghans who have outgrown over the last 17 years reject, and what the sponsors of reconciliation talks abroad themselves would not accept.

Connectivity

Fourth, Afghanistan is being better connected with its neighbours and the region and beyond, opening prospects for trade and investment as never before. The upgrading of the Chabahar Port in Iran permitting trade with Afghanistan from India and other countries bypassing and reducing Afghanistan's dependence on Pakistan has been a major breakthrough. Several consignments of donations of Indian wheat have already been shipped through this route and the Zaranj-Delaram highway built by the blood, sweat and tears of Indians (the Border Roads Organisation and Indo-Tibetan Border Force) and Afghans alike. Similarly, an air corridor between India and Afghanistan, launched in June 2017 for the export of Afghan agricultural produce to India, has enabled over 2,000 tons of fresh and dry fruits and 'hing' valued at over US$ 40 million to be air-freighted from Kabul and Kandahar to Delhi and Mumbai over 82 flights by March this year.

To these have been added major new initiatives such as the five-nation Lapis Lazuli Agreement signed by Afghanistan, Turkmenistan, Azerbaijan, Georgia and Turkey late last year connecting Afghanistan by land and sea to Europe, and the long anticipated inauguration of the laying of the Turkmenistan-Afghanistan-Pakistan-India (TAPI) gas pipeline from Turkmenistan via Afghanistan and Pakistan to India.

China too has proposed projects that link the China-Pakistan Economic Corridor (CPEC) to Afghanistan through various offshoots that would connect Afghanistan to Gwadar Port. Though this adds to the challenge posed by the CPEC to us, it is a tempting and attractive prospect for Afghanistan. China is also leading a Five-Nation Railway Corridor (FNRC) running from China through Kyrgyzstan, Tajikistan, Afghanistan to the Iranian ports of Chabahar and Bandar Abbas the memorandum for which was signed in Dushanbe in 2014 though it is behind schedule, as is another 7,200 km multi-modal International North South Corridor (INTC) backed by India intended to reduce transport time between India and Moscow from 40 days (through the Suez Canal) to 20 days that will also benefit Afghanistan and Central Asia. Taken together, these projects have the power to change Afghanistan's economic future.

India's Role in Afghanistan's Future

India's policies in its neighbourhood are often criticised for being reactive, Pakistan-centric, and lacking strategic perspective and direction. There is a feeling that despite the deep historical ties, strategic importance and the successful rebuilding of India's relationship with Afghanistan post-Bonn, India has not been able to convert its intrinsic weight, positive attributes and political capital in Afghanistan into hard political influence as other countries are able to do with much less.

To some extent, this is valid. To overcome this, India will have to go beyond its current security-dominated vision of Afghanistan to one based on more long-term, fundamental and enduring attributes and goals—Afghanistan's strategic location, its economic potential, its territorial integrity, its political unity and regional realities.

First, the connectivity projects and initiatives described above are creating pre-conditions to unlock Afghanistan's strategic location and economic potential, as also that of Central Asia, based on sustainable development of its natural resources including minerals, hydrocarbons and hydropower, agro-horticultural and livestock processing, and new markets. India should be the first mover in developing these. India should also be prepared to look at China's Belt and Road Initiatives (BRI) connecting Central Asia and Afghanistan to the Arabian Sea that do not impinge on India's territorial integrity, augment access to and from Afghanistan and Central Asia especially through Chabahar, and contribute to its viability and economic prospects in this light as also the April 27 Modi-Xi Jinping informal summit in Wuhan where Afghanistan was identified as an area of India-China cooperation.

Second, India will have to move beyond its current largely trade and development based relationship with Afghanistan to encourage, incentivise and cover risks associated with commercial Indian investment in Afghanistan (and our extended neighbourhood in general) as an arm of foreign policy especially along emerging connectivity routes, building on its pioneering 2013 initiative to organise the 1st International Investment Summit for Afghanistan in Delhi.

Indian industry should particularly develop, process and add value to Afghanistan's and the region's natural resources and not merely extract or market it) and primary agro-horticultural and related produce on which the majority of its people depend for livelihood, and enhance its presence in the daily life of the Afghan people. Small investments in small enterprises in light industries on a large scale through sustainable financing arrangements that do not lead to debt traps would generate employment, promote entrepreneurship, build a broad ownership base, raise productivity and revenues, and catalyse a virtuous cycle of investment, growth and sustainable development in Afghanistan in mutually beneficial partnerships that should bring incalculable political dividends. India should also be prepared to invest in first and last mile connectivity to trunk routes and environmental and water management to avoid and offset environmental damage. Security concerns should not deter such investments and will have to be factored into the strategy.

Third, any reading of India's history should make it clear that India will have to continue to invest in its security and defence on its western frontier for the near future, and in the security and defence of Afghanistan including the security of its own investments. Central Afghanistan, where India has an iron ore concession (that has still to be developed), can serve as a strategic 'fortress' for Indian investments westwards towards Iran as well as in other directions. We will also have to make a clear-eyed assessment of the implications of the appearance of China in Afghanistan and its various BRI routes through it via Pakistan and Central Asia to the Arabian Sea, for our security.

Fourth, we may have to be prepared to play a larger role in Afghanistan's politics, not interfering in its internal affairs but as a catalyst in preserving Afghanistan's internal unity in the face of external and internal threats.

Fifth, India should also complement its bilateral diplomacy with the USA with diplomatic initiatives on Afghanistan with all of its neighbours, especially Iran, Russia and China who are all more active in Afghanistan now. The recent Modi-Xi Jinping agreement to cooperate in Afghanistan could be built upon.

Conclusion

India's strategic vision for Afghanistan been somewhat limited by contingent political and security factors including Pakistan's attempts to keep India away from Afghanistan and use it against us. So far, India has responded to recent challenges posed by Pakistan, the Taliban and its aftermath remarkably well despite handicaps of 'geography, military capacity and excessive caution' through the skilful use of soft power. But as India seeks to occupy its place in the 'Asian century', it must look outward, beyond its immediate horizon, to more long-term objectives and assets in its extended neighbourhood.

Afghanistan has been a formative factor in India's history. In the absence of ethnic, tribal, kinship, and past cultural ties, the strategic core of India's Afghanistan policy should be its location and economic potential that could serve as a hub and spoke in various directions, not just a 'bridge' or 'roundabout'. Recent advances in regional connectivity offer the opportunity for India to go beyond its development and trade vision of Afghanistan to the use of outward investments as an arm of India's strategic thinking and foreign policy benefiting both India and its partners. These should be explored and exploited.

(Gautam Mukhopadhaya is a former diplomat who served as the Ambassador of India to Syria, Afghanistan and Myanmar. Lt. Gen. Ravi Sawhney, PVSM, AVSM (Retd), is a former Deputy Chief of the Army Staff and Director of Military Intelligence. He is presently a Centre Head & Senior Fellow at the VIF)

*

11

INDUS WATER TREATY: AN APPRAISAL

Maj Gen A.K. Chaturvedi

Voices on Indus Water Treaty at Different Points in Time

"No armies with bombs and shellfire could devastate a land so thoroughly as Pakistan could be devastated by the simple expedient of India's permanently shutting off the source of water that keeps the fields and people of Pakistan green."

—*David Lilienthal, former Chairman of the Tennessee Valley Authority and of the U.S. Atomic Energy Commission.*

"Blood and Water cannot flow together."

—*Narendra Modi, Prime Minister of India, 26 Sep 2016.*

"The 1960 Indus water Treaty between India and Pakistan has survived disputes between the two countries, providing a framework for resolving disagreements over water use."

—*Amina Mohammed, UN Deputy Secretary General, 27 Aug 2018.*

ABSTRACT

Water from the Indus River and its tributaries in the Indus River basin is the lifeline of people living there. However, there is a wide variation in the availability of water between various rivers of the basin and that is why from the late nineteenth century efforts were made to create an irrigation infrastructure in the forms of link canals and head works to transfer water from surplus to deficient regions and rivers through an integrated canal system. However, this was essentially limited to Eastern Rivers, namely, Ravi, Sutlej and Beas, and benefitted those areas which were along these rivers and canals. Gradually a fertile strip emerged along these canals.

At the time of Partition water sharing between India and Pakistan could not be arrived at because of a peculiar situation wherein two of the major headworks, namely,

Ferozepur and Madhopur Headworks, were in India and the canal system was in Pakistan. After sustained negotiations, water sharing in terms of river sharing could be achieved finally when the Indus Water Treaty (IWT) between India and Pakistan, brokered by the World Bank, could be signed in 1960. Although both the countries felt that they were short-changed in the distribution of water-bearing assets, the Treaty has survived wars and hostilities between the two countries over 58 years. In the aftermath of the Uri terror incident, the Government of India has decided to review the treaty.

Thus, there is a need to appraise the opportunities and threats that such a review will bring in its wake.

Introduction

The above statement by David Lilienthal brings out the reality of agrarian societies. In fact, in the absence of adequate availability of water even industries are also likely to suffer badly. That is why it is important that water resources which are finite in nature are preserved, shared and optimally used particularly in the case of those water channels which have more than one riparian state along its course.

The four thousand-year-old Indus Valley civilisation has its roots in agriculture based on a river drainage system which is unitary in nature and man-made boundaries make it quite difficult to work out a fair and just sharing formula. The geography of the Indus River Drainage System is a highly unified spread over an area of 1.2 million square km. The north-western part of the Indian subcontinent always had adequate water but the geography of the area is such that these resources are monolithic in nature and can be optimally utilised only when used in an integrated manner. While overall there was no shortage, there were pockets which had less availability of water and simultaneously there were areas which were well endowed with it. After the integration of Punjab into British India, Punjab had a taste of the first controlled round-the-year irrigation in 1859 when the Upper Bari Doab Canal (UBDC) emanating from Madhopur was completed. Over the next 70-80 years a comprehensive canal network came up to provide year-round irrigation facilities in unified Punjab. However, post-partition, a more intricate problem as compared to the political division of Punjab came up, in the form of distribution of water resources, which were unified from time immemorial, and were now required to be divided between the two legatee states.

19 September 1960 is an important date in Indo-Pak Relations, as on that day India and Pakistan signed the historic Indus Water Treaty (IWT) at Karachi. The relevance and importance the two countries attached to this treaty is quite evident from the fact that the then Indian Prime Minister, the Late Pandit Jawaharlal Nehru and the then President of Pakistan the Late Field Marshal Mohammed Ayub Khan, HPk, NPk, HJ, MBE, signed the treaty personally, which was brokered by the World Bank (then the International Bank of Reconstruction and Development). The aim of the Treaty was to create a framework for sharing control of the waters of the Indus River and its eastern tributaries, namely, Jhelum, Chenab, Ravi, Sutlej and Beas, between India and Pakistan.

Historical Background

The Indus River rises in the high mountains of Tibet (south-western China), traverses through Tibet, India and Pakistan including Pakistan Occupied Kashmir (PoK) and empties into the Arabian Sea, south of Karachi, after traversing a distance of 3,180 km. It is joined by the Dhar River near the Indo-China border. After entering Jammu & Kashmir (J&K) it flows between the Ladakh and Zanskar ranges. It flows through the regions of Ladakh, Gilgit-Baltistan. The average elevation at which the Indus flows through J&K is about 4,000 m above sea level. It is joined by the Zanskar River at Leh, near Skardu and in PoK it is joined by the Shyok River. The Gilgit, Gartang, Dras, Shiger and Hunza rivers are the other Himalayan tributaries of the Indus from the west.

Kabul River from Afghanistan joins the Indus near Attock from the west. Thereafter it flows through the Potwar plateau. Some of the important tributaries which join the Indus below Attock include the Kurram, Toch and the Zhob-Gomal. Just above Mithankot, the Indus is joined by Panned (Panchnad) from the east, which is formed due to the accumulated waters of the five eastern tributaries—Jhelum, Chenab, Ravi, Beas and Sutlej. The river empties into the Arabian Sea south of Karachi after forming a huge delta.

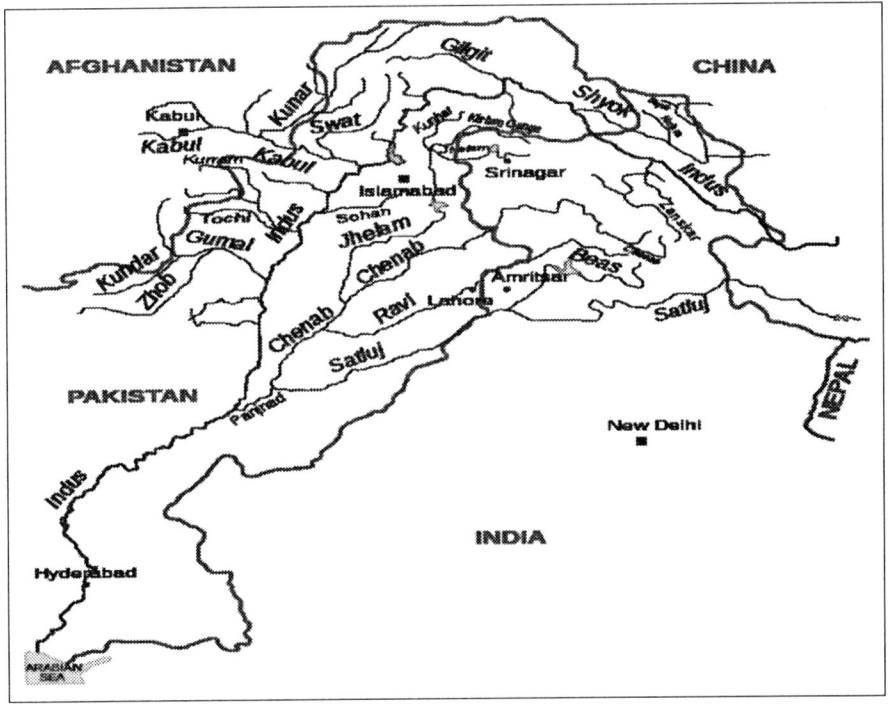

Figure 1: Indus River Basin (Source: http://www.en.wikipedia.org)

The total area of the Indus River Basin (IRB) is 1,165,000 km² and of this area, 60 per cent lies in Pakistan and Pakistan Occupied Kashmir (PoK), 22 per cent lies in India, 10 per cent in China and 7 per cent in Afghanistan. Most of the rivers are glacier and rain-fed. The waters of the tributaries of the Indus in the Indus IRB begin in Tibet, Afghanistan, the Himalayas, and the states of Jammu and Kashmir and Himachal Pradesh. The annual rainfall in the IRB ranges from less than 100 mm in parts of the lower Indus Region above the Arabian Sea to more than 750 mm in the northern foothills below the Himalayan mountains. The geography of the area of the IRB is such that initially there was only a narrow strip of irrigated land along these rivers.

Towards the last quarter of nineteenth century, it became apparent that the water resources of the individual rivers were not in proportion to the potential irrigable land. The supply from the Ravi, serving a large area of Bari Doab, was insufficient, while the Jhelum and Chenab rivers had a

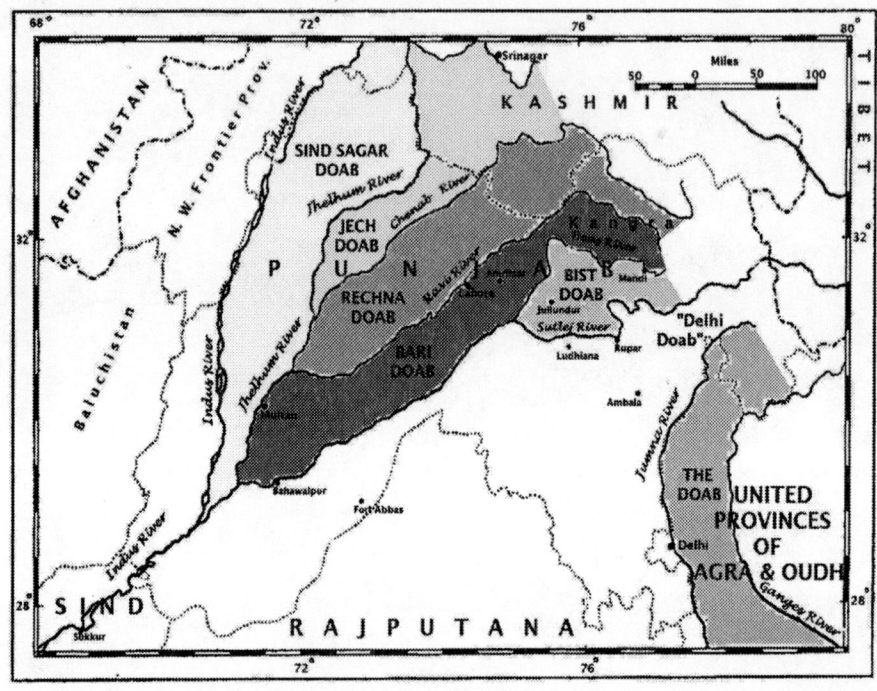

Figure 2: Doabs in IRB in 1947
(*Source:* http://www.en.wikipedia.org)

surplus. The first major canal, the UBDC, came up in 1859. An innovative solution, the Triple Canal Project, was constructed during 1907-1915. The project linked the Jhelum, Chenab and Ravi rivers, allowing a transfer of surplus Jhelum and Chenab water into the Ravi. The Triple Canal Project was a landmark in integrated inter-basin water resources management. All these efforts of the developments over the last century have created a large network of canals, 34,000 miles of major canals through 13 additional canals and storage facilities that provide water for more than 26 million acres (110,000 km^2), the largest irrigated area of any one river system in the world. More than 50 million people are dependent on these waters.

Evolution of Conflict

The conflict between the stakeholders commenced as early as in 1874. Initially it was between British India and the princely states, wherein solutions were such that the princely states had no choice but to accept them. Later in 1942, it was between various states of British India. Solutions generally were in the form of executive orders. Due to lack of storage facilities, competition for the run-of-river flow increased and led to a dispute between Sind and Punjab in the 1930s. In 1942, a judicial commission was set up by the British Government to study Sind's concerns over Punjab's plans to exploit the water resources of the IRB. The commission's report was not found acceptable by either of the states, despite sustained efforts through 1943-45. The issue was finally referred to the Imperial Government at London for a decision in 1947.

However, before the decision could be made, the British Parliament passed the Indian Independence Act on 18 July 1947 and a Boundary Commission under Sir Cyril Radcliffe was formed to decide the boundary between the two resultant sovereign dominions. When it came to deciding the boundary in the state of Punjab, the Boundary Commission realised that the issue was problematic due to the existence of the integrated canal system and the high dependency of agriculture upon canal water. Thus, the nature of the integrated canal system exacerbated the difficulties in deciding the new boundary and there was a need to arrive at an arrangement which could provide a mechanism for the equitable sharing of the water from various rivers and canals located in the IRB.

In this situation, Radcliffe contacted the leaders who were likely to lead their respective countries, namely, Pandit Jawaharlal Nehru and Mr. Muhammad Ali Jinnah, and suggested to them that the Punjab irrigation system should be a accepted as a joint venture, and that the headworks at Madhopur and Ferozepur be run by an independent agency formed jointly by both the countries. However, both Muhammad Ali Jinnah as well as Jawaharlal Nehru did not appreciate the criticality of the decision. Jinnah told him to get on with his job and stated that he would rather have a Pakistan full of desert rather than with fertile fields, watered by the courtesy of the Hindus of India. Jawaharlal Nehru on the other hand curtly informed him that what India did with India's rivers, was India's internal affair.

When no decision could be taken with respect to the division of the water available within the IRB, the matter was referred to a committee, called Committee B, formed by the Government of India. Both the governments were required to place their respective problems regarding the distribution of water before it. The report of Committee B came up before the Punjab Partition Committee, chaired by the Governor of Punjab and consisting of equal representation of East Punjab and West Punjab. The Partition Committee accepted the points on which Committee B was in agreement, "that the pre-partition shares of West Punjab and East Punjab in the canal waters would be maintained." But the Partition Committee, like Committee B, was unable to agree on the valuation of the canal system. As such, finally, the Punjab Partition Committee decided to refer the case to the Arbitration Tribunal. This Tribunal was headed by the then Chief Justice of India, Sir Patrick Spense, and its tenure was up to 31 March 1948. As per the terms of reference of this tribunal, disputes and difficulties between the two countries over the division of assets or liabilities formed by Partition could be placed before the Tribunal until December 1947.

In regard to the equitable water sharing, there were two different views from the two disputing states. N.D. Gulhati, the then chief engineer of East Punjab, summed up the issue and by 30 November 1947, five issues were placed before the Arbitration Tribunal. All of these related to financial adjustments and referred to the following:

(a) Irrigation system,
(b) Crown wastelands,
(c) Irrigated forest plantations,
(d) Seigniorage charges for canal use in transporting water around the IRB,
(e) The general ratio for calculating the financial adjustment needed.

With the chairman's permission, on 22 December 1947, West Punjab (Pakistan) submitted its claim for the Mandi hydro-electric plant. Chaudhary Muhammad Ali, who was heading the Pakistan side, stated that the most vital national interest, water, was not placed before the Arbitration Tribunal because of the agreement reached by Committee B and the Punjab Partition Committee where the view was that the pre-partition shares of water would be maintained. The dispute arose between East Punjab and West Punjab over the continuation of water supply from the Ferozepur Headworks (in East Punjab) to the UBDC (West Punjab), when the East Punjab (India), as an upstream user of the three eastern rivers, claimed that the property rights in the waters of East Punjab's rivers were vested with India and that West Punjab (Pakistan) could not make a claim on them as its right (under the Punjab Partition-appointed Assets and liabilities Order, 1947, and the Arbitral Award of Property Rights).

In contrast, West Punjab's standpoint was that the Arbitral Award protected its rights and also as per International Law and justice, West Punjab had rights to the waters of the Eastern Rivers. The real problem behind this spiralling dispute was that out of 26 million acres of land irrigated annually by the IRB canal system, 21 million acres of land and ten canals were in Pakistan and 5 million acres of land and only two canals were left in India. Most of the developed canal system and the famous canal colonies, the granary of the Punjab, went to West Punjab (Pakistan). India, as the middle/upper riparian, wanted to develop new irrigation facilities for those areas in India which were not under irrigation, while Pakistan's claim was based on its argument that the objective of the canal system, when it was developed, was to provide water to those areas in the pre-Partition days which were now located in Pakistan, and therefore supply from the Eastern Rivers should be maintained as earlier in the existing canal network.

According to Michel, the water sharing dispute became critical between East and West Punjab when monsoon flows receded in the autumn of 1947 with a likely impact on the standing rabi crop. To resolve it, the chief engineers of East and West Punjab met and signed a 'Standstill Agreement' on 18 December 1947, which froze water allocations at the existing level, allowing discharges from head works on the UBDC, the Dipalpore canal and the Bahawalpur canal systems. This Standstill Agreement was to continue till 31 March 1948, and it was clearly stated that any kind of agreement for sharing water, post the period stipulated would have to be negotiated. Both the parties agreed to the Standstill Agreement with the hope that a permanent solution to the problem would be found within the stipulated period of aforesaid agreement.

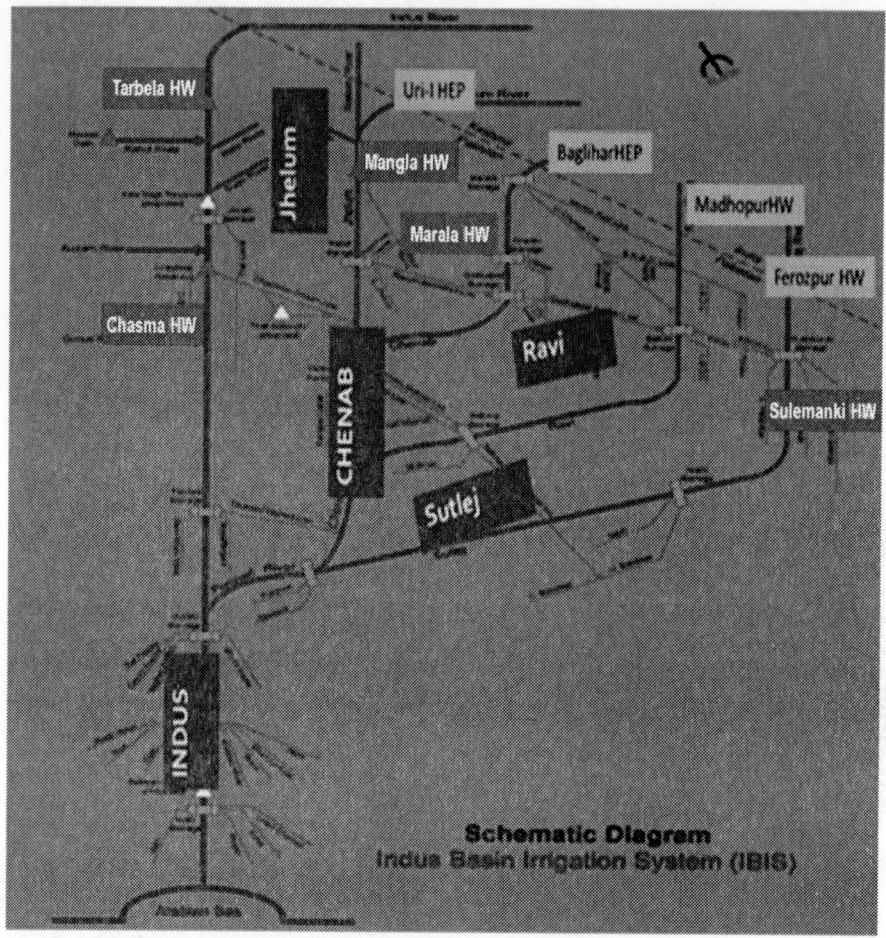

Figure 3: Canal layout in Indus River Basin

Source: Victor Miguel Ponce, "Link Canals in Indus Basin Irrigation System, Uploaded on http://www.ponce.sdsu.edu

However, either deliberately or circumstantially, West Punjab (Pakistan) did not take any initiative till 31 March 1948 to resolve the issue, the date of expiry of the agreement. A situation for a full-blown water conflict between the two countries developed on 1 April 1948 when East Punjab discontinued the delivery of water from the Ferozepur Headworks to the Dipalpore canal and two main branches of the UBDC within its territory. Pakistan had not anticipated an action of this kind and as such there was a clamour in Pakistan for going to war on this issue. As a consequence of the development, post 31 Mar 1948, in the absence of any formal water agreement with West Punjab (Pakistan), East Punjab (India) acquired legal rights on the use of water of the 'Eastern Rivers'. The shutting off of the canal's water in West Punjab (Pakistan) resulted in strained political relations between the two countries.

To resolve this dispute, East Punjab (India) invited the chief engineer of West Punjab (Pakistan) to meet his East Punjab counterpart at the province's new headquarters at Shimla on 15 April 1948, to re-negotiate resumption of the water supply. After due deliberations, an interim Standstill Agreement was signed on 18 April 1948. Discussions and deliberations continued and finally an 'Inter-Dominion Agreement', popularly referred as the 'Delhi Accord', was signed by India and Pakistan on 4 May 1948. On behalf of India, Pandit Jawahar Lal Nehru, Sardar Swaran Singh and Sri N.V. Gadgil signed the Accord and for Pakistan the signatories were Jenab Ghulam Mohammad, Jenab Shaukat Hayat Khan and Mia Mumtaz Daultana.

As per this Accord, India was required to resume water supply through the canals originating at Madhopur and Ferozepur and Pakistan was required to pay for the cost of the water. As per the provisions of the Accord, the water supply would continue till Pakistan found alternate means to compensate for the loss of water. No solution could however, be found post the accord, because neither side was willing to compromise its stated positions and negotiations reached a stalemate. From the Indian point of view, there was nothing that Pakistan could do to prevent India from undertaking any of the planned schemes to divert the flow of water in the rivers to areas which, in its assessment, needed it. Pakistan wanted to take the matter to the International Court of Justice, but India refused, arguing that the conflict was between India and Pakistan and as such, required only a bilateral resolution.

It is worth appreciating that the Partition indeed had internationalised the dispute. Pakistan felt that its livelihood was threatened by the prospect of Indian control over the Eastern Rivers, namely, the Ravi, Sutlej and Beas of the Indus Drainage System (IDS) that fed water into the canal system in the Pakistani portion of the basin, which was vital for the irrigation of its cultivable land. It is relevant to note that at that point in time, the canal system to exploit the waters of the western rivers, namely, the Chenab, Jhelum and Indus of the IDS, was not well developed. On the contrary, India felt that it was its right to harness the water resources available in that part of the Indus River Basin (IRB) that she had inherited consequent to Partition, and that Pakistan's insistence on its historical rights, in view of the new ground realities, was not justified.

The Indian argument was based on the ground situation as existing in the IRB during the early part of the decade of the 1940s. In this context, India, using the 1941 Census, claimed that although 21 million people lived in Indian Punjab and 25 million people lived in Pakistani Punjab, yet, out of 105,000 km^2 irrigated annually in the IRB, less than 20 per cent or 21,000 km^2 was meant for the East Punjab territory. This imbalance needed correction. Therefore, India now wanted to correct the situation by establishing its own claim to the waters of Eastern Rivers. Another relevant aspect in the entire consideration was that Pakistan was missing the point that the geography of Partition was such that not all the sources of rivers of the IRB were in India. The Indus and Sutlej had their origin and sources in China; Kabul River, a western tributary, had its origin in Afghanistan, and only Jhelum, Chenab, Ravi and Beas originated in India. This made China and Afghanistan becoming upper riparian states in cases of the Indus, Sutlej and Kabul, respectively, with attendant implications for the availability and control of the water for the lower riparian states. Thus, the insistence of both India and Pakistan that the dispute was bilateral was flawed from the very inception.

In 1948, David Lilienthal, formerly the chairman of the Tennessee Valley Authority and of the US Atomic Energy Commission, visited the region to write a series of articles for *Collier's* magazine. Lilienthal had a keen interest in the sub-continent and was welcomed by the highest levels of both the Indian and Pakistani governments. Although his visit was sponsored by *Collier's*, Lilienthal was briefed by the State Department and executive branch officials, who hoped that Lilienthal could help to bridge the gap between India and Pakistan and also gauge the severity of the hostilities between the two newly-created sovereign states within the Indian sub-continent. During the course of his visit, it became clear to Lilienthal that the tensions between India and Pakistan were acute. In this context it is relevant to note that whatever the expansion and modernisation of the irrigation system in Punjab had happened during British Rule, it had actually happened in the territory that later went to West Punjab (now Pakistan). East Punjab (Punjab in post-Partition India), regarded this as an injustice, especially as any future development would now need expensive storage facilities.

Like Radcliffe earlier, Lilienthal also recommended that India and Pakistan should work out a plan, which entails development and operation of all water resources available within the IRB system and the infrastructure to exploit them jointly. The scope of such a plan would be to build new dams and irrigation canals to get additional yield from the Indus and its tributaries. The financial support to this plan could be provided by the International Bank of Reconstruction and Development (predecessor of the World Bank). Lilienthal's idea was well received by the officials at the World Bank, and, subsequently, by the Indian and Pakistani governments. India's previous objections to third-party arbitration were remedied by the Bank's insistence that it would not adjudicate the conflict, but would rather work as a conduit for the agreement.

However, hopes for a quick resolution to the Indus dispute were premature. Neither India nor Pakistan seemed willing to compromise their stated positions (Pak's historical 'Rights' argument versus India's argument based on 'Needs' due to the new geopolitical reality). While Pakistan insisted on its historical right to the waters of all the Indus tributaries because of the fact that in the absence of adequate water supply in the canal network, half of West Punjab which was dependent on water supply from the canal network, was under threat of desertification, the Indian side argued that the previous distribution of waters should not prejudice the future allocation based on the newly emerged political landscape (Partition of the country) and new social and economic needs that had emerged. The Indian side argued to set up a new benchmark for distribution of water within the IRB.

The main point of the proposed distribution plan entailed that the waters of the western tributaries should be allocated to Pakistan and those of the eastern tributaries be allocated to India. Pakistan decided to renege from the Inter Dominion Agreement in July 1950, stating that the agreement had been accepted under 'compulsion' and signed under 'duress' and as such it decided to give notice of its termination (*It needs to be noted that probably it was the beginning of a pattern wherein Pakistan has mastered the art of reneging on agreements which it gets into when under duress and goes back on them when it suits it*). Pakistan stopped depositing the amount (which was fixed in the agreement of 4 May 1948) and stated it would be paid only after the dispute was taken to the International Court of Justice or the UN Security Council or any other international organisation.

The Treaty

After nearly two years of negotiations, in 1954, the World Bank offered its own proposal. It entailed the following:

(a) India to get water from the three eastern tributaries of the basin and Pakistan to get it from the three western tributaries.
(b) Canals and storage dams were to be constructed to divert water from the 'Western Rivers' and replace the current system of supply of water from 'Eastern Rivers' lost by Pakistan.

The Indian side was amenable to the World Bank proposal because it was eager to settle the Indus waters issue as a large number of developmental projects had been put on hold due to the slow progress of the negotiations. Pakistan, on the other hand, found it unacceptable as it thought that it was unfair. It threatened to withdraw from the negotiations. The Pakistani Press reported rumours of an end of the negotiations with talk of increased hostilities between the two countries. However, notwithstanding the high domestic hysteria, the Pakistan Government was ill-prepared to go for a violent conflict with India and could ill-afford to forgo talks; as such, it was forced to reconsider its position. The negotiations continued based on the World Bank proposals for the next six years. Finally the Treaty was signed by the supreme leaders of both the countries, Pandit Jawaharlal Nehru, Prime Minister of India and Field Marshal Ayub Khan, President of Pakistan, and Mr. W.A.B. Iliff of the World Bank on 19 Sep 1960 at Karachi, to be effective from 1 April 1960.

The Treaty has 12 Articles; serially numbered from I to XII and eight Annexes; serially numbered from A to H. The details can be accessed from the Treaty documents but the broad headings are as below:

Table 1: Articles

Article-I	Definitions
Article-II	Provisions regarding Eastern Rivers
Article-III	Provisions regarding Western Rivers
Article-IV	Provisions regarding Eastern rivers and Western Rivers
Article-V	Financial Provisions
Article-VI	Exchange of Data
Article-VII	Future Cooperation
Article-VIII	Permanent Indus Commission
Article-IX	Settlement of Differences and Disputes
Article-X	Emergency Provisions
Article-XI	General Provisions
Article-XII	Final Provisions

Table 2: Annexures

Annexure-A	Exchange of Notes between Government of India and Government of Pakistan
Annexure-B	Agricultural Use by Pakistan
Annexure-C	Agricultural Use by India from the Western Rrivers
Annexure-D	Generation of Hydro-electric Power by India on the Western Rivers
Annexure-E	Storage of Water by India on the Western Rivers
Annexure-F	Neutral Expert
Annexure-G	Court of Arbitration
Annexure-H	Transitional Arrangements

Source: siteresources.worldbank.org

It needs to be noted that the original plan of the International Bank of Reconstruction and Development (predecessor of the World Bank) for the utilisation of the Indus waters could not be pursued as both India and Pakistan refused to budge from their respective stances on "Need" and "Historic Rights" based division. In fact that would have helped both the nations to meet their needs as well as the historic rights. This plan was, as mentioned on page 122 of Gulati, akin to the plan put up by India for the most effective utilisation of the rivers in the IRB. It talked of joint management of the water resources of the IRB. Pakistan, however, did not agree to the proposal and that is why a crude division of the rivers was resorted to. In hindsight, it appears to have been a blessing in disguise because the later experiences of dealing with Pakistan suggest that the joint management would have been a non-starter due to congenital anti-Indian mindset of Pakistan.

Salient Points of the Treaty

The Indus system comprises three Eastern Rivers, namely, Indus, Jhelum and Chenab, and three Western Rivers, namely, Ravi, Sutlej and Beas. The Treaty, under Article 5.1, envisages the sharing of waters of the Ravi, Beas, Sutlej, Jhelum and Chenab which join the Indus River on its left bank (eastern side) in Pakistan. According to this treaty, Ravi, Beas and Sutlej were declared as the 'Eastern Rivers' and Indus Jhelum and Chenab as 'Western Rivers'.

Some of the important provisions of the Treaty are as follows:

(a) Under the Treaty, the waters of Eastern Rivers were allocated to India. Pakistan for agricultural purposes could withdraw from certain tributaries of the Ravi, located downstream of the Madhopur Headworks, namely, Basantar, Bein, Tarnah and Ujh—a total of 45,400 acres of water (Article II of the Treaty).

(b) India would be under obligation to allow the flow of the waters of the Western Rivers except for the following usage (Article-III):
   (i) Domestic use;
   (ii) Non-consumptive use;
   (iii) Agricultural use as specified;
   (iv) Generation of hydro-electric power as specified.

(c) India was permitted to construct storage of water on the Western Rivers (Annexure-E) up to a maximum of 3.6 million acre feet (MAF) for various purposes. No storage was developed so far (this was the state at the time of the signing of the Treaty).

(d) India was permitted 'Agricultural Use' (Annexure-C) of 701,000 acres, over and above the irrigated cropped area (ICA) as on 1 April 1960. Out of this additional ICA of 701,000 acres, only 270,000 could be developed (i.e., a total ICA of 912,477 acres including that on 1 Apr 1960) till adequate storage facilities were constructed and 0.5 MAF of water was to be released from there every year. ICA during 2011-12 was 784,955 acres.

(e) Under the Treaty, India and Pakistan were required to create permanent posts of Commissioner for Indus Waters (Article-VIII). They would constitute the Permanent Indus Commission (PIC) which is entrusted with the implementation of the Treaty. The PIC is required to hold meetings and tours. It is required to submit reports on its work to the two governments every year. It has held 117 tours and 111 meetings so far.

(f) Both sides are required to exchange information related to river flows observed by them not later than three months of their observation, and to exchange specified information on Agricultural Use every year (Article-VI).

(g) India is under obligation to supply information of its storage and hydroelectric projects as specified.

(h) India communicates as a gesture of goodwill, flood data to Pakistan from 1 July to 10 October every year, to enable them to undertake advance flood relief measures. The arrangement is reviewed every year.

(j) The Commissioners may discuss questions arising out of the issues covered by the Treaty under the provisions of Article IX of the Treaty related to Settlement of Differences and Disputes, and in the case of non-resolution, take further action under this Article for resolution through a Neutral Expert, (Annexure-F) negotiators or a Court of Arbitration.

(k) A transition period of 10 years was permitted in which India was bound to supply water to Pakistan from the Eastern Rivers. During this period Pakistan was required to build the necessary canal system for the utilisation of the waters of the Jhelum, Chenab and the Indus itself, as allocated to it under the Treaty. After March 31, 1970, when the 10-year moratorium would end, India would secure full rights for use of the waters of the three Eastern Rivers allocated to it (Annexure-H).

(l) Pakistan will receive one-time financial compensation for the loss of water from the Eastern Rivers. India will pay a sum of Pound Sterling £ 62,060,000 in 10 equal instalments on 1 Nov each year starting from 1 Nov 1960 (Article-V).

Analysis of the Treaty

The Treaty had few problems even when it was signed. Some of the issues were as enumerated in the following paragraphs:

The Treaty is highly unbalanced

(a) Despite the IRB being a monolithic geographical entity, the IWT crudely divided the five rivers from the east and the Indus along the longitudes.

(b) Also, it did not take into account that two of the rivers, namely, Indus and Sutlej, originate in the Tibet Autonomous Region of China, with its implications on availability of water in these rivers.

(c) The treaty does not take into account other rivers joining the Indus from the west like Kabul, which has a bearing on the availability of water in the Indus.

The Treaty does not cater for the changing social, economic, technical and environmental issues

(a) Increased urbanisation in the region from a population of 485 million in 1961 to 1.39 billion in 2011 has affected the demand. This has also led to massive deforestation, increased pollution and the drainage system getting blocked due to squatters, which has further adversely affected the water availability and consequent demand supply gap on either side of the border. In fact, water availability was 5,000 cubic feet in West Punjab (Pakistan) in 1960 which has come down to 1,500 cubic feet in 2016 during the same period and water availability in East Punjab (India) came down from 6,000 cubic feet to 1,600 cubic feet. During the same period, the population of Pakistan rose from 50 million to 175 million. It was a double whammy for Pakistan because on one side the water availability had reduced and on the other, demand has grown. No wonder Pakistan is looking to grab more water than what it is entitled to as per the provisions of the IWT.

(b) The impact of global warming is affecting the availability of water and that is making the 'Rights versus Needs' debate shriller. Regional climate change is reducing the flow in the rivers located in the IRB. It is anticipated that by 2040 the Indus is likely to become a seasonal river. Because of global warming, consequent melting of glaciers and the resultant water flowing down from great heights of the Himalayas will bring a tremendous amount of silt with them; the reservoirs at Tarbela, Trimmu and Mangla in Pakistan and Salal in India have substantially been silted and almost 25 per cent of their holding capacity is now unavailable.

(c) The Treaty clubs J&K with India and PoK with Pakistan, and as such the aspirations and needs of the people of J&K have not been taken care of.

(d) A sizeable number of canals in Pakistan are unlined and almost 41 MAF of water per year is lost due to seepage. This aspect needs to be flagged when Pakistan raises the unfair deal as per the provisions of the IWT.

Allocation of Water is Interpreted Differently

Both countries consider it unfair because Pakistan argues that its demand should have been considered based on traditional 'Rights' (prior to Independence the canal system on the Eastern Rivers was made for those areas which now form part of Pakistan) but India wants it to be interpreted on the basis of 'Needs' (this point has been explained earlier). In this connection it needs to be noted that although Pakistan accepted the distribution, it was with a grudge, which is quite evident from Field Marshal Ayub Khan's statement after the signing of the Treaty. He said, "*Every factor was against us. The only sensible thing to do was to try and get a settlement, even though it might be second best, because if we did not, we stood to lose everything. The very fact that Pak had to be content with waters of three western rivers underlined the importance of having physical control over the higher reaches for max utilisation of the growing needs of West Pakistan. In my mind, therefore, the only solution of the Kashmir issue acquired a sense of urgency on the conclusion of the Treaty.*"

IWT does not conform to the UN Convention on the Law of Non-Navigational Uses of International Water Courses, 1997

This Convention though it came much later puts the rights of lower riparian states in the case of international water channels in perspective. In the instant case, for Indus and Sutlej, China, and for the Kabul River Afghanistan are the upper riparian states. Since China and Afghanistan are not part of the Treaty, their activities related to water utilisation without the consent of lower riparian states have a bearing on the availability of water in the river channels, and as such, the assumed quantum of water does not remain the same. The IWT does not take into account this kind of revised water availability. Probably there is a need to explain to Pakistan this aspect and try working out a common cause in conjunction with Pakistan against China. As far as the Afghanistan-Pakistan issue with respect to availability of water in the Kabul river is concerned, Pakistan can take its own call.

The Treaty has too many engineering provisions, which give Pakistan undue advantage to vet the designs of the Indian projects on the Western Rivers

No wonder none of the proposed Indian projects are getting cleared easily. The Salal Hydro Power Project (a run of the river power project), and the Baglihar Hydro Power Project (also run of the river) earlier, had faced many problems during the planning and design phase; even the Kishenganga Hydro-electric Project, a 330–a MW run of the river project which was inaugurated in May 2018 is still being resented and resisted by Pakistan at every international forum though India has met all the conditions that were stipulated by the International Court of Arbitration.

As per the Award, the Court had allowed India to go ahead with the construction and upheld India's right under the provisions of the IWT to divert waters from the Kishenganga for power generation; however, India was required to release a minimum of nine cubic metres per second into the river at all times to maintain environmental flows. Pakistan is now raising questions about Pakal Dul (1,000 MW), Lower Kalnai (48 MW), Ratle (a 850 MW run of the river Hydroelectric project, cleared by the World Bank in 2017) and Tulbul Navigation Projects—all have been facing

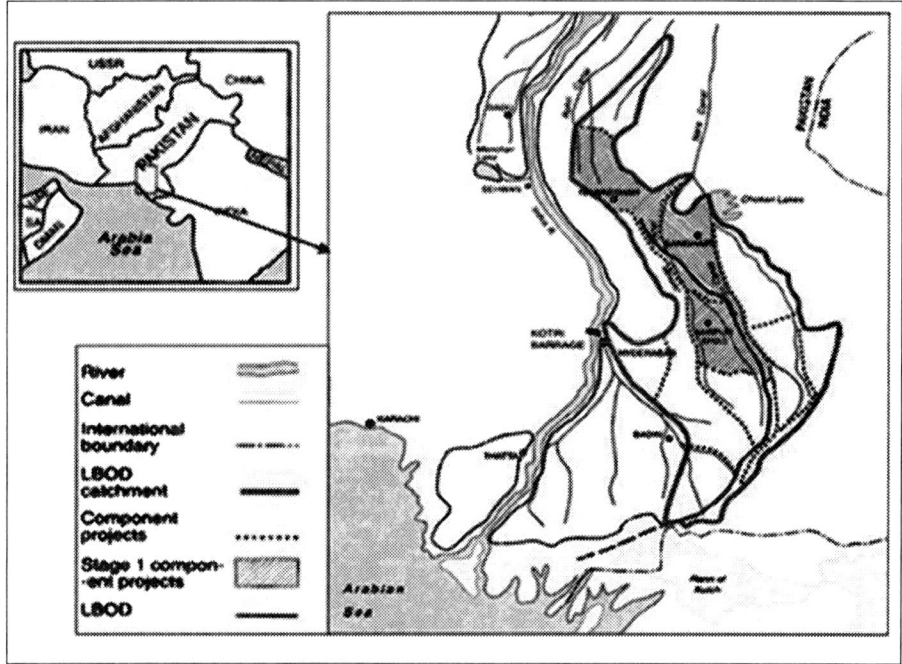

Figure 4: Layout of Left Bank Outfall Drain (LBOD)

Source: Kori *et al* 2013, extracted from Researchgate.net

problems for clearance. It is worth noting that as against 3.6 MAF which India can store on the Western Rivers, till date the total storage capacity that has been created is a mere 0.5 MAF. And Pakistan is crying itself hoarse that India is stealing Pakistan's water!

Rights of Gujarat were totally missed out while negotiating on IWT
IWT negotiations were steered by David Lilienthal at the behest of the World Bank (then the International Bank of Reconstruction and Development). In this connection, almost forgotten is that the right of Gujarat had not been addressed—Kutch vs Sind rights over Indus waters in pre-Partition British India is worth recalling. India needs to flag the issue to highlight the conduct of Pakistan in not getting design concurrence for its Left Bank Outfall Drain (LBOD); this Drain passes through the Great Rann of Kutch, over areas adjacent to India's Kutch and causes floods besides contaminating water bodies on the Indian side, in violation of Articles VI and IX of the IWT.

The Review System is almost non-workable
As per Article XII of the IWT, it can be modified only when both the parties agree.

The Case of Jammu & Kashmir: J&K, through which the Chenab, Jhelum, Indus and part of Ravi and its tributaries flow, has no special provisions in the Treaty. Thus whatever provisions with respect to the Western Rivers are made about storage and hydro power generation, these are not being permitted by Pakistan. For example, in 2007 the Water Ministry of the Government of India had estimated that J&K could increase its Integrated Crop Area (ICA) by 425,000 acres, but out of 600,000 hectares of cultivated land in J&K only 150,000 hectares is under irrigation. Further, the hydro-power potential of the water resources available in the J&K is 20,000 MW but as on date a mere 25,00 MW is being harnessed, all because of the dilatory tactics of Pakistan on projects like Tulbul Navigation Project, Ratle Run of the River Project, Kishenganga Hydro-electric Project and a large number of other projects which are either not being progressed, like the Tulbul Navigation Project, or have not even started (in a recent decision to review the suspension on this project, the Indian Cabinet has decided to resume work notwithstanding Pakistan's objections.

In fact, the Hydro-electric Policy of J&K, 2011, stipulates setting up of 28 projects in both public and private sectors. Sixteen of these projects are under various stages of execution and when all these are completed, it will add a total of 1,872.26 MW of capacity. In addition, there are 12 projects which are under planning and will add another 5,756.5 MW of capacity. It is significant to note that completion of these projects will not violate the provisions of the IWT for storage as far as the Western Rivers are concerned. Yet, exploiting the provisions of Articles VIII and IX with respect to the dispute redressal mechanism, Pakistan is placing impediments in their execution. No wonder, in 2003 the J&K Assembly passed a resolution to review the IWT. This kind of double-speak on the part of Pakistan needs to be highlighted to the people of J&K so that the dissatisfied locals can be apprised of the facts.

Fresh Evaluation of Treaty Provisions

The Uri Incident and Subsequent Developments

On 18 Sep 2016, Pakistani militants attacked an army administration base near the town of Uri in North Kashmir when 23 (19 security personnel and four militants) fatal casualties were reported. In addition, another 19-30 non-fatal casualties were also reported. The nation was enraged and the Prime Minister of India on 27 Sep 2016 told top officials who had gathered to review the implementation of the 56-year-old IWT, *"rakt aur paani ek saath nahin beh sakte"* (blood and water cannot flow together). Moving to mount pressure on Pakistan in the wake of the Uri attack, the Government decided that the meeting of the Indus Water Commissioners of the two countries can "only take place in an atmosphere free from terror." This meant that the meetings of the Commissioners, held twice a year, stood suspended since that date—since 1960, the water Commissioners have met 112 times.

New Delhi has also decided to maximise, within the overall ambit of the provisions stipulated vide Article III of the IWT, the potential of India's use of water on the three Western Rivers, namely, Indus, Chenab and Jhelum in the areas of hydro-power, irrigation and storage. It also decided to withdraw the earlier agreed goodwill gesture of 'unilateral suspension' of the Tulbul Navigation Project on the Jhelum in Kashmir. The Government has further decided to "move expeditiously" on the three power projects on the Chenab River, namely, Pakaldul (1,000 MW) which is under construction, and Sawalkot (1,856 MW) and Bursar (800 MW) which are in advanced stages of planning. Pakistan has raised objections with respect to Kishenganga and Ratle Hydro Energy Project (HEP) and both sides have approached the World Bank to find a solution and stipulate the procedure to be adopted. The World Bank, on 13 Dec 2016 had paused the two separate mechanisms for dispute resolution—neutral expert as asked for by India, and Court of Arbitration (COA) as asked for by Pakistan.

Fresh Look on IWT

The Government of India in the meantime has formed an Inter-Ministerial Task Force, to be headed by the Principal Secretary to the Prime Minister, to look into all the strategic aspects of the Indus Water Treaty (IWT) with

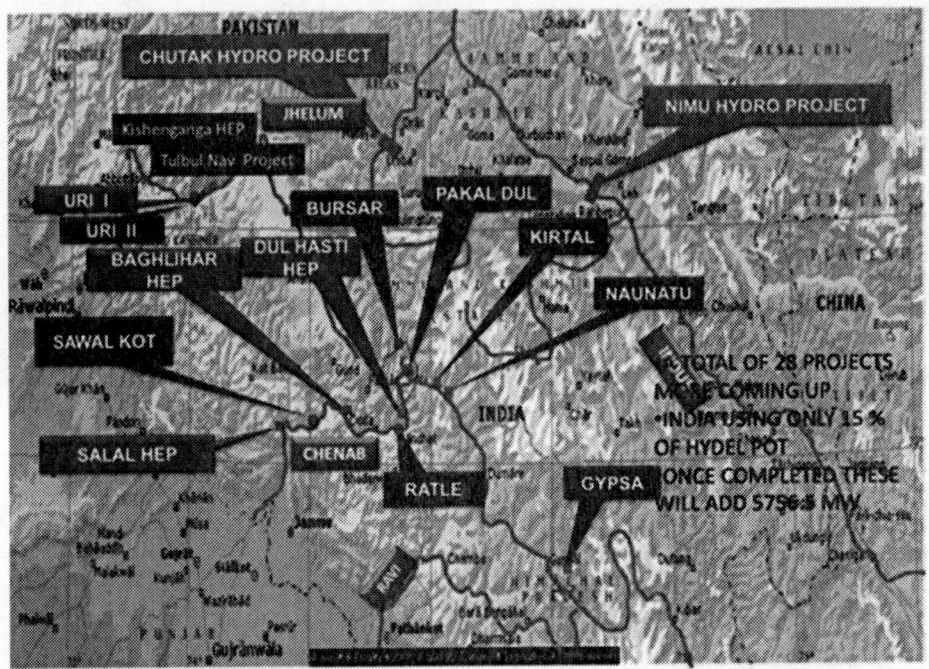

Figure 5: Existing/Under Construction/Proposed Hydro Projects/HEP

Source: Developed by the Author: The markings in red are those which have already been completed, dark blue are either under construction or under planning and light blue are those which will be taken up subsequently. It may be noted that Kishenganga HEP has already completed but is being questioned by Pakistan.

Pakistan. Other members of the team include the National Security Advisor, Foreign Secretary and secretaries in the ministries of finance, environment, power, water resources and chief secretaries of Punjab and J&K. The first meeting of the Task Force was held on 23 Dec 2016. It was decided to speed up Sawalkot, Pakal Dul and Bursar projects for completion in a time-bound manner.

India has decided to fast track three projects to reduce the wastage from the Eastern Rivers. These include dams and reservoirs at Shahpur Kandi in Punjab, Ujh in J&K and expediting work on the Sutlej-Beas Link in Punjab. The three projects will help save a lot of water from the 0.58 million acre feet of water wastefully flowing to Pakistan. It will also help to generate 198 MW of power from Ujh Hydro Electricity Project. The main beneficiary will be J&K. The proposal has already been forwarded by the Government of J&K to the Advisory Committee of the Ministry of

Water Resources for clearance. In September 2018, the Punjab and J&K governments signed an agreement to resume work on the Shahpur Kandi Project. When completed it will enable the upstream dam project power station to act as a peaking station, besides having its own Ranjit Sagar generation capacity of 206 MW and irrigation benefit for 37,173 hectares to Punjab and J&K. The Government of India has also asked the Punjab Government to prepare a Ravi-Beas link to further enhance utilisation of the share of India from the Eastern Rivers.

An Appraisal of the Future of the Treaty

Pakistan, despite its protestations, is unlikely to ever abrogate this Treaty because of its own vulnerabilities caused by the increasing shortage of water within Pakistan. The shortage is due to various factors many of which are of Pakistan's own making. But it will keep making noises to claim victimhood. India, due to the geography of the IRB, is indeed in a position to influence the flow in the downstream. No wonder, in view of the current state of tension between the two countries, many of the strategic thinkers in India are of the view that the Treaty needs to be abrogated or at least reviewed, and they feel that the water can be used as a weapon to restrain Pakistan from its inimical behaviour. However, there is a need to take a call on either abrogation or maintaining the *status quo ante* based on rational thinking rather than as knee-jerk reaction. In this regard the aspects meriting consideration are discussed below.

The IWT does not contain a provision for either party to unilaterally suspend or terminate the provisions of the Treaty. Article XII(4) of the IWT provides that *"The provisions of this Treaty or the provisions of this Treaty as modified under the provisions of Paragraph (3), shall continue in force until terminated by a duly ratified treaty concluded for that purpose between the two Governments"*.

All treaties and agreements, bilateral or multilateral, are signed on the basis of the *Pacta Sunt Servanda Principale*, i.e., 'agreements must be kept'. Although Pakistan's own record on this account is not very good, but India which prides itself in being a responsible country should not do it, lest it affects her credibility and moral high ground.

India also needs to take into account its position vis-a-vis China, where it is a lower riparian state. Although no water treaty exists as yet with China, unilateral abrogation of the IWT will definitely have a bearing on the credibility and as such on future negotiations, particularly in view of the Zangmu Dam on the Brahmaputra, the dam on the Indus at Nagri opposite Eastern Ladakh, and the Pari Chu incident in 2004-05 which caused devastation in Himachal Pradesh. Additionally, India is likely to make its position weak while challenging Pakistan's ceasefire violations which are also acts of violation of certain agreements.

Pakistan is almost a water scarce-country whose problems on account of water are extremely daunting. Lack of water in the lower reaches in the Indus has resulted in flow speed reducing to the extent that sea ingress into the Sukkur bowl (main rice production area) has taken place fairly deep, which is likely to affect Pakistan's food security. Lack of water, absence of consensus amongst various states and shortage of funds are substantially affecting Pakistan's power generation capacity and aggravating dissension among various provinces. In such a situation, closing the tap on Pakistan may result in a human rights violation charge against India. It may also be noted that the worst affected areas in such a scenario will be Sind and Baluchistan where presently disaffection against the central authority is substantial and India is seen by these groups as someone who can help them in the long run. Abrogation of the IWT may alter that equation.

Pakistan's water woes are of its own making. It is worth noting that currently Pakistan does not have sufficient water storage reservoirs; it is currently 10 per cent below the global water storage capacity of 40 per cent. In terms of days, it works out to only 30 days of storage. Whatever capacity exists is also not being optimally utilised. In this connection, a reality check reveals that the live storage capacity of Tarbela Dam which once was at 11.95 BCM in 1974 has eroded to 7.82 BCM and might further plummet to 6.49 BCM by 2025. Likewise, storage capacity in Mangla dam has gone down to 5.50 BCM of water from 6.58 BCM in 1967 and is prone to reduce further to 4.93 BCM by 2025. And in Chashma Barrage, the live storage capacity is likely to reduce to 0.55 BCM. This is basically due to silt accumulation. To add to it, as mentioned earlier, about

41 MAF of water every year is lost due to seepage from unlined canals. With these problems, India need not do anything to disturb the existing arrangement; Pakistan is set to commit enough mistakes on its own.

Currently, through leakage from India's various water storage facilities —due to not fully stopping the flow of the tributaries of the Ravi south west of Madhopur Headworks, namely, Ujh, Basantar, Bein and Tarnah, and not utilising its full quota of the Western River storage—plenty of water which belongs to India under the provisions of the IWT is flowing into Pakistan. India currently has a water storage capacity of only 220 days. Although that is better than Pakistan but it is much less as compared to capacities of some other countries—Egypt 1,000 days alone on the Nile River, America 900 days, Australia 600 days, South Africa has carry-over capacity of 500 days on the Orange River. In case India decides to abrogate the treaty without creation of adequate storage capacity, it would be absolutely impractical, rather disastrous, particularly during the monsoon seasons. India appears to have realised the mistake and is planning to construct an additional 2,500 dams by 2050 to add 180 BCM of storage. Silting is also an issue with India and a technical solution needs to be found to ensure that reservoirs like Salal are rejuvenated and dams like Baglihar are not allowed to get silted, and that all future dams have built-in arrangements to get the silt cleared as part of the maintenance arrangements.

It is also pertinent to consider the geo-political implications of any abrogation. The IWT was brokered by the World Bank (International Bank of Reconstruction and Development) but the fact of the matter is that it was at the behest of the United States of America, and therefore it will be naïve to think that the USA would not try to resist its abrogation. In such a scenario, Pakistan will claim victimhood and may find support from USA which would be detrimental to the geo-political aspirations of India. Closer home, it will send a wrong message to Bangladesh, a lower riparian state for a large number of common rivers (54 in number) and Nepal, a upper riparian state, having 6,000 common water channels. It will also have an adverse impact on Indo-Chinese water relations where China is the upper riparian state for the Indus, Sutlej and Brahmaputra rivers. China has not signed the UN Convention on the Law of the Non-Navigational Use of International Water Courses of 1997. The ramifications of this point have already been discussed earlier in the paper.

The Way Ahead

While it may not be prudent to unilaterally abrogate the treaty, a review of the IWT, to use it as an important element of national strength and as part of the strategy to deal with Pakistan is highly desirable. The following aspects are relevant in this connection:

(a) **Early Completion of Water Retaining Structures and Power Projects.** This would be essential to ensure that the infrastructure which needs to be developed to fully harness the capacity as provisioned under the IWT with respect to both western and eastern rivers should be completed expeditiously in a time-bound manner. Neither the kind of generosity which India showed earlier in case of the Tulbul Navigation Project (stopped work in 1987, unilaterally, in deference to the objections raised by Pakistan), nor the lack of commitment by the Project Team and the State Administration shown in the Ratle Hydro-Electric Project to progress land acquisition and construction should be acceptable. In this connection, it would be necessary that Pakistan's effort to delay the projects based on the rights it has been granted vide Article VIII of the Treaty ("India is under obligation to supply information of its storage and hydroelectric projects as specified") needs to be addressed on high priority and disposal of the cases as required vide Article IX is completed as quickly as possible. Pakistan's design of putting impediments in the progress of legitimate projects on the Western Rivers, as evident in the case of Baglihar, Tulbul and Kishenganga, should not be allowed to sabotage India's efforts to build these structures in a time-bound manner. Although never used as a weapon and nor is likely to be ever used as such, completion of all the proposed structures will definitely provide an option to India to regulate the flow of water in the Western Rivers.

(b) From the point of view of India's overall interests, factoring in the power sector development and agricultural and allied sectoral needs of J&K, it may be appropriate to plan to exploit the provisions of the IWT for more effective water usage arrangements, and thereafter, adhere to our stand determinedly in defence of the measures taken in consequence. It is of essence to reckon that any project of water regulation and usage in a state like J&K requires at least a ten-year time span to be successfully operationalised. In this connection, it is worth noting that Pakistan too has certain sane voices who admit that India has not violated the provisions of the IWT. In April 2008, Pakistan's Indus Water Commissioner, Jamaat Ali Shah, in a frank interview conceded that the water projects undertaken by India do not contravene the provisions of the Indus Water Treaty of 1960. He said that "in compliance with the IWT, India has not so far constructed any storage dam on the Indus, the Chenab and the Jhelum rivers (rivers allotted to Pakistan for full use). The hydro-electric projects India is developing are from the run-of-the-river waters, projects which India is permitted to pursue according to the treaty." Such sane voices in Pakistan need to be supported to counter the misinformation campaign which the Pakistani establishment has been deliberately spreading. It also needs to be appreciated that ameliorating the deficient power situation and increasing the ICA will go a long way to reduce disaffection among the people of J&K.

(c) Afghanistan's authorities, with the help of Indian experts, have completed the feasibilities and detailed engineering designs of 12 hydro-power projects with the total capacity to generate 1,177 MW of electricity to be built on the Kabul river. If the 12 projects are completed, they will store 4.7 MAF of water. That would squeeze to some extent the flow in the river and have an impact on the availability of water in the lower reaches of the Indus, and that could have a bearing on the production of paddy in Pakistan's Sukkur bowl. Therefore, Pakistan, rather than inciting trouble and funding its aggressive behaviour, needs to be more serious in managing its waters. In any case, India needs to continue its engagement with Afghanistan, notwithstanding protestations by Pakistan.

(d) There is a need to complete the Shahpur Kandi Dam at the earliest so that waters of the Ravi which are so desperately needed in Kathua district of J&K reach their destination and the desired benefit to the locals start accruing. It is relevant to note that recently J&K and Punjab have agreed to fast-track completion of the dam. Besides augmenting supply in the Ravi-Tavi irrigation complex, it will also provide much needed 206 MW of power. Also, this arrangement will substantially reduce the leakage from Madhopur. There is also a need to harness the water of the Ujh, Basantar, Bein and Tarnah rivers on which Pakistan has only limited entitlement.

(e) From the Eastern Rivers, presently almost 3 MAF water is going un-utilised. If harnessed fully, besides providing better irrigation facilities in the Kathua-Sambha area, it will also help in restricting the waters allocated to India as per the provisions of the IWT going across the border, where one of the major usages of this water is in filling of Pakistan's ditch-cum-bund (DCB) defences; it is ironical that India buys battle tanks to cross the same DCBs! There is a definite need to save this water for domestic use, besides limiting Pakistan's capacity to create formidable defence positions.

(f) India's diplomatic efforts need to be gingered up to explain to the world in general and Pakistan in particular that for the Indus and Sutlej rivers, India is a middle riparian state, and as such, China, which is an upper riparian state, needs to be brought to the discussion table so that the rights of middle and lower riparian states, India and Pakistan, are not usurped. Although that sounds a little far-fetched at this stage, may be some day Pakistan will see the merit in the argument that joint diplomatic pressure can ensure that China does not unilaterally use India's and Pakistan's share of the Indus and Sutlej waters. Secondly, Chinese help in the Aimer Bhasha project in the Gilgit-Baltistan area of the PoK needs to be contested, because that area is a sovereign part of India and presently is in illegal occupation of Pakistan. Simultaneously, efforts need to be made to highlight the ill-effects of this project on local ecology and cultural heritage. Ways need to be found to make locals aware of that, so that they protect their interests and resist its construction.

(g) Issue of the construction of the LBOD in the Great Rann of Kutch needs to be taken up with Pakistan. This construction is a violation of the provisions of the IWT, as it has already been discussed earlier in this paper.

Conclusion

The formation of a task force to review the IWT is a good move and hopefully it will help India in creating adequate water management infrastructure in a time-bound manner so that it is able to utilise all the water that it is entitled to harness. The unending debate over 'Rights of Pakistan vs Needs of India' may be left to continue without having to abrogating the IWT.

REFERENCES

1. Col Harjeet Singh, "Water availability in Pakistan," *Indian Defence Review*, Vol. 25, 04 Oct-Dec 2010/23 Sep 2016.
2. Doab refers to the area between two rivers. Upper Bari Doab Canal is between the Ravi and Beas rivers.
3. The Indus is loaded on Wikipedia.
4. Gulhati, *Indus Water Treaty: An Exercise in International Mediation*.
5. Muhammad Ali Choudhury, *The Emergence of Pakistan* (Lahore: Research Society of Pakistan, 1989).
6. Internet upload at http://www.simple.wikipedia.org, shodhganga.inflibnet.ac.in/bitstreams/10603/14384/chapter_4.pdf, www.fao.org/nr/water/aquastat/basins/indus/index.stm
7. Palijo, Sindh-Punjab Water Dispute 1859-200, 22.
8. Tabassum, River Water Sharing Problem between India and Pakistan: Case Study of Indus Water Treaty,
9. J. S. Mehta, "The Indus Water Treaty: A Case Study in Resolution of an International River Basin Conflict," *Natural Resources Forum*, Vol. 12 (1988).
10. Michel, The Indus Rivers: A Study of the Effects of Partition.
11. Asit K. Biswas, "Indus Water Treaty: The Negotiation Process," *Journal of Water International*, (1992): 203.
12. Extracts from the Media Centre of the Ministry of External Affairs uploaded on https://mea.gov.in/bilateral-documents.htm?dtl/5198/InterDominion+Agreement+ on+ Punjab+ Canal+Waters
13. Internet upload on www.internationalwaterlaw.org/documents/.../punjab-canal.html: Inter-Dominion Agreement Between the Government of India and the Government of Pakistan, on

the Canal Water Dispute Between East and West Punjab.
14. 'What Indus Water Treaty Means' by Dr. Adam Nayyar, *Dawa*. Archived May 11, 2012, at the Wayback Machine.
15. Mason, Edward Sagendorph and Asher, Robert E. (1973). *The World Bank Since Bretton Woods* (First ed.). Washington: The Brookings Institution. p. 612.
16. "Indus Waters Treaty: View From Kashmir". 2006. Retrieved 22 September 2016.
17. "Indus water treaty". http://web.worldbank.org. World Bank. Retrieved 28 October 2014.
18. "Indus water Treaty 1960" pdf. Site Resources; World Bank pp. 1-24, up loaded on www.site resources.worldbank.org
19. Internet upload: http://wrmin.nic.in/writereaddata/internationalcooperation/induswatertreaty196054268637.pdf

Shreyan, Sengupta. "Transboundary water disputes" (PDF). ETH Zurich. Retrieved 24 September 2013.
20. Garg, Santosh Kumar (1999), *International and Interstate River Water disputes*, Laxmi Publications. Pp.. 54–55.
21. "Indus Waters Treaty 1960," Site Resources, World Bank. pp. 1–24.
22. Sarfraz, H., "Revisiting the 1960 Indus water Treaty" pub in *Water nternational*, 38 (2) during 2013.
23. M. S. Gill, "Water Crisis of East and West Punjab," pub in *The Hindu* dated 15 Dec 2016.
24. Faris S., "The Last Straw: If You Think These Failed States Look Bad Now, Wait Until The Climate Changes", pub in *Foreign Policy*, available at http://www.foreignpolicy.com/articles/2009/06/22/failed_states_index_the_last_straw. Accessed on 15 Jan 2010.
25. Internet upload: http://www.un.org/esa/population/publication/wpp2008/wpp2008_text_tables.pdf. Accessed on 15 Jan 2010.
26. Maj Gen A. K. Chaturvedi, *Water A Source Of Future Conflicts*, p.160, pub by Vij Books India Pvt Ltd.
27. PTI Report, "India Pakistan to resume talks on Indus Water Treaty in Lahore this week," published in *Economic Times* dated 27 Aug 2018.
28. Internet upload: http://timesofindia.indiatimes.com/india/india-permitted-to-construct-kishanganga-ratle-projects-worldbank/articleshow/59874464.cms
29. "Wular Lake," uploaded on en.wikipedia.org
30. Amitabh Sinha, "Turning off Indus tap easier said than done", *Indian Express,* 3 Oct 2016.
31. "Wrangles over water: Pakistan wages a water war on India". Retrieved 22 September 2016.
32. Iftikhar Gilani, "Explained: How the Indus water Treaty Affects India and Pakistan", pub in *DNA* dated 27 Sep 2016.
33. IANS Report, "Reviewing Tulbul Navigation Project can put Pakistan on Backfoot: Officials" pub in *Business Standard* dated 26 Sep 2016.
34. Jayant Jacob, "Why Indus Waters Treaty is a Bad Bargaining Chip for India," pub in *Hindustan Times,* 29 Sep 2016.
35. Internet upload: www.indianenvironmentalportal.org.in/…/ 1_j&k%20state%hydroelectric, "Jammu & Kashmir State Hydro Electric Projects Development Policy," given as Annexure to Government Order No 205 PDD dated 07 Jul 2011.
36. Brahma Chellaney, "Securing the Indus treaty," pub in *The Hindu* dated 05 Aug 2016.
37. Shubhajit Roy and Amitabh Sinha, "Blood and water can't flow together, says PM Modi at Indus Water Treaty meeting, Govt plans cross-border river strategy", *The Indian Express,* 27 Sep 2016.

38. PTI, "Government forms high level task force on Indus Water Treaty" dated 17 Dec 2016.
39. "Indus Water Treaty meet: Issues of fast-tracking hydropower projects in J&K discussed", pub by *Indian Express* on 23 Dec 2016.
40. PTI Report, "Govt to expedite 3 Projects to stop share of Indus Waters forgoing to Pak," pub in *Business Standard* dated 25 Nov 2018.
41. Navneen S. Garewal, "2nd Ravi-Beas Link forgotten," *The Tribune* dated 18 May 2018.
42. Gautam Sen, "Deactivating the Permanent Indus Waters Commission," IDSA Comment dated 3 Oct 2016 uploaded on http://www.idsa.in/taxonomy/term/1509.
43. The Vienna Convention on the Law of Treaties, signed at Vienna on May 23, 1969, entered into force on January 27, 1980, art. 26, and the Vienna Convention on the Law of Treaties between States and International Organisations or between International Organisations, signed at Vienna on March 21, 1986, *not yet entered into force*, art. 26.
44. Abdul Rasheed Azad, "Water Storage Capacity far below Global capacity," *Business Recorder,* dated 07 Dec 2017.
45. Imran Rana, "Pakistan's Water Storage Capacity Falling Continuously," *The Express Tribune,* dated 22 Jun 2018.
46. Internet upload: http://en.wikipedia.org/wiki/sharing_the_water_of_the_Ganges; http://www.thethirdpole.net/en/2017/05/02/india-nepal-border-plagued-by-water-troubles/
47. Sameer Yaasir, "Indus Water Treaty, the Tulbul Project and its Implication on India-Pakistan Relations," *First Post,* dated 27 Sep 2016.
48. Dr. S. Chandrasekharan, "The Indus Water Treaty In Post Uri Situation – Analysis", *Eurasia Review,* dated 26 Sep 2016.
49. Khalid Mustafa, "India Out to Damage Pakistan's Interests on Kabul River," *International: The News* dated 5 Jun 2016.
50. Pawan Sharma, "Shahpur Kandi Dam: Punjab, J&K agree to sign Fresh Pact", *Hindustan Times,* dated 03 Oct 2015.

(Maj Gen Ajay Kumar Chaturvedi (Retired) has been a Sapper officer, who post his retirement has been working on issues related to non-traditional threats to National Security and Disaster Management. He has written extensively on water and energy security issues)

*

12

STRATEGIES FOR ENHANCING INDIA'S COMPREHENSIVE NATIONAL POWER

Brig Rahul Bhonsle

Comprehensive National Power: Concept and Utility

National power is defined as the ability of a nation to attain its strategic objectives by directed action. The use of power would be based on the overall national vision based on the aspirations of the people at large and the capability of the leadership to fulfill the same. Given people-centric envisioning of goals and objectives national power is no longer restricted to the military but also includes a multiplicity of factors such as strength of the economy, human resources, availability of national resources, knowledge and science and technology. Thus the concept of Comprehensive National Power (CNP) which includes all these factors has assumed significance. The model of CNP is not alien in India, in ancient times, the sage and administrator Kautilya in his widely read treatise Arthashastra Book VI states, "The King, the Minister, the Country, the Fort, the Treasury, the Army and the Friend, and the Enemy are the elements of Sovereignty."

In modern times, Hans Morgenthau, the leading international relations exponent, in 1954 proposed that national power should include geography, food, raw materials, industrial capacity and military preparedness, technology, leadership, quantity and quality of armed forces, population, national character, morale, diplomacy and governance. In China the concept of CNP gained greater acceptance after propagation by Deng Xiaoping, the doyen of modern reforms in the country. Deng said, "In measuring a country's national power, one must look at it comprehensively and from all sides." The Chinese define CNP as, "comprehensive capability of a country to pursue its strategic objectives by taking the necessary actions internationally," or it is mobilization and utilization of strategic resources of a country, to realize national objectives.[1]

To obtain an accurate perspective of national power an analytical exercise to measure CNP quantitatively and in comparison with other countries is felt necessary. American intelligence analyst, Ray Cline was the first to do such a study evolving a comprehensive index of power in the United States in 1977. The Cline formula was extensively used by Chinese scholars in their study of comprehensive national power. In India a National Security Council Secretariat supported study has published a National Security Index from time to time since 2002. Past studies and analysis of CNP have considered a number of factors varying from economy and military the most common to human resources, national will and leadership. A review of these studies reveals that while using the CNP as a tool for enhancing national power essential factors which need to be considered are as follows:

(a) Economy,
(b) Military,
(c) Internal Security and Social Harmony,
(d) Human Capital,
(e) Governance,
(f) Knowledge and Information,
(g) Science and Technology,
(h) Geography and Natural Resources,
(i) Foreign Policy and Diplomacy,
(j) National Will and Leadership.

A recent exercise on comparative quantitative measurement of 30 countries [hereinafter referred to as CQM exercise] with the highest per capita GDP including India provides a good indicator of the status of countries with reference to their comprehensive national power holistically.[2]

The CQM exercise examines economy, military, human capital, science and technology and natural resources quantitatively and ranks countries in each. This provides additional indicators for enhancing components of national power and where applicable relevant tables have been included in the Paper.

The CNP so derived whether from a quantitative perspective or analytically has to be seen from the point of view of impact on achievement of national goals and objective by utilising the power of the sum of the whole rather than disparate strengths in varied domains. Nations which are able to use the sum total of their national strength to achieve strategic objectives would be seen to have used their CNP to effect. Conversely the CNP model can also be used to identify strengths and weaknesses critically in each element of national power by examining sub-components of the same. Such an exercise should lead to identifying critical interventions for enhancement of value of each factor to generate a holistic self enhancement model. This is the focus of this Paper. A brief discussion of various elements of national power and strategies that can be taken for enhancement of each is therefore outlined as per succeeding paragraphs.

Economy

The importance of economy as a key factor of national power needs no elaboration; the focus is the size, growth and mitigation of risk factors. A standard measurement of economic strength is Gross Domestic Product (GDP). As GDP is linked with a number of primary indicators of the economy focus on enhancing GDP assume significance. Consistent double digit growth of GDP is seen to contribute substantially to the economy as a whole. The CQM exercise on economy includes factors as Nominal GDP, Gross National Savings as a percentage of GDP, Foreign Exchange (Forex) Reserves, Public Debt as a percentage of GDP and Nominal GDP per Capita. The conclusions of the CQM exercise reveal that China, USA, Australia, Saudi Arabia, and South Korea figure in the top five. India is mid way in the index.

The table containing top five countries and India is as shown in next page.

Economy Index

Country	GDP Nominal US$ Million[3]	Index	Gross National Savings (%age of GDP) Year[4]	Index	Forex Reserves US$ Billion[5]	Index	Public Debt as %age of GDP[6]	Index	Per capita Nominal GDP World Bank[7]	Index	Total Economy Index
China	9240270	54.36	52.37	100	3,213	100	43.5	82.15	6091.01	7.3	68.76
United States	16800000	100	11.64	0	148	4.08	67.8	69.83	49965.27	74.04	49.59
Australia	1560597	7.99	22.85	27.54	46.83	0.91	26.7	90.67	67035.57	100	45.42
Saudi Arabia	745273	3.07	37.69	63.96	541.1	16.38	12.6	97.82	20777.67	29.64	42.17
South Korea	1304554	6.45	31.92	49.31	306.4	9.04	33.6	87.17	22590.16	32.4	36.97
India (Rank 14)	1876797	9.9	33.74	54.27	297.9	8.77	50.5	78.6	1489.24	0.3	30.37

The areas in the sphere of economy which need to be addressed for attaining higher GDP growth are as follows:

(a) **Enhancing National Savings Rate (NSR).** National Savings Rate is percentage of GDP that is saved by households across a country. Household saving is one of the primary sources of capital investment in the country. The Government has to create schemes for encouraging National Savings. This could be achieved by reducing the spread of the interest rate of saving to borrowing in favor of saving apart from a number of incentives with structural benefits to participants in the NSR schemes while contributing to the national savings kitty.

(b) **Expanding Gross Capital Formation (GCF).** GCF formation reflects the total value of a producer's acquisitions, less disposals of fixed assets, during the accounting period, plus certain additions to the value of non-produced assets realised by the productive activity of institutional units. Statistically it measures the value of additions to fixed assets purchased by business, government and households less disposals of fixed assets sold off or scrapped. Capital formation includes drive towards savings, setting up financial institutions, fiscal measures, public borrowing, and development of capital markets, privatisation of financial institutions and development of secondary financial markets. Apart from these measures India could encourage GCF by opening up economy and infrastructure for private participation as also foreign direct investment.

(c) **A Diversified Trade Basket.** India needs to improve its manufacturing capacity to move towards finished product higher up in the value chain. This aspect is highlighted by Prime Minister Mr Narendra Modi through the Make in India campaign. India needs to exploit and expand trade, primarily exports, by seeking new partners and increase export volumes. India needs to enlarge the list of export commodities, from restricted basket comprising Tea, Fabric, Spices, Iron ore and concentrates and Gems, to also include finished industrial goods by moving up the value chain. This will provide considerable boost to the economy.

(d) **Balancing Sectoral Growth with Focus on Manufacturing.** Diversifying large pool of workforce presently concentrated mainly in the agriculture sector into Industry and Services is necessary. Also the focus of industry and agriculture sector should include raw production as well as value addition in equal measure. There is inescapable need for India to revamp its rural economy and provide strong incentives for locating new industrial and infrastructure projects into rural areas for inclusive growth.

(d) **Foreign Direct Investment (FDI) Growth.** India could also focus on FDI in export oriented labour intensive industries and encourage creating parallel infrastructure, through FDI to facilitate exports.[8] The FDI in defence industry could also be considered for enhancement as despite recent increase to 49 percent flow of FDI has remained stagnant.

(f) **Public Debt – Expanding Government Revenue.** India needs to bring down its public debt to manageable levels in the coming decade. One of the methods could be to carry out revenue and tax reforms and disinvestment of public sector to generate more revenues for the Government. There is need for India to revisit the issue of subsidies, and eliminate (as in case of fuel) and /or ensure optimal utilisation (in case of food and fertilizers), to reduce public liability. Most countries use public debt for GCF and infrastructure development rather than to meet revenue expenditure. A gradual reduction in public debt from the current levels of 75 percent to 30–40 percent of GDP needs to be worked at.

(g) **Private Industry and Labour Reforms.** Privatisation and labour reforms have to go hand in hand. Opening up more areas of industry for private participation and permitting up to 100% FDI in non-core industries, labor reforms for export oriented industries and spread of infrastructure base towards rural areas with a view to incentivize the private industry to transit to these areas are some other strategies to be looked at.

Military

Military remains one of the primary factors in determining a countries overall security and ability to defend territorial integrity, national sovereignty as well as safety and security of its people. In the Indian context, with disputes on the boundary with two nuclear powers, growing competition for resources, and control of Sea Lines of Communications, military will require substantial accretions to develop adequate combat potential in varied dimensions, nuclear conventional and sub conventional as well as cyber and space. In the CQM exercise which measured defence expenditure, the amount spent per soldier, and the nuclear factor revealed that top five countries are USA, China, UK, Australia and Russia while India is sixth. The Table is as shown on next page.

Military strength can be enhanced by the following:

(a) **Greater Investment in Defence Capital Budget.** Allocations to defence have remained stagnant at below 2 percent of the GDP which is not considered adequate to make up hollowness and acquire state of the art modern weapons systems. Alternately for enhancing capital budget corpus without substantial accretion to the defence budget restructuring the ratio of revenue and capital budget in the coming years from the current ratio of approximately 60:40 to 50:50 and then improving it further to 40:60 which is considered an ideal one. Similarly savings in manpower costs are called for by cutting back on numbers with accretion of force multipliers is recommended.

(b) **Human Resources Pool in the Security Sector.** Optimising manpower holistically in the security sector by adopting an integrated manpower policy wherein the armed forces are able to shed those superannuating from the services at a relatively young age profile between 35 to 40 to the police and para-military is the way ahead for generating internal resources without loss of efficiency apart from reducing cost of training police personnel for tasks such as counter terrorism and will also optimise the exservicemen pool and talent.

Military Index

Country	Total Armed Forces[9]	Armed Forces Index	Defence Expenditure Millions of $US[10]	Defence Expenditure Index	Defence Expenditure per soldier $ US[11]	Per Soldier Expenditure Index	Total Military Index[12]
United States	1458219	63.2	668841	100	458669.8	100	100**
China	2285000	100	157603	23.32	68972.87	13.35	56.95**
United Kingdom	197780	7.09	59795	8.65	302330.9	65.24	33.74**
Australia	59023	0.92	25555	3.52	432966.8	94.29	32.91
Russia	1027000	44	90646	13.28	88262.9	17.64	31.22**
India	1325000	57.27	48255	6.92	36418.87	6.12	29.29**

** Indicates accretion of 25% to basic military index for nuclear weapon states.

(c) **Creating Usable Capability in Capital Acquisitions.** The focus on capital acquisitions has to be on creating usable capabilities for a multi-spectrum conflict environment ranging from the sub-conventional to the conventional. Priority for acquisitions would have to be thus given to Force multipliers, joint usable assets such as fighter aircraft, helicopters gunships and Unmanned Aerial Vehicles (UAV), transport and utility helicopters so that existing resources are converted into usable assets and capabilities.

(d) **Fast Tracking Make in India in Defence Sector.** There is an urgent need to build the country's strategic industrial base to begin local manufacturing of aircraft, tanks, artillery guns, UAVs, Night Vision Devices (NVD) and a variety of defence equipment in India. Joint ventures on BrahMos model is one route there are other dynamic processes which have to be adopted for timely acquisitions through a concerted push at all levels as a national priority.

(e) **Triad and Ballistic Missile Defence (BMD).** Nuclear weapons will continue to remain a *sine qua non* for security in South Asia despite much talk of global disarmament. India will have to build a more robust, multi-dimensional deterrent in addition BMD has become equally important and progression in this direction needs to be undertaken at a rapid pace for operationalisation of a system by 2022 to cover all strategically vulnerable areas of the country with exothermic and endothermic BMD cover.

(e) **Annual Measurement of Combat Readiness State.** There is a perception in the strategic community at present in India of low combat readiness levels of the forces due to deficit in state-of-the-art equipment as well as ammunition, 'hollowness', officer deficiencies and low rate of modernisation. A realistic assessment has to be made each year to identify capacity deficits which impact combat readiness and gaps in war waging capability or deterrence. Such a report should be presented to the Cabinet Committee on Security (CCS) by the Chairman Chiefs of Staff Committee each year and relevant unclassified portions discussed with the Parliamentary Standing Committee on Defence and released to the public.

Internal Security

India continues to face a number of challenges in the internal security domain in varied forms, which include insurgency in the North East and Naxal infested States of Central India, terrorism in Jammu and Kashmir and the challenge posed by religious extremist terror in the hinterland loosely categorised as Jihadi terror. In addition political violence in the country is also a major challenge which is triggered by socio-economic and communal factors. No quantified assessment of the factor of Internal Security is available. The strategies for improving Internal Security are summarised as follows:

(a) **Police Capacity Building Numbers and Effectiveness.** The challenge in police capacity building is two-fold, numbers and effectiveness. There is a need for addressing both aspects. The All India Police-Population Ratio as per the National Crime Records Bureau for 2013 is 141 per 100,000 population against an ideal UN recommended 220. The overall deficiency is 24.5 percent. Making up the same on priority is necessary. On the other hand efficiency and effectiveness needs to be enhanced by improving the quality of intake, basic and refresher training, provision of modern equipment and upgrading the available training infrastructure. The 'SMART' policing model unveiled by Prime Minister Narendra Modi is the way ahead, there are likely to be a challenge in transition to the same which have to be overcome by effective supervision and allocation of budgetary resources

(b) **Skill Development to Enhance Employment Opportunities.** To optimally utilise the youth bulge in the country apart from education skill development is necessary. This will ensure that the educated young men join the mainstream and are not veered away by radical ideology. For this extensive skill building, focus on vocational training, expansion of the services sector where jobs at a lower skill level are easier to create, rural infrastructure, Information Technology Enabled Service (ITES) processing are some of the areas which need attention. The largest demand for jobs is in the rural areas, working out a model for creation there would be necessary alternatively effective urban migration policies should be evolved. A massive skill development programme in multiple dimensions as launched by the National Skill Development Agency needs to be fast tracked and sustained over the long term. The overall objective of the skill development programme has to be to enhance the rate of employability to 6 percent from the current rate of 2.8 percent.

(c) **Inequality Reduction.** Economic growth should not be restricted to niche sectors such as Information Technology but has to be spread to those employing large number of persons such as agriculture to reduce the gap between the rich and the poor, the rural and the urban. This will prevent disaffection by reducing the marginalised and preventing a sense of victimisation. At the same time, inequality has to be seen holistically thus social and political empowerment is as important as economic for reduction of sense of deprivation. This is an important factor in the information age where youth who feel disempowered politically may be looking at alternate avenues including extremist ideologies and thus needs consideration.

Human Capital

Enhancing the value of human capital (HC) will impact all other sectors of national growth to include the economy, military and governance. In the CQM exercise which measured Human Capital six sub-factors were considered to include size of population, ratio of economically active population to total population, expenditure on health as a percentage of GDP, physicians per 10,000 of population, literacy and public spend on education as a percentage of GDP. USA, Belgium, Netherlands, Spain and Germany figure in the top five countries India is amongst the bottom five. The Table is as shown in next page.

Strategies for enhancing human capital should focus on improving two primary areas of significance—education and literacy as well as health. These are recommended as follows:

(a) **Literacy and Education.** There is a need for enhancing the rate of

Human Capital Index

Country	Population[13]	Index	Physicians per 10,090[14]	Index	Expenditure on Health Care as Percentage of GDP[15]	Index	Economically Active Population as ratio of total population[16]	Index	Public Spending on Education as Percentage of GDP[17]	Index	Literacy[18]	Index	Overall Index
United States	313847465	22.76	24	54.76	16.2	100	0.52	68.75	5.43	70.79	99	98.66	69.29
Belgium	10438353	0	30	69.05	11.8	68.12	0.45	48.95	6.57	100	99	98.66	64.13
Netherlands	16730632	0.47	29	66.67	10.8	60.87	0.52	70.03	5.94	83.91	99	98.66	63.43
Spain	47042984	2.75	40	92.86	9.7	52.9	0.49	60.11	5.01	59.92	97.7	95.75	60.71
Germany	81305856	5.32	36	83.33	8.1	41.3	0.52	68.97	5.06	61.06	99	98.66	59.77
India [Rank 26]	1205073612	89.63	6	11.9	2.4	0	0.42	37.88	3.21	13.42	61	13.65	27.75

literacy to 99 percent by end of the decade from the present 74.04 percent as per the 2011 census. This will imply a growth by 25 percent in 5 years or 5 to 6 percent per year. At the same time there is a need for increasing the High School Life Expectancy from the current rate of .32 per year to further increase to .41–.5 per year. Essentially an increase in allocations to education as percentage of GDP as a broad guideline is recommended from the 2013 allocation of 3.9 percent to over 6 percent for progressive development of human resources in a holistic manner. The use of ICT based education tools can overcome the bane of teacher deficiency particularly in rural areas. Thus digital education interventions would provide the way ahead.

(b) **Health Sector Allocations.** Allocations in the health sector need to be categorised in terms of savings rather than expenditure given the benefit that is accrued from healthy citizens who can contribute to the economy consistently. India's health expenditure as percentage of GDP public and private is 4 percent. Of this the share of public expenditure is 32 percent and private correspondingly 68 percent. There is a need for enhancing the public expenditure on health as this is the main area which can contribute to enhanced human resource development at the grass roots and overall contribution to the betterment of life and thus the economy. Enlarging capacities in medical colleges, para medical institutes and exploiting avenues in alternate medicine such as ayurveda, homeopathy and so on is also essential.

Science and Technology

For a nation with an aspiration to be on the global high table there is a need for enhancing science and technology (S&T) capabilities which in turn will have a multiplier effect on the economy and military amongst others. India can achieve domain specific competencies in S&T such as in Information Technology, pharmaceuticals and bio-technology within a short period of time while gradually increasing potential in other spheres. The CQM exercise on science and technology to include sub factors as expenditure on science and technology as a percentage of GDP, number of personnel involved in research and development, and the number of patents produced in a given year reveals that top five countries in this index are USA, Japan, China, Germany and South Korea while India is in the middle ranking sixteenth. The Table is as given below:

S&T Index

Country	R&D Percentage of GDP[19]	Index	No. of R&D Personnel[20]	Index	No. of Patents[21]	Index	Total S&T Index
United States	2.9	76.98	1412639	44.32	53916	100	73.77
Japan	3.36	89.59	1152787	36.16	40411	74.95	66.9
China	1.7	44.29	3183687	100	18557	34.42	59.57
Germany	2.82	74.95	774271.5	24.26	24430	45.31	48.17
South Korea	3.74	100	500124	15.64	10935	20.28	45.31
India [Rank 16]	0.76	18.45	391149	12.21	1329	2.46	11.04

Some of the strategies for enhancing science and technology potential of the country are as follows:

(a) **GERD.** R&D is a resource intensive domain which requires considerable financial investment. This is measured in terms of Gross Domestic Expenditure on Research and Development or GERD. India will have to increase GERD from an average of $ 1.696 million PPP per year to at least 4 times or $ 7 million to achieve viable progress in the field of S&T.

(b) **Institutes and Research Pool.** Expanding the capacity and quality of S&T institutes is an accepted intervention. This in turn will lead to an increase in the number of researchers and add to the overall S&T potential of the country.

(c) **Patents.** Patents are an important benchmark of S&T work that is being carried out in the country. A twofold strategy is necessary the first being increasing the number of patent registration and secondly rate of actualisation of patents into manufactured goods and products.

(d) **High Technology Exports Base.** High technology exports are another area that would enhance S&T potential of the country and will also contribute substantially to value added exports as well as trade and economy. Joint ventures and partnerships with advanced technology nations is necessary for this purpose.

Knowledge and Information

Increasingly advanced nations in the global society are basing their capabilities on Knowledge and Information (KI) marking a shift from the industrial to the information age. This adds to overall development by transforming goods and services more efficiently, generate better institutional capacity, enhance civil society and invite positive outside intervention. A comparative quantified model is not available for KI. Three main areas need to be considered to ensure expansion of India's KI base as follows:

(a) **Higher Education Mass and Quality.** Enhancement of the university infrastructure which is the base for higher education is imperative for the country. While focusing on the numbers there is also a necessity to ensure quality and may appear challenging but with greater participation of the private sector, investment of resources and rationalisation of university structures growth as well as quality can be achieved. Inviting quality foreign faculty is another intervention that needs consideration.

(b) **Expanding Base of Tertiary Education.** The Gross Enrolment Ratio in tertiary or post-secondary education is very low in India and more importantly declines substantially from 100 percent in primary to just 9 percent in the tertiary. So far there has been focus on primary education enrolment, now the emphasis has to increase on tertiary education as this will lead to enhancement of the overall knowledge base in the country by creating well educated individuals.

(c) **Reaping Digital India and Smart City.** The focus of the government on Digital India and Smart City projects can be reaped to advantage by extension of computer penetration and broad band reach through mobile connectivity. The possibility of leaping from the computer to the digital era exists for a large portion of the population which needs to be exploited by sustaining investments in Digital India and Smart City programmes to building K&I. At the same time investments should be made in transforming personnel to the digital age through education and training as laying out the infrastructure for digitisation alone will not lead to corresponding dividends in this sphere.

Primary Natural Resources

India is blessed by a favourable geography astride the primary sea lanes of the Indian Ocean, with a sufficiently large land mass and size of EEZ. There is a deficit of primary resources such as arable land, water, oil and gas and minerals. In the CQM exercise three sub factors have been included for natural resources to include total area of the country, per capita arable land and per capita availability of renewable fresh water, Canada, Russia, Australia, Brazil and USA figure amongst the top five. India is in the 10th position. The Table is as given below.

Size and Intrinsic Resources Index

Country	Area in sq kms[22]	Index	Arable land (1000 ha) per capita[23]	Index	Per capita Water Resources[24]	Index	Total Index
Canada	9984670	58.32	1.314866	60.78	82969	100	73.03
Russia	17098242	100	0.85428	38.95	30195	36.38	58.44
Australia	7741220	45.18	2.142165	100	21764	26.21	57.13
Brazil	8514877	49.71	0.307042	13.01	27551	33.19	31.97
United States	9826675	57.4	0.518567	23.03	9001	10.83	30.42
India [Rank 10]	3287263	19.08	0.131048	4.66	1165	1.38	8.37

Strategies for enhancing utilisation of natural resources are suggested as follows:

(a) **Effective Water Management.** Water management is a critical area for a country in which a major portion of the population is based on rain fed agriculture. At the same time a large portion of the water is wasted due to flooding. Enhancing water storage capacity exponentially through rain water harvesting programmes, restricting the drawal of ground water, encouraging dry land farming and drip water irrigation, expanding the irrigation network, river linking are some of the strategies which need consideration. In Gujarat reviving small and big water bodies has been a major success which needs to be replicated across the country.

(b) **Productivity of Arable Land.** Arable land is a premium resource in the country. The pressure on land is likely to increase with requirement for industrialisation conflicting with that of agriculture. Enhancing productivity of the available arable land is the only viable option. Agriculture extension, dry land farming, cropping, research and seed diversity are some of the key measures necessary to be undertaken to overcome the problem. Wasteland management is another area which needs active consideration. Improving agricultural output using better technology and investments in infrastructure and other areas such as dry land farming as a mission and utilising all available land gainfully remain alternatives.

(c) **Energy Enhanced Production and Energy Mix.** A mix of renewable and non-renewable energy is the way ahead. Natural gas is more efficient, thus cheaper long term LNG contracts, re-gasification plants of bigger size than at Hazira, investment in clean coal technology R&D, energy efficient nuclear and thermal power plants, assured supply using hydro power potential of Bhutan and Nepal, cutting down of transmission and distribution losses, energy grading of machines and daily use items and non-grid solar/wind energy for isolated rural and tribal areas are the multiplicity of options available in this sphere.

(d) **Transportation – Project Implementation.** India has the advantage of a favourable physical geography for building infrastructure. Project implementation remains a problem area which needs to be overcome with synergy and coordination between state and central government, environment agencies, public and private sector partnerships, optimal cost management, accountability for delay and financial evaluation. Speedy completion of freight corridors, completion of gauge conversion, and electrification of tracks and extension of railways to frontier areas is the way ahead for railways.

(e) **Strategic Minerals – Assured External Sources.** The availability of strategic minerals in the country especially Uranium is limited. There is however scope for exploration which needs to be undertaken on priority. India has to sign long term agreements with Australia, France, Russia, Canada, Kazakhstan, Uzbekistan and Namibia amongst others to ensure supply in the long term. Completion of the Thorium fuel cycle should also be given a priority so that domestic availability of this resource can be effectively exploited.

Governance

Governance is dictated by political stability, effectiveness of the government in delivery of services as well as law and order, quality of regulations, acceptance of rule of law by the people, level of corruption in society, internal security, and management of government affairs, decision making, foreign policy and diplomacy and so on.

(a) **Political Consensus.** As a vibrant democracy and a Union of States there are challenges to build political consensus in India. The aim should be to focus on larger issues of governance such as development goals and economic objectives through multiple consensus building mechanisms taking all political parties and sections of society on board. Education of masses on policies and consultative federalism in polity is the need of the hour.

(b) **Focus on Districts.** Delivery of governance at the district level which is the most proximate face of Government to the masses should be the focus. Down streaming the same, Panchayat empowerment and village adoption schemes need to be encouraged so that visible change can be brought about at the grass roots. There is a need for fixed tenures for district magistrates and superintendents of police of two to three years wherein their performance can be assessed and evaluated. This should be supplemented by similar performance appraisal of other district officials such as health, revenue and so on. This appraisal system will have to be quantitative and 360 degree including public perception thereby focusing on accountability to the people rather than the hierarchy alone.

(c) **Regulation of Industry.** Regulatory bodies in activities such as telecommunications, IT, energy, aviation and defence production are necessary to prevent exploitative monopolies be it public or private. This will establish a level playing field for all players which will be controlled by the regulatory bodies by promoting transparent growth, speedy settlement of disputes and removing bottlenecks.

(d) **Improving Judiciary.** Just as in policing India has one of the lowest judges to population ratio at ten judges to a million. A huge backlog of cases reflects poorly on the dispute resolution systems in the country and creates a high degree of frustration with resort to alternate means including use of crime. Thus an urgent focus on enhancing the judicial numbers needs consideration.

(e) **Transparency and Empowerment**. The Right to Information Act has had a salutary effect on controlling corruption in some areas. There is need for all government organs, the legislature, executive and the judiciary to be brought under its ambit the fastest and without exception. Appointment of Lok Ayuktas and a whistle blowers act with protection for witnesses also needs consideration.

Foreign Policy and Diplomacy

Foreign Policy enumerates the overall framework within which a nation conducts relationship with other countries and is built around its bilateral, regional and international aims and ambitions. Implementation of Foreign Policy is achieved through diplomacy. Some of the key recommendations for enhancing efficiency and effectiveness of foreign policy and diplomacy are as given below:

(a) **Public Articulation of Foreign Policy**. Public articulation of foreign policy through instruments such as White Papers periodically will create greater transparency thereby improving the quality of interaction with states and international institutions alike. The present practice of restricting the same to speeches and statements or annual reports lacks coherence and continuity. Consolidation through the process of white papers may provide greater visibility of the vision and the vectors which are driving India's interaction with the World at large.

(b) **Smart Power**. There is a general agreement that in meeting challenges of the 21st Century, Smart Power, a combination of Soft and Hard power is necessary. India has been able to leverage soft power to advantage as was evident in acceptance of Prime Minister Narendra Modi's proposal for declaring 21 June as International Yoga Day. This is an example where visional leadership was combined with effective diplomacy to achieve consensus on a platform as large as the United Nations. At the same time hard power provides the necessary umbrella of security which can is essential for sustain economic growth and development. A combination of the two termed as smart power is the way ahead.

(c) **Decentralisation and Delegation.** Within the overall ambit of foreign policy laid down by the Central Government through the Ministry of External Affairs, decentralisation and delegation for conduct of diplomacy economic, trade or military to respective ministries and State governments is the need of the hour. This will cut down time in decision making and empower Ministries/States to follow a vibrant policy of engagement with counter parts across the globe in various domains.

(d) **Numbers and Resources.** It is commonly acknowledged that India's foreign policy establishment is hampered by numbers, budgetary resources and research inputs. There is a need for enhancing the numbers in a gradual manner without creating turbulence. Recent move to rope in consultants should be another form. Encouraging study of international relations in universities and think tanks, improving the quality of education in this stream and investing in policy research is necessary so that this can provide the knowledge pool to the policy makers.

(e) **Expanding the Field of Ambassadors.** Able and articulate people from all walks of life should be picked up for diplomatic assignments while within the service Ambassadorship should be earned based on ability and a proven track record.

(f) **Expanding Economic Diplomacy.** Geo-economics is increasingly dictating geo-politics. Strengthening the economic arm of diplomacy has assumed importance. At the apex level a separate minister of state for economic diplomacy may have to be nominated to give an impetus to the same who should be able to coordinate between the Ministry of External Affairs and the Ministry of Commerce and Industry as well as other ministries to give an impetus to trade, use development aid and assistance effectively while contributing to overall engagement of nations at large.

(g) **Expanding Military Diplomacy.** Military diplomacy is a major tool for attaining foreign policy goals. A systematic effort to develop military diplomats is necessary to include foreign language courses during initial cadet training, mid-career exposure to global and regional affairs by attending seminars and conferences and enhancing representation on foreign missions. A specialist cadre of military diplomats also needs to be considered as this field requires a high degree of experience and expertise.

National Will and Leadership

Hans J. Morgenthau has highlighted the importance of national will and leadership particularly during a crisis. He states, "A nation's will tends to manifest itself most clearly in times of national crisis, when the existence of the nation is at stake or an issue of fundamental importance must be decided." Good leadership can convert strength of a nation into power while poor leadership will remain inhibited by deficits. There are three constituents of National Will follows:[25]

(a) Level or degree of cultural integration of the people in a feeling of belonging to a nation, which includes assessments of both cultural uniformity (ethnicity, language, religion) and popular identification with a territory (with cultural integration weighted three times as heavily as territorial integration).

(b) Effective strength of national leadership, comprising equal parts of governmental policy capability and level of social discipline.

(c) Relevance of strategy to national interest.

Some recommendations for developing National Will and Leadership are as follows:

(a) Study of India's glorious historical legacy and inherent strengths of India as a civilisation.

(b) Identification and articulation of national goals and objectives.

(c) Emphasising cultural cohesion, common national values, justice and fairness in society.

(d) Developing collective will to face national challenges peace as well as war.

(e) Developing strategic culture and vision.

(f) Youth should be groomed to be community, national and global leaders by providing opportunities for interaction at an early age.

Conclusion

The concept of CNP is not new to India. As highlighted the roots lay in the works of Chanakya's elements of sovereignty and circle of states which determine the strength of a nation and thus are the source of a six fold policy. Chanakya highlighted that a strong state can follow an independent policy of engagement with neighbours while a weak state will remain a vassal. India's aspirations for leadership in the World can be met by enhancing the CNP potential for which exists. By articulating a national vision and adopting a structured program with identification of critical strategies in each domain of the entire spectrum of national power CNP can be enhanced and goals achieved within a reasonable time frame of a decade or so.

NOTES

1. Hu Angang. The Rising of Modern China: Comprehensive National Power and Grand Strategy. Center for China Studies at Tsinghua University. Available at http://www.irchina.org/en/pdf/hag.pdf. P 3, 4. Accessed on 10 August 2014
2. Satish Chandra, Rahul Bhonsle National Security: Concept, Measurement and Management Strategic Analysis. Vol. 39, Issue. 4, 2015. IDSA. New Delhi.
3. GDP at purchaser's prices is the sum of gross value added by all resident producers in the economy plus any product taxes and minus any subsidies not included. It is calculated without making deductions for depreciation of fabricated assets or for depletion and degradation of natural resources. Data are in current U.S. dollars. Dollar figures for GDP are converted from domestic currencies using single year official exchange rates. For a few countries where the official exchange rate does not reflect the rate effectively applied to actual foreign exchange transactions, an alternative conversion factor is used. Data is for 2013. The details are as per World Bank 2013 World Development Indicators Available at http://data.worldbank.org/indicator/NY.GDP.MKTP.CD. (Accessed August 12, 2014).
4. Gross savings (% of GDP). Gross savings are calculated as gross national income less total consumption, plus net transfers. World Bank national accounts data, and OECD National Accounts data files. Data is for 2010.
5. Reserves of Foreign Exchange and Gold for 2011. This entry gives the dollar value for the stock of all financial assets that are available to the central monetary authority for use in meeting a country's balance of payments needs as of the end-date of the period specified. This category includes not only foreign currency and gold, but also a country's holdings of Special Drawing Rights in the International Monetary Fund, and its reserve position in the Fund. Available at https://www.cia.gov/library/publications/the-world-factbook/rankorder/2188rank.html. (Accessed February 21, 2013).

6. Public Debt as percentage of GDP for 2011. This entry records the cumulative total of all government borrowings less repayments that are denominated in a country's home currency. Public debt should not be confused with external debt, which reflects the foreign currency liabilities of both the private and public sector and must be financed out of foreign exchange earnings. Available at https://www.cia.gov/library/publications/the-world-factbook/rankorder/2186rank.html?countryName=China&countryCode=ch&regionCode=eas&rank=75#ch. (Accessed February 21, 2013).
7. GDP per capita is gross domestic product divided by midyear population. GDP is the sum of gross value added by all resident producers in the economy plus any product taxes and minus any subsidies not included in the value of the products. It is calculated without making deductions for depreciation of fabricated assets or for depletion and degradation of natural resources. Data are in current U.S. dollars. Available at http://data.worldbank.org/indicator/NY.GDP.PCAP.CD. (Accessed February 22, 2013).
8. Chasing the Dragon, Mohan Guruswamy and Zorawar Daulet Singh, Dorling Kindersley (India) Pvt. Ltd., 2010, p. 125.
9. Active military personnel represent those ready to fight. Available at SIPRI 2010 as indicated in Wikpedia List of countries by number of military personnel which include Active forces only. http://en.wikipedia.org/wiki/List_of_countries_by_number_of_military_and_paramilitary_personnel. Data has also been counter checked with other sources. (Accessed June, 22 2013).
10. Defence Expenditure 2012 at 2011 constant Prices. Available at SIPRI Military Expenditure Database 2012, http://milexdata.sipri.org. Defence of some countries including China is SIPRI estimates and may vary with actual. Data is for 2012. (Accessed on June 22, 2013).
11. Defence Expenditure per soldier is calculated by dividing the total defence expenditure for 2012 by the number of armed forces personnel.
12. Nuclear weapon states, China, France, India, Pakistan, Russia, UK and United States have been given a 25 % accretion in the basic military index due to possession of higher capability.
13. Population Data for 2012. This entry gives an estimate from the US Bureau of the Census based on statistics from population censuses, vital statistics registration systems, or sample surveys pertaining to the recent past and on assumptions about future trends. Available at CIA Gov. https://www.cia.gov/library/publications/the-world-factbook/rankorder/rawdata_2119.txt. (Accessed December 07, 2012).
14. Physicians (Per 10,000 Population). Available at http://www.globalhealthfacts.org/data/topic/map.aspx?ind=74. (Accessed December 13, 2012) Physicians per 1000 http://data.worldbank.org/indicator/SH.MED.PHYS.ZS used in case of countries where the data is not available for 10,000 citizens. (Accessed December 13, 2012).
15. Total expenditure on health as a percentage of GDP. Health expenditures are broadly defined as activities performed either by institutions or individuals through the application of medical, paramedical, and/or nursing knowledge and technology, the primary purpose of which is to promote, restore, or maintain health. Available at CIA Country reports available at https://www.cia.gov/library/publications/the-world-factbook/rankorder/2225rank.html?countryName=Afghanistan&countryCode=af&regionCode=sas&rank=67#af. (Accessed December 15, 2012). Variation of 0.20 in UK not corrected as minor.
16. The economically active population is taken as a proportion of total population. The economically active population comprises all persons of either sex who furnish the supply of

labour for the production of goods and services during a specified time-reference period as per the International Labour Organisation. (ILO). Data is to be multiplied by 1000 and is for 2011. Available at FAO http://www.fao.org/nr/water/aquastat/data/query/results.html. (Accessed March 10, 2013).

17. Public spending on education, total (% of GDP). Public expenditure on education as % of GDP is the total public expenditure (current and capital) on education expressed as a percentage of the Gross Domestic Product (GDP) in a given year. Public expenditure on education includes government spending on educational institutions (both public and private), education administration, and transfers/subsidies for private entities (students/households and other private entities). Available at http://data.worldbank.org/indicator/SE.XPD.TOTL.GD.ZS for 2009. (Accessed December 15, 2012). Some data is for other years and from other sources where data is not available in main source. For instance China 2008 Data from http://www.oecd.org/china/48677215.pdf. (Accessed December 15, 2012). Figures for Nigeria GDP %age Edn are NA hence that of India used based on same level of literacy but will not be accurate indicator.

18. Literacy as percentage of population implies age 15 and over can read and write. Available at https://www.cia.gov/library/publications/the-world-factbook/fields/print_2103.html. (Accessed December 15, 2012). India literacy is as per 2001 Census and has been retained for uniformity with other countries parameters even though new census 2011 has been published.

19. GERD or General Expenditure on R&D as a percentage of GDP. Data of 2009 unless otherwise indicated, partial data not included. Available at http://stats.uis.unesco.org/unesco/TableViewer/tableView.aspx?ReportId=2656. (Accessed December 16, 2012). Provisional or Partial Data is not take nearest full data available has been taken.

20. Total R&D personnel by sex (Headcounts - HC) Data is of 2009 but in some cases of earlier years. In some cases date may have been derived from full time equivalents as given in the source Head count Available at http://stats.uis.unesco.org/unesco/TableViewer/tableView.aspx?ReportId=5472. (Accessed December 16, 2012).

21. International applications via the PCT, Madrid and Hague systems by origin, Data is for 2011. A patent is a set of exclusive rights granted by law to applicants for inventions that are new, non-obvious, and commercially applicable. It is valid for a limited period of time (generally 20 years), during which patent holders can commercially exploit their inventions on an exclusive basis. In return, applicants are obliged to disclose their inventions to the public in a manner that enables others, skilled in the art, to replicate the invention. The patent system is designed to encourage innovation by providing innovators with time-limited exclusive legal rights, thus enabling the innovators to appropriate the returns on their innovative activities. World Intellectual Property Organisation. WIPO 2011. WIPO Publication No. 943E/2012. wipo_pub_943_2012 Patents.pdf. (Accessed December 15, 2012). Annexure page 39. Data for Brazil is 564 but erroneously reflected as 584 and is not corrected being comparatively marginal error.

22. Data is for 2012 Available at https://www.cia.gov/library/publications/the-world-factbook/rankorder/rawdata_2147.txt. (Accessed February 21, 2013).

23. Arable land is per capita and Data is for 2009. Available at http://www.fao.org/nr/water/aquastat/data/query/results.html. (Accessed December 07, 2012). Separate source for Japan only.

24. Total internal renewable water resources per capita (m^3/inhab/yr). Available at http://www.fao.org/nr/water/aquastat/data/query/results.html . (Accessed December 07, 2012). Data for 2011.

25. Richard L. Merritt. Dina A. Zinnes. Alternative Indexes of National Power in Richard J Stoll. Michael D Ward. Ed. Power in World Politics. Lynne Rienner Publications. Boulder, CO. 1989, p. 20.

(Brigadier Rahul K. Bhonsle (Retd.) is managing a strategic risk and knowledge management consultancy-security-risks.com focusing on strategic culture and security trends in South Asia, future warfare and human security. The author acknowledges the guidance by Ambassador Satish Chandra and Lt Gen R K Sawhney in conceptualizing the research for this article and formalizing recommendations along with study team members).

*

Contemporary: Japan

13

Japan's Changing Security Discourse through the Prism of its Deterrence Imperative

Prerna Gandhi

> "In strategy, it is important to see distant things as if they were close, and to take a distanced view of close things"
>
> —Miyamoto Musashi, Book of Five Rings, 1645.

ABSTRACT

All international relations experts contend that the US-Japan alliance is the cornerstone for Japan's security and its deterrence. However, most miss out as to why despite conflicts of interests and intermittent tensions, Japan has never sought to replace the alliance with its own defence capabilities. Though Japan's strategic policies underwent a massive change with the beginning of the 2000s, its security policy for deterrence has not shifted from resting on the US-Japan alliance. In this paper, through the prism of the changing dynamics of the alliance-arms substitution argument in regard to the US-Japan alliance, we will study Japan's Changing Security discourse to meet its deterrence imperative and efforts to formulate new security frameworks to suit changing times.

Introduction

Bernard Brodie, in his pioneering work '*The Absolute Weapon: Atomic Power and World Order*' in 1946, wrote that the world before 1945 was fundamentally different from the world that would follow. Up to that point, he argued, "the chief purpose of our military establishment [had] been to win wars. From now on, its chief purpose must be to avert them. It can have almost no other purpose." For Japan, the essence of deterrence has formed the underlying theme of its security policy since the adoption of its Peace Constitution in May 1947. The Peace Constitution led Japan to give up its right to belligerence as a means of settling international disputes, while not maintaining any offensive war armaments. As a result, Japan's concept of deterrence has focused more on the conceptualised end of deterrence (prevention of war) rather than the means necessary for deterrence (military preparations to deter).

Over the decades, Japan has maintained three bright lines with regard to its security policy. First, it will pursue an exclusively defence-oriented policy. Second, it will not become a military power that poses a threat to other countries. Third, it will follow the three 'Non-Nuclear Principles' of not possessing nuclear weapons, not producing nuclear weapons, and not permitting nuclear weapons to be brought to Japan. The Security Treaty of 1951 and Treaty of Mutual Cooperation and Security of 1960 with the USA have been the underpinning of its territorial and external military security till date. These security treaties entitling the USA to station military bases in Japan and extend nuclear deterrence to Japan have been pivotal to not only Japan's post-war security policy but also to the strategic-military balance of power in the region.

Extended Deterrence

Vesna Danilovic writes in her 2002 book, *'When the Stakes Are High: Deterrence and Conflict among Major Powers,'* that the outcome of extended deterrence is determined by two factors—retaliatory capability and threat credibility. Retaliatory capability is linked to the analysis of relative power distribution between the 'challenger' and 'defender' in regard to defending the third party. On the other hand, threat credibility is a function of three factors: (1) the intensity of linkages between a major power and the region in which a conflict occurs (an extension of inherent credibility theory); (2) the domestic incentives for not backing down; and (3) the pursuit of a costly signalling strategy intended to develop an international reputation for strong resolve in honouring commitments (i.e., the core of commitment theory). The author also notes that the power shift argument is inconsistent that wars are likely to result from an uncertainty of power parity and emphasizes it is important to differentiate between balance of power and balance of interests, as they can have reverse effects on deterrence outcomes.

In view of the rapidly changing security environment in the region, Japanese policymakers note an increase in and prolongation of so-called 'gray-zone' situations that can be considered neither pure peacetime nor contingencies over territory, sovereignty and maritime economic interests. Gray-zone coercions also involve show of physical presence frequently in an attempt to make changes to the status quo to the extent that it does not constitute armed attack. In the context of shifting balance of power and insufficient institutionalisation of security frameworks in the region, the increasing number of gray zone situations especially in the maritime domain—East China Sea and South China Sea—have led to a negation of diplomacy and the established rule-based order.[1] In addition, the very countries involved in gray-zone coercion like North Korea and China have sought to rapidly reinforce their military capabilities and intensify their military activities. In view of the growing entanglements of the USA with North Korea and, more specifically, China, it is difficult to predict what regional issues and interests in Japan will determine USA's willingness to get involved in a conflict on behalf of Japan.

All international relations experts contend that the US-Japan alliance is the cornerstone of Japan's security and its deterrence. However, most miss out as to why despite conflicts of interests and intermittent tensions, Japan has never sought to replace the alliance with its own defence capabilities. Though Japan's strategic policies have undergone massive change with the beginning of the 2000s, its security policy for deterrence has not shifted from resting on the US-Japan alliance.

Table 1: Japan's Defence Budget

Year	Defence Budget (in US$ bn)	Defence Budget as Percentage of GDP
2000	45.402	0.9
2001	46.197	0.9
2002	46.427	1.0
2003	46.486	1.0
2004	46.300	0.9
2005	46.216	0.9

(Contd.)

Year	Defence Budget (in US$ bn)	Defence Budget as Percentage of GDP
2006	45.627	0.9
2007	45.034	0.9
2008	44.601	0.9
2009	45.436	1.0
2010	45.595	1.0
2011	46.209	1.0
2012	45.653	1.0
2013	45.459	1.0
2014	45.944	1.0
2015	46.754	1.0
2016	46.471	0.9
2017	46.556	0.9

Source: SIPRI[2]

In this paper, through the prism of the changing dynamics of the alliance-arms substitution argument in regard to the US-Japan alliance, we will study Japan's Changing Security discourse to meet its deterrence imperative and efforts to formulate new security frameworks to suit the changing times.

Alliance-Arms Substitution

As mentioned by Robert Rothstein in his 1968 seminal work *'Alliances and Small Powers'*, alliances with other countries may substitute for arms (i.e., national defence capabilities), if an 'alliance' increases the probability of successful deterrence by making the deterring state stronger. Through an alliance, a state is able to acquire a reliable promise of support from an ally and translate that promise into a credible threat, though at the prospective cost of having to moderate conflicts with the ally. In the case of Japan, a number of reasons, from its constitution and historical legacies, to increasingly severe security environment with various challenges and destabilizing factors, have led it to substitute arms with the US-Japan alliance to pursue its national interests and national security objectives. Thus, it is no surprise that many of Japan's official policy documents when talking about strengthening Japan's own deterrence include strengthening the extended deterrence of the deeply-embedded US-Japan alliance.

One must note that arms or national defence capabilities and alliances are also complements rather than water-tight substitutes for one another. Substitution or complementary effects of alliances on arms spending depend on alliance types, prevailing defence burdens, and numbers of allies. Increases in a state's relative capabilities allows for increases in both arms and alliances, leading a state to rely on increases in both because they help to obtain the same good. While the costs of arms and alliances are usually internal, arms and alliance benefits tend to be external. The internal costs of arms are that they necessitate dealing with domestic political opposition, especially to increases in taxation and extra-territorial military involvement. The internal costs of alliances are that they necessitate dealing with domestic political opposition to certain policy concessions required to placate alliance partners. The external benefits of arms are that they are more reliable than alliances in improving a state's international security environment, although arms build-ups generate security more slowly than alliance ties. The external benefits of alliances are that they improve a state's international security environment more quickly than arms build-ups, although alliances are less reliable than arms in generating security.[3]

States evaluate the gains they would receive from an alliance in terms of the trade-offs they would make that arise from the risks of 'abandonment' and 'entrapment'. Abandonment occurs when a state's allies fail to come to its assistance. Entrapment occurs when a state is drawn by an ally into a conflict it otherwise would have avoided. Evaluating alliance costs thus means comparing the risks of abandonment and entrapment to the gains in security or autonomy that a state expects to receive from its alliance. Thinking of alliance costs in terms of abandonment and entrapment puts arms-alliance substitution into a meaningful context. In the case of Japan, its alliance with the USA provides it with additional strength and a more effective deterrent posture. However, similar to asymmetric alliances for security, Japan is more likely to be concerned about the risks of abandonment than the risk of entrapment. In fact, much of its changing security debate is based on strengthening Japan's contribution to the US-Japan alliance in fear of abandonment by the USA. Entrapment on the other hand, tends to be more important to a state whose alliance is intended to increase its autonomy, or to a member of symmetric alliance in which the military capabilities of both states affect the other's security. Thus, on the issue of sovereignty of the Senkaku Islands, the official US position on its security involvement has only been reiteration of Article 5 of the US-Japan Security Treaty that limits the scope of the Treaty's application to "territories under the administration of Japan."[4]

For the USA, Japan holds a unique position among its allies, and very rightly so, owing to Japan's unique geopolitical position of bordering on the maritime front with Russia, the Korean Peninsula, and China. In its 2017 National Security Strategy, the USA clubs Russia and China as 'revisionist powers' and North Korea as a 'rogue power' in its three categories of prime challengers (third being 'transnational threat organisations') to US security. Commander Fleet Activities Yokosuka (CFAY) located in Tokyo Bay is home to 55 tenant commands and is strategically the most important US naval installation in Western Pacific. It houses the headquarters of both the US Seventh Fleet and Naval Forces Japan. The Americans have been at Yokosuka since 1945 and not so surprisingly Yokosuka is the home to the only forward deployed US aircraft carrier USS Ronald Reagan and one of the two Blue-Ridge class command ships of the US Navy. Yokosuka Naval Base was the heartbeat of the Imperial Japanese Navy for its ship-repair facilities which are considered better than even on the US mainland. Yokosuka today is the second largest US fuel storage depot which can keep the US Seventh Fleet operating for six months. Even with the Trump Administration in the USA and its 'America First' strategy, Japan will thus continue to remain the core of US access and influence in the Asia-Pacific region, while housing its second largest number of overseas bases.

Further, unlike the mutual defence agreement with South Korea or collective defence agreement such as the North Atlantic Treaty Organization (NATO), Japan is heavily reliant on US military protection for defence, with total dependence upon US nuclear deterrence. Japan provides the US with "facilities and areas" and "Host Nation Support" in return for a US commitment to defend Japan and ensure the security of the region. Though, unlike Japan that seeks alliance to increase security, the USA with a high level of security seeks this alliance to increase autonomy and its leverages to serve as its substitute for arms. The unique bilateral defence relationship between the USA and Japan is also cemented by close trade and investment relations.

Background to Japan's Security Debate

In a paper, Sorokin (1994)[5] illustrates how states tend to rely on their allies' arms when allied support is relatively cheap and their allies are militarily strong, whereas they tend to rely on their own capabilities when allied support is relatively costly and their allies are militarily weak. To this dynamic, one could further add the non-military cost of mitigating differences and managing conflicts of interest with the ally.

Though over the course of decades post World War II, even when alliance costs went up for Japan, rapidly changing external security variables led it to continue to substitute pursuing arms with the continuation of the alliance. In its costs and benefits analysis, allying with the USA provided it substantial remuneration beyond security for a resource-scare nation. The USA allied security support was not only cheap, but also entailed Japan's access to the US domestic market, international re-acceptance, access to a world-class intelligence and surveillance network, technology, international legitimacy with USA being the leader of the free world, etc. After its horrendous defeat in World War II, strong public aversion to war and historical legacies that made relations with nearly all its neighbours difficult, the militarily strong USA led Japan to contentedly reduce its defence spending as it gained security at almost nil rate.

Yoshida Shigeru, one of the most powerful figures in post-war Japan and prime minister from 1946-47 and then 1948-1954, influenced much of post-war Japan's strategic–military policy. He promulgated the 'Yoshida Doctrine' built on three pillars of 'seikei-bunri' or economics first policy, Japan's adherence to the Peace Constitution and reliance on the USA for security. Japan's first post-war official document, the Basic Policy on National Defence (1957), defined Japan's strategic-military role as to resist direct and indirect aggression against Japan's national security pending the arrival of assistance from the US/UN forces. This approach was reinforced in the second official document on Japan's defence policy, the National Defence Policy Outline (NDPO), that for the first time defined mission and force structure for Self Defence Forces (SDF) in 1976. Yoshida's landmark quote, *"If you like shade, find yourself a big tree"*, was to remain a defining theme in Japan's post-war strategic-military culture until the 1970s.

Thereupon it was challenged by multiple international events such as Nixon visiting China in 1972, the oil crisis, withdrawal of American troops from Vietnam in 1975, increased trade friction with the USA and continuous US pressure after the Nixon-Sato Communiqué in 1969 to take up greater military responsibilities.[6]

Post-war Japan had assumed that the international security environment was given which could not be affected by Japan. By 1968, Japan surpassed West Germany to become the world's second largest economy after the USA. But the breakdown of détente and intensification of the Cold War in the late 1970s, led to a new comprehensive security concept that security went beyond military issues where Japan could also influence the international environment. In 1974, Japanese Prime Minister Kakuei Tanaka's tour of Southeast Asian capitals was met by vehement anti-Japanese demonstrations especially in Bangkok and Jakarta. To resolve tensions, Prime Minister Takeo Fukuda in his 1977 tour of the Association of South East Asian Nations (ASEAN) member states enunciated the Fukuda Doctrine. The Doctrine pledged that Japan would never become a military power, two that it would build up a relationship of mutual confidence and trust with Southeast Asian countries in wide-ranging fields, and that Japan would cooperate positively with ASEAN and its member countries in their own efforts, as an equal partner. The Doctrine itself became "a symbol of amity and cooperation between Japan and Southeast Asia."

In fears of US military withdrawal from Asia, the Guidelines for Defence Cooperation were signed in 1978 when Japan started contributing 10 per cent to the maintenance of US forces in Japan. Thus, even though Japan had adequate economic resources, the unresolved historical legacies and increasing instability in the international and regional strategic environment led it to continue with the alliance-for-arms substitution after alliance support costs went up. The 1978 Defence Cooperation Guidelines between Japan and the USA provided division of responsibilities and the foundation for joint planning and crisis response to defending an armed attack against Japan. Subsequently, after 20 years, the 1997 Guidelines for Japan-US Defence Cooperation would introduce the Bilateral Coordination Mechanism (BCM) to provide formal structures for joint planning and crisis response in response to an armed attack against Japan, and cooperation in situations surrounding Japan. The BCM, however, could not be activated unless an armed attack commenced. Thus in 2015, the Revised Defence Guidelines outlined the need for whole-of-government coordination. They stated that the Alliance Coordination Mechanism (ACM) will be utilised in "any situation that affects Japan's peace and security or any other situation that may require an Alliance response."

Japan, in its efforts to support the US-Japan alliance, expanded its Official Development Assistance (ODA) policy in the 1980s to countries deemed as "strategically important" by the USA.[7] More changes came along under Nakasone's term as prime minister as he removed the ban on Japan's export of dual military technology to the USA. Under him, Japan also increased cooperation on military front with the USA. Japan agreed to cooperate with the USA in its Strategic Defence Initiative (SDI) and entered into joint production of the advanced fighter aircraft, FSX. Nakasone also broke the 1 per cent ceiling on defence expenditure (though it amounted to only 1.013 per cent) to strengthen military capability.[8] Nakayamo Taro's (foreign minister at the time of the Gulf War) quote, *"peace has its price, and we have to pay it"*, was a radical departure from Yoshida. It lay down the tone for the 1990s marked by the Gulf War, North Korean nuclear and missile crises, Taiwan Strait rises and an increased threat perception from China.

In fact, it was the Gulf War in the beginning of the 1990s decade that raised the alliance support costs for Japan tremendously. Japan though it initially declined US/UN requests for participation in the war on grounds that it did not want to involve in a middle-eastern crises, it later contributed about $13 billion to the war effort. However, its contribution was derided as "check book diplomacy" and it was excluded from Kuwait's congratulatory message to US/UN forces. The fear of alienating the USA provoked Japan to seriously question its pacifist policy. While in the 1950s, Japan used the UN as a shield for its minimalist security policy; decades later in the 1990s, the UN once again became the legitimising institution to overcome domestic constraints so as to carve a responsible role in international security affairs. With the enactment of the International Peace Cooperation Law

(IPCL) in 1992 that allowed Japan to send not just civilian personnel but even its SDF, Japan cooperated in numerous peacekeeping operations and international humanitarian relief operations such as in Angola, Cambodia, Rwanda and Iraq.

Japan's participation in the UN peacekeeping operations (PKO) and its anti-piracy measures in Somalia by guarding commercial ships with military escorts won it much international acclaim and praise. Owing to the Gulf War debacle, after the 2001 terrorist strike on US soil, Japan was quick to show solidarity and passed the Anti-Terrorism Special Measures Law in September 2001, following which the SDF was deployed to assist the US-led international coalition through rear end and logistics support. Former Prime Minister Koizumi justified the decision to send the SDF to Iraq with the following three points: To send SDF to Iraq is to help Iraqi people and support international cooperation; the SDF would be offering humanitarian assistance and would not be using force; it is important for Japan's international relations with the USA. Further in the Diplomatic Bluebook 2004, the Japanese government stressed that the instability in Iraq would have a direct impact on Japan due to its extensive reliance of almost 90 per cent on Middle Eastern oil and hence it was necessary that Japan make efforts towards ensuring peace and stability in this region. Japan withdrew from Iraq in 2006.

After North Korea withdrew from the Non-Proliferation Treaty (NPT) in 2003, Japan announced its decision to build a missile defence system through joint-efforts with the USA and introduced the Aegis Ballistic Missile Defence (BMD) capability of the Sea-Based Midcourse Defence System as an upper-tier capability, and Patriot PAC-3 for lower-tier Ground-Based Terminal Defence. 2004 saw the beginnings of both the East China Sea Conflict and the rapid ascent of the China-Japan bilateral trade relationship. In 2004, China with Hong Kong became Japan's largest trading partner. 2005 saw Tokyo and Washington's Two-Plus-Two meeting in February 2005 and issuing of a joint security statement that placed the Taiwan Strait under Japan-US joint defence. This indicated that Japan might intervene in a future cross-strait scenario and thus interfere in what China deemed a domestic matter. The next month, UN Secretary General Kofi Annan declared his support for adding Japan to the permanent members of the UN Security Council. Additional anger arose when the Japanese Ministry of Education approved a supposedly nationalist textbook which glossed over Japan's war record. All this led to the largest anti-Japanese demonstrations in China since the two countries normalised diplomatic relations in 1972.[9]

What is truly interesting is that when across China, businesses with connections to Japan, billboards advertising Japanese goods and stores stocking Japanese made products were vandalised by protesters, the same year Japan became the largest overseas supplier of products to China with $79.9 billion in exports. China's displacement of the USA as the largest destination for Japanese exports highlighted the growing dependence of the world economy on China as it helped to keep the then world's second-largest economy from falling back into recession. Also by the end of 2005, Japan's accumulated investment in China had reached over US$ 70 billion to make it the main source of foreign investment in China. To add further insult, Japan was soon surpassed by China as the world's second largest economy in the last quarter of 2010. Ironically, when the ruling Democratic Party of Japan was engaged in a vehement conflict in 2010 with the USA to move the US Futenma military base unpopular with many locals from Okinawa, China became a saving factor in the weakening alliance. In September 2010, Japan seized a Chinese trawler and its crew after it collided with two coast guard vessels near the islands, sparking a serious diplomatic row. Small anti-Japanese protests were held in several cities in China. In the end, Japan released the trawler's crew.

In the aftermath of the boat collision incident near the Senkaku/Diaoyu islands, Chinese Customs officials reportedly stopped shipments of rare earth minerals to Japan. Japan was China's largest purchaser of the minerals, which have a wide variety of applications in high tech machinery, especially in clean energy and military technologies. Therefore, the drop in rare earth shipments, which reportedly lasted until the end of November 2010 and then resumed at less than previous amounts, was keenly felt in Japan's high-tech industry. In August 2012, the Japanese government's purchase of three of the disputed islands from a private landowner, in order to preempt their sale to Tokyo's nationalist governor Shintaro Ishihara, sparked massive Chinese protests and a marked drop in Sino-Japanese trade. This led to military escalation in the East China Sea by both the countries, leading to scrambling of fighter jets, locking of radars followed by undue display of naval warships which further precipitated suspicion rather than calming the conflict.

On 23 November 2013, a Chinese Air Force spokesperson, Shen Jinke announced that, "any aircraft flying through the newly designated East China Sea Air Defence Identification Zone (ADIZ) must seek prior permission from the Chinese authorities in advance and follow instructions from its air-traffic controllers". He further stated that "China's armed forces will adopt 'defensive emergency measures' to respond to aircraft that do not cooperate in the identification or refuse to follow instructions".[10] This sudden declaration from the Chinese side was vehemently opposed by Japan and the USA, which are strong proponents of freedom of navigation in international waters. While Japan's Prime Minister Shinzo Abe expressed his discontent by terming China's action to create a new ADIZ over the disputed islands as dangerous, US President Barack Obama responded swiftly by sending two unarmed B-52 bombers in a 'routine exercise' to fly over the new ADIZ without informing China. The USA is bound by the US-Japan Security Treaty to protect "the territories under the Administration of Japan" and has asserted that Japan administers the Senkaku (Diaoyu, for the Chinese) Islands. Yet though Japan is assured of US help through the treaty, its anxiety remains over Washington's commitment to defend Japanese territory if it risks going to war with China.

The islands conflict in East China Sea goes beyond mere questions of territorial sovereignty of three uninhabitable islands and five rocks (which, in total, amount to only 2.7 square miles in the East China Sea). The conflict spills over to clashing Exclusive Economic Zones (EEZ) and continental shelves based on the inconclusive UN Convention on the Law of Sea (UNCLOS), fisheries, shipping routes and logistics. The uncertainty of exact scope and scale of natural resources of the East China Sea which were last explored in 1968, and a derisive desire to perpetuate the conflict as a nationalist agenda by building upon historical wounds and memories by both countries exacerbates the matter. China's increasing demand for energy has prompted intense interest in resource extraction from the continental shelf that runs under the East China Sea. Also, the strategic shipping routes for China in the Yellow Sea Economic Basin (YSEB), catering to 57 per cent of China's trade[11] north of the East China Sea lead to more reasons for China's controlling interests in the Islands. For Japan, its stake in those Islands assume even more strategic importance beyond oil and fish as they form its first line of defence and are a mere 410 kilometres or 220 nautical miles away from Okinawa which is strategically important for both Japan and the USA. Despite a brewing debate in Japan and lack of stable domestic political government later, the Koizumi administration had prevented the steering of security policy-making in a distinct direction. From 2007 to 2013, no party in Japan enjoyed majority in both the Lower and Upper Houses of the Diet for more than a few months. In fact, since 2007, Japan saw six prime ministers, including Prime Minister Shinzo Abe who came to office in late 2012 after holding the office previously in 2006-2007 with a landslide victory for his Liberal Democratic Party (LDP). Abe's statement of *"Japan will never be a tier-two country"*, during his famous 'Japan is Back' speech at the Centre for Strategic and International Studies (CSIS) in 2013, greatly sums up his vision for Japan. There has been a growing pressure on Japan from the USA in recent years to participate in joint efforts for peace and stability and take on a larger security role commensurate with its national capabilities. Japan is now at the crossroads of having to deal with new power realities associated with the dramatic rise of China—both economically and militarily. Since surpassing Japan to become the world's second largest economy, China has also begun infringing on the economic leadership enjoyed by Japan in the Asia-Pacific region. China-led initiatives such as the Belt and Road Initiative (BRI) and Asian Infrastructure Investment Bank (AIIB) rival Japanese initiatives such as the Official Development Assistance (ODA) and the Japan-led Asian Development Bank (ADB).

At this stage, the power differential between China and Japan has widened considerably, whereas continuing with the alliance-for-arms substitution is Japan's only pragmatic choice to deter aggression. As the leeway of Japan's free-ride on the USA's arms declines and as the USA becomes militarily stronger, the disparity in contribution to the alliance has increased the price of alliance support on Japan. Yet, any efforts by Japan to offset the controversial aspects of shifting its arms-alliance in favour of arms build-up will still need to be done under the auspices of the US-Japan alliance. The alliance offsets the controversial aspects that could fuel a regional arms race and alienate the neighbours of Japan it enjoys good ties with such as the ASEAN-member states and South Korea. Arms build-up under the umbrella of alliance will also cushion the domestic resistance where economics plays a dominant role and historical memories of World War II have not yet faded.

Nuclear Deterrence

In modern international relations discourse, deterrence is more often than not referred to as nuclear deterrence. It is not an understatement to say that there is probably no country which shows more dislike for nuclear armaments than Japan which suffered the trauma of nuclear attacks twice. Japanese public opinion polls consistently reveal that public opinion is overwhelmingly opposed to nuclearization. Concurrently, Japan has been active in encouraging and strengthening multi-lateral non-proliferation and disarmament regimes since the early 1990s and submitted disarmament resolutions to the United Nations General Assembly every year since 1994. However, Japan's nuclear deterrence is provided in entirety by a country that dropped two atomic bombs on it. In a paper, Satoh (2017)[12] mentions that Japan lacks strategic depth, as its population is heavily concentrated in a few major cities along the coasts. Thus, the only credible deterrent it might consider would be the one deployed at sea—nuclear submarines carrying nuclear-tipped ballistic missiles. Being a US ally, Japan is ensured of a very credible extended nuclear umbrella, evident through the US's major Trident II SLBM program and the global deployment of US surface ships and submarines.

Japan's nuclear and non-proliferation policy is composed of four main pillars: Atomic Energy Basic Law of 1955, restricting Japan's nuclear energy use exclusively to peaceful purposes; the 'Three Non-Nuclear Principles', of not possessing, producing or introducing nuclear weapons on Japanese soil; compliance with the NPT; and reliance on US nuclear umbrella for external security.[13] However, Japan's role as a spokesperson for nuclear disarmament has been complicated between its contradictory positions of nuclear abstinence and ensuring the credibility of the US extended nuclear deterrence. In 2010, Japan acknowledged a Cold War secret pact with the USA, concluded in 1969, that US ships carrying nuclear weapons could stop at Japanese ports as it was not tantamount to passage of nuclear weapons on Japanese soil, and that nuclear weapons could be stationed in Okinawa during an emergency. The 'No Confirm-No Denial' policy deferred questions over US Forces in Japan (USFJ) without creating tensions in the region and implicating Japan.[14]

The National Defence Policy Guidelines (NDPG) documents of Japan from 1976, 1995, and 2004 left it to the USS entirely to deter nuclear threats. The first NDPG of 1976 simply stated, "Against nuclear threats, Japan will rely on the nuclear deterrent capability of the United States." The second NDPG of 1995 qualified reliance on US nuclear deterrence with an emphasis on Japan's diplomatic efforts for nuclear disarmament. By contrast, the NDPG of 2004, adopted by the Koizumi government, separated reliance on US nuclear deterrence from efforts for international nuclear disarmament. It also underlined the importance of BMD as Japan's own efforts to supplement reliance on US extended deterrence. This NDPG also stressed Tokyo's preparedness to play an active role in international disarmament and non-proliferation efforts, including Japan's participation in the Proliferation Security Initiative (PSI) proposed by US President Bush a year earlier in 2003.[15]

Against this backdrop, the NDPG of 2010 reflected a major shift in Japanese leadership views of the US extended deterrent. It recognised that US' 'extended deterrence, with nuclear deterrent as a vital element' would be indispensable as long as nuclear weapons exist, and stated that Japan would closely cooperate with the USA in order to maintain and improve the credibility of extended deterrence. Thus, the Extended Deterrence Dialogue (EDD) was instituted in 2010 to strengthen policy coordination on extended deterrence and the nuclear umbrella, Dialogue, and has happened every year since then. Surprisingly, the Dialogue has aroused little backlash in public and political opinion, testifying to the increased public awareness of the need to ensure the effectiveness of that umbrella. The major shift reflected in the 2010 NDPG was also reflected in Japan's first-ever National Security Strategy, as crafted by Abe government and released in 2013. On the topic of extended deterrence, it argued, "with regard to the threat of nuclear weapons, the extended deterrence of the US with nuclear deterrence at its core is indispensable. In order to maintain and enhance the credibility of the extended deterrence, Japan will work closely with the US, and take appropriate measures through its own efforts, including BMD and protection of the people."

In 2014, the world was stunned when Japan agreed to turn over more than 700 pounds (320 kg) of weapon-grade plutonium and highly enriched uranium (HEU) back to the USA that it had received for research and development (R&D) purposes. Japan already has 9 tons of plutonium in Japan and an additional 35 tons stored in Europe. This amount is sufficient to produce 1000 nuclear weapons.[16] Japan was one of the earliest countries to participate in 'Atoms for Peace', and has utilised research reactors and critical assemblies powered by HEU since the 1960s. However, the country became an early participant in civil HEU minimisation efforts. Since 1992, Japan Nuclear Fuel Ltd. has produced low-enriched uranium (LEU) at Rokkasho for Japan's extensive nuclear power program. Japan is in the final stages of conversion and shutdown of most HEU-powered facilities. All new research reactors in Japan have been designed to use LEU fuel. However, Japan's policy on how to handle its HEU materials has been less clear, and there are simultaneous and interlinked concerns regarding Japan's policy on plutonium. There have been some shipments of HEU spent fuel to the USA, but other HEU spent fuel remains in Japan.[17]

Further, Japan also has an active commercial space launch program using several types of solid-fuel rockets, which could provide the basis for a long-range ballistic missile program. Under the conditions set by the Allied Powers following World War II, Japan was forbidden to develop rockets until 1955. Some experts suggest that Epsilon, an advanced three-stage, solid fuel rocket with its shortened pre-launch timeline, could allow it to be converted to an Inter-Continental Ballistic Missile (ICBM); numerous technological modifications would be necessary, however, specifically in the area of guidance and payload delivery.[18] Further, Japan's quest for reusable launch vehicles (RLV) technologies for space programs (OREX, HOPE-X) has allowed the country to successfully develop and test re-entry and advanced guidance technologies applicable to ballistic missile programs.[19] Toshiyuki Shikata, a government adviser and former lieutenant general, indicated that part of the rationale for the fifth M-V Hayabusa mission, from 2003 to 2010, was that the re-entry and landing of its return capsule demonstrated "that Japan's ballistic missile capability is credible."[20] Therefore, Japan inherently possesses both an extended nuclear and existential nuclear deterrence. Its *de-facto* nuclear readiness state has the potential to be translated from capability to ability in a short span of time.

Shinzo Abe Administration

Morrow (1991) argues that states use alliances less to aggregate capabilities but to exchange security. It is important to consider arms-alliance trade-offs, because national military capabilities differ from allied military capabilities in their restraint over involvement in armed conflict. A state has no direct control over allied military capabilities, unlike national military capabilities. Allied involvement depends on its allies' national interests and on a state's own ability to shape those interests. Sabrosky (1980), reports that allies honour their agreements reliably in less than 30 per cent of war opportunities. By contrast, when considering the specific obligations mentioned in alliance treaties, Leeds, Long, and Mitchell (2000) find that alliance reliability amounts to 74.5 per cent. Still, even this increased reliability figure is clearly below the aforementioned 100 per cent reliability of national military capabilities.

A number of new legislations under the present Shinzo Abe administration have started to slowly unshackle Japan of its historical remorse and constitutional restrictions. Shinzo Abe's agenda and policy intentions are well known. With his overwhelming priority on security policy, his foremost desire is to revise the Japanese Constitution to seek legitimacy for the SDF. Abe feels an amendment of Article 9 is necessary to rejuvenate Japan on both domestic and international platform, and enable it to be a security provider for itself and in the region. However, along with the Japanese populace, Japan's neighbours such as China and South Korea remain highly wary. Doubts remain as to whether Abe seeks to amend the unconstitutionality of the SDF or expand the role of the forces. In a bid to calm domestic and international fears over his new security reforms, Abe has transformed from an erstwhile historical revisionist to a pragmatic nationalist in his second innings as Prime Minister. Abe's visit to Pearl Harbour in December 2016 indicates his desire to settle the ghosts of Japan's World War II history once and for all and ensure that future generations are not burdened by having to apologise for Japan's World War II history.

It was during Abe's first stint as the prime minister that the Defence Agency was elevated (after 53 years) to the level of Defence Ministry in 2007. In his second and third stints, Abe instituted the National Security Council that centralised security policy of Japan under the prime minister. This was followed by the first National Security Strategy that outlined a 'Proactive Contribution to Peace' on Japan's part and even discarded the sacrosanct one per cent ceiling of Gross Domestic Product (GDP) on defence spending. Abe further introduced the most extensive legislation in Japan's security policy, the National Security Legislation, which allowed the SDF to operate overseas for collective self-defence. Abe also lifted the total ban on arms exports and passed the State Secrets Law that had been abolished under the Allied Occupation period.

Rebooting Indigenous Defence Industry

The defence production and technological bases that Japan's defence industry possesses contribute to latently enhance its deterrence, by possessing industrial capability sufficient to build up defence forces in a timely manner at Japan's will. Japan's domestic foundations for strengthening its military posture, its defence production and technological bases, face challenges in the changes in the international security environment through realignment of European and US defence industry. However, Japan has massive advantages in certain technologies such as high tensile steel, thin plate technology, welding technology and varieties of sensors systems for building of destroyers, submarines and general shipbuilding. Japan also has internationally advanced guidance and propulsion technology, semiconductors, infrared sensors and solid rockets due to joint R&D with the USA.[21] However, its inability to resolve its historical legacies has led Japan to constantly reiterate its pacifist stand by prohibiting manufacture and export of complete weapons-systems.

In the years following World War II, Japan's military industries were totally shut down during a period of internationally rapid development, particularly in the case of the aircraft industry. Japan's defence industry was kept in quasi-isolation by its own government under a ban on arms exports in keeping with 'The Three Principles' formulated at the 1967 session of the Diet. The Three Principles prohibited export to communist bloc countries, countries subject to arms exports embargo under the United Nations Security Council resolutions, and countries involved or likely to be involved in international conflicts. In February 1976, the Government of Japan announced the collateral policy guideline at the Diet session that arms exports to other areas not included in the Three Principles would also be restrained in conformity with Japan's position as a peace-loving nation.[22] However, despite the isolation, the domestic defence industry transformed into a dominant player in design and manufacture of defence components. Japan began as a supplier of defence components and later began to build and produce various indigenous aircraft such as the C-1 and PS-1 to the more recent P-1 and F-2. Though Japanese industry went on to make great progress, building components for the most advanced civilian aircraft such as Boeing 767s/777s/787s and co-producing advanced military aircraft such as the Lockheed P3Cs and F-15s, it was handicapped by restrictions placed on exports of military technology or products.[23]

On December 27, 2011, the Japanese government officially eased the ban allowing Japanese defence contractors to take part in the joint development of weapons with other countries (and not only the USA) and to supply military equipment for humanitarian purposes. While defence equipment has become more advanced and complex, the defence industry in Japan has been exposed to harsh conditions by a decrease in the number of units procured caused by Japan's severe financial conditions and an increase in imports of foreign-made equipment when other countries are aiming to acquire advanced military capabilities utilising the latest technologies. In order to ensure the quality of defence capabilities and to enhance deterrence as well as response capabilities in a situation when rapid technological innovations have significant influence on the global security environment, it is crucial that Japan acquires due technological superiority. Hence, it is indispensable for Japan to work on strategic research and development, maintenance and strengthening of defence production and technological bases, and promotion of defence equipment and technology cooperation.

On April 1, 2014, the Government of Japan, in accordance with the National Security Strategy adopted on December 17, 2013, set out 'The Three Principles of Transfer of defence Equipment and Technology' as a set of new principles on overseas transfer of defence equipment and technology, which replaced 'The Three Principles on Arms Exports and their Related Policy Guidelines'. According to the new principles, an appropriate overseas transfer of defence equipment and technology contributes to "active promotion of the maintenance of international peace and security through timely and effective implementation of contribution to peace and international cooperation…to strengthening security and defence cooperation with the United States as well as other countries."[24] The new principles lay out that the Japanese government will make a comprehensive judgment in the light of the existing guidelines of the international export control regime and based on the information available will analyse the extent the overseas transfer of such equipment and technology will raise concern for Japan's security.

With a more capable indigenous defence technology base, Japan has the potential to reduce its reliance on imports of defence products as indigenously developed technologies can be tailored to Japan's specific needs. This has the added benefit of increasing economic activity at higher levels of the value chain, including design and R&D. Since defence technology can often be applied to the electronics, computing or commercial aerospace industries, Japan's edge in robotics can also be multiplied by leveraging technology and processes developed in the defence industry.

New Agenda: Upgrading the SDF and BMD

The Air SDF is steadily reinforcing Japan's defence posture through measures such as creating one new squadron in the Air Warning Unit at Naha Air Base in 2014, and establishing the 9th Air Wing by increasing the number of fighter squadrons to two in 2016. In 2017, based on the importance of its missions and roles, it is tasked with, the South-western Composite Air Division, which was historically positioned as a sub-unit to air defence forces and was upgraded and reorganised into the South-western Air Defence Force for enhancing the defence posture in the south western region.[25] In March 2018, Japanese Ground SDF underwent its most significant structural reform since its formation in 1954 with the creation of a unified command and the launch of an Amphibious Rapid Deployment Brigade (ARDB) tasked with defending Japan's remote islands.

On June 20, 2017, the Research Committee on Security within the ruling LDP released an interim report with recommendations for Japan's next NDPG and Mid-Term Defence Program (MTDP) for fiscal years 2019-2023. The interim report supported the increase of the Japanese defence budget to 2 per cent of GDP (similar to NATO) and pushed for acquisition of counter-attack capabilities such as the Cruise missiles.[26] A study released in redacted form by Japan's Ministry of Defence on April 27, 2018 asserted that the helicopter destroyer JS Izumo, along with its sister ship, JS Kaga, can be turned into fully fledged aircraft carriers. With certain modifications, the Izumo-class can operate the F-35B, capable of vertical or short take-offs and vertical landings (STOVL) without requiring a catapult launcher from the warship's flight deck.[27] The Japanese Maritime SDF is also expected to acquire 22 submarines by the mid-2020s as specified in the NDPG 2014. While the maritime capabilities of its ally, the USA, is unsurpassed, the priority on security lines of communication has led Japan to pursue a strong, independent maritime capability to hold certain decision autonomy as well as to support the USA.

North Korea fired two missiles over Japan in 2017, as well as three inter-continental ballistic missiles on steep trajectories into the Sea of Japan. The unprecedented and high number of ballistic missile and nuclear tests from North Korea forced Japan to fast track the installation of two land-based Aegis Ashore missile defence systems. Japan's position east of North Korea means that missiles fired by the North toward the USA, including its Pacific military base in Guam, would (almost certainly) have to fly over Japanese territory. In 1999, the USA and Japan had signed a memorandum of agreement to cooperate to develop the SM-3 Block IIA interceptor, and began the SM-3 Cooperative Development Project with a revised Memorandum of Understanding in 2006. The December 2014 Mid-Term Defence Plan mandated the Maritime SDF to purchase two new Atago-class guided missile destroyers. These are scheduled to enter the fleet in 2020-21 and will be armed with the SM-3 Block IIA interceptor.

Japan's missile defence system inter-connects Japan's domestically owned and operated missile defence systems and sensors, as well as those hosted from the USA. Also, Japan already hosts two US Army-Navy Transportable Radar Surveillance Systems, or AN/TPY-2, that are deployed in Kyogamisaki and Shariki. The USA has also deployed its own PAC-3 battery and a Ticonderoga-class missile cruiser in Japan since 2006. The PAC-3 unit was deployed to Kaduna Air Force base in Okinawa in October 2006 after the North Korean nuclear test and subsequent missile launches in July of that year. The USA currently deploys six Aegis BMD-capable ships at Yokosuka as part of the Seventh Fleet.[28]

Revision of Article 9 of Japanese Constitution

"Aspiring sincerely to an international peace based on justice and order, the Japanese people forever renounce war as a sovereign right of the nation and the threat or use of force as means of settling international disputes. In order to accomplish the aim of the preceding paragraph, land, sea, and air forces, as well as other war potential, will never be maintained. The right of belligerency of the state will not be recognised."

—*Chapter II, Article 9 of Japanese Constitution.*

Japan has the world's 21st largest army where most of its neighbours China, Russia, North Korea and South Korea rank in the world's top ten largest armies. Despite the constraints—constitutional, legal, political, and societal—the SDF has been operating under this Constitution. Since its establishment, the SDF has evolved into one of the most sophisticated defence forces in the world.

Abe, in his second administration has already passed new legislations that re-interpret the pacifist constitution to allow Japanese troops potentially to fight overseas, eased curbs on military exports and erased the sacrosanct defence-budget ceiling of 1 per cent of the previous administrations. Abe's winning the 2016 Upper House national elections and obtaining the critical two-thirds majority in both houses with coalition partner Komeito now gives him the mandate to start the Diet processes for constitutional revision. In a bid to calm domestic and international fears over his new security reforms, Abe has transformed from an erstwhile historical revisionist to a pragmatic nationalist in his second innings as Prime Minister since 2012. Abe's visit to Pearl Harbour in December 2016 indicates his desire to settle the ghosts of Japan's World War II history once and for all and ensure that future generations are not burdened by having to apologise for Japan's World War II history. This makes constitutional revision a realistic possibility for the first time in its 70-year history.

Critical constraint on an actual amendment to the Constitution, however, lies in the public referendum mandated by Article 96 that specifies the process for amendment. It states that after concurring vote of two-thirds or more of all the members of each House, an amendment shall require the affirmative vote of a majority of all votes cast at a special public referendum. While Japanese public opinion has a strong anti-militarist distrust even after more than seven decades post-World War II, it also has an attitudinal defensive realism indicated by overwhelming support for missile defence systems and enhancing capabilities of the coast guard. However, support for overseas deployment of Japan's SDF still remains an issue with the public evidenced by the recent scrapping of the South Sudan mission for Ground SDF even under UN auspices.

Developing New Neighbourhood Allies

In a bid to expand its autonomy and leverage to influence strategic equations in the region, Japan has strongly expanded its security cooperation along with diplomatic engagement with many of its neighbours. Some of these are elaborated in succeeding paragraphs.

ASEAN

The *Vientiane Vision*[29] is a guiding principle for Japan's defence cooperation with ASEAN, as announced by Defence Minister Inada at the second ASEAN-Japan Defence Ministers' Informal Meeting held in Vientiane, Lao PDR on 16 November 2016. Practical defence cooperation is conducted by combining the sharing of understanding and experience regarding international law, Maritime Domain Awareness (MDA), conducting capacity building cooperation in various fields such as HADR, PKO, landmine and unexploded bomb clearance, cyber-security, etc., transferring technology, developing human resources and multi-lateral joint training and exercises, etc. Japan supplied frontline coast guard cutters to the Philippines and Vietnam in May 2017. It also agreed to supply to Vietnam six patrol boats in January 2017. In May 2017, Japan sent its Izumo helicopter-carrier to the South China Sea for three months of port visits in Southeast Asia under the Japan-ASEAN Ship Rider Cooperation Program.

India

During the 2015 Annual India-Japan summit, both the countries signed two major agreements aimed at enhancing defence and security cooperation. One of the agreements focused on transfer of defence equipment and technology transfer. The second was an agreement concerning security measures for the protection of classified military information. Concurrently, these agreements have paved the way for robust India-Japan cooperation in the avenues of intelligence exchanges between the Indian Armed Forces and the Japanese SDF as well as in defence technology. Earlier during the Sixth Strategic Dialogue in April 2012, Foreign Ministers also agreed to launch a bilateral cyber security dialogue at the diplomatic, national security, and technical levels. Recently, we also see the re-emergence of Shinzo Abe's 'Diamond Concept', evidenced by the first Indo-Pacific consultations in Manila in the Philippines, in November 2017. As part of a 'Quad', the USA, Japan, Australia and India have instituted a coordinating mechanism to consult on regional challenges, in particular, in dealing with 'gray-zone' maritime emergencies and security threats like piracy.

Russia

Abe has held almost 20 Japan-Russia summits with Russian President Putin in his two terms as Japanese Prime Minister. A lingering territorial dispute over the four islands of Etorofu, Kunashiri, Habomai and Shikotan (called the Northern Territories by Japan and Southern Kuril Islands by Russia) has led to Japan and Russia being unable to negotiate a peace treaty even after 7 decades post-World War II. Abe's perseverance is remarkable since he held more summits with Putin (almost double) than with US President Obama during his tenure. The proposal of joint sovereignty has been mooted, with Japan and Russia agreeing to expand joint economic engagement under an eight-point cooperation plan proposed by Abe totalling around ¥300 billion and covering over 60 projects from the energy sector, tourism, transfer of cutting-edge Japanese technologies to higher human exchanges and the industrialisation of the Russian Far East. Even if there is no breakthrough in the Kurils dispute *per se*, the process of Japanese-Russian rapprochement can be said to be more important than the outcome.

Limitations

Japan, after World War II, believed peace was 'domestically generated', that there would be no international peace unless the countries of the world were themselves peaceful. After a self-described increasingly severe security environment, Japanese policymakers now consider that no nation can maintain its own peace and security alone. Thus, they seek to prevent the emergence of threats by making proactive efforts to improve the international security environment and expand its ability to cooperate on international security operations. However, population aging and decline reduces Japan's capacity to absorb soldier casualties. There is strong public aversion to Japanese SDF engaging in anything that looks like combat activity. Even the former Chief of Staff of Maritime SDF, Admiral Koichi Furusho, warned that any further collapse involving insufficient manpower resources for recruitment, education and training (schools), and rear end support could weaken the combat capabilities of the MSDF as a whole.[30] The 2014 NDPG also talks of a number of measures to increase the forces strength such as promoting the perception that the SDF is an attractive job option and making more effective use of female SDF personnel, expansion of re-appointment, and measures related to honours and privileges.[31]

The SDF earned widespread recognition and appreciation from the

Japanese public following its prompt disaster relief and reconstruction activities after the earthquake and tsunami in 2011. Ironically, its image as a disaster relief force rather than one for national security dominates the discourse in Japanese security policy regarding its role and organisation. The first rush clause added for the UN Peacekeeping Operation in South Sudan in November 2016 saw a strong public backlash when the unrest in South Sudan became public. Japan withdrew in March 2017.

Conclusion: Anxieties with Trump Administration

The inter-operability between US forces and the SDF has been dramatically advanced after the revision of Guidelines for the US-Japan Defence Cooperation in 2015. The USA and Japan continue to meticulously consult with each other on joint-exercises and other issues through the Alliance Coordination Mechanism. In case US forces exercise the Flexible Deterrent Options (FDO) by deploying aircraft carriers and strategic bombers around the Korean Peninsula, based on the 2015 revised Guidelines, the Japanese SDF would also join and support the FDO. Besides, the SDF can also make a more proactive contribution to US forces such as protecting the US forces' assets.[32] In May 2017, JS Izumo escorted a US naval supply ship following increasing tensions with North Korea.[33]

Despite reiterations, Japan has reservations against the continuity of the American commitment to Japan's security. The US attitude of special engagement with security partners especially Japan has undergone a dramatic change in the Trump era. US President Trump's 'America-First', led to the USA walking out of the Trans-Pacific Partnership (TPP), a US-Japan led regional trade deal. Japan was also informed later about Trump consenting to talks with Kim Jong-un. Further, Japan and the USA are at loggerheads on how to frame future trade talks, with Tokyo resisting US calls to enter negotiations for a bilateral FTA that could force Japan to open its highly protected agricultural markets. To appease the increasing demands by Trump for more alliance support, Japan markedly stepped up its defence purchases from the USA. The Japanese defence budget fiscal 2018 will total a record high of $45.91 billion, marking the sixth consecutive increase since fiscal 2013. We can expect similar hikes in 2019. Japan will purchase about

$4.24 billion worth of equipment in fiscal 2018 that will include the Aegis Ashore, a land-based system to intercept missiles, Lockheed Martin's extended-range Joint Air-to-Surface Standoff Missile (JASSM-ER), F-35A fighter planes, Global Hawk unmanned reconnaissance planes manufactured by Northrop Grumman, and Osprey tilt-rotor transportation aircraft produced by Bell and Boeing from the USA.

In summary, it is the anxiety over US security commitment in Japan that has triggered the recent warming of ties between China and Japan. But, as shown throughout history, Japan will never accept a subordinate role to China's. To cope with the North Korea crisis, Abe has often emphasised the importance of the US-Japan alliance. However, increasing power differential between Japan and its neighbours and the inability to predict US short and medium term interests in the region (for the long term, the USA is definitely not retreating), will force Japan to increase the proportion of its own defence capabilities in its arms-alliance balance, for its deterrence to be effective in the future.

NOTES

1. http://www.mod.go.jp/e/publ/w_paper/pdf/2017/DOJ2017_1-1-1_web.pdf
2. SIPRI- https://www.sipri.org/sites/default/files/1_Data%20for%20all%20countries%20from%201988%20E2%80%20932017%20in%20constant%20%282016%29%20USD.pdf
3. Diehl, P. (Ed.). (2004). *The Scourge of War: New Extensions on an Old Problem*. Ann Arbor: University of Michigan Press. doi:10.3998/mpub.17556
4. Sorokin, G. (1994). Arms, Alliances, and Security Tradeoffs in Enduring Rivalries. *International Studies Quarterly*, 38(3), 421-446. doi.10.2307/2600740
5. Ibid.
6. Singh, Bhubhindar, 2013. *Japan's Security Identity: From a Peace State to an International State*, Routledge.
7. Miyashita, Akitoshi, 2003. *Limits to Power: Asymmetric Dependence and Japanese Foreign Aid Policy*, Lexington Books.
8. Singh, Bhubhindar, 2013. *Japan's Security Identity: From a Peace State to an International State*, Routledge.
9. June Tuefel Dreyer, "Sino-Japanese Rivalry and Its Implications for Developing Nations", *Asian Survey*, Vol. 46, No. 4, July/August 2006, pp. 538-557 from http://www.jstor.org/stable/10.1525/as.2006.46.4.538.
10. "Announcement of the Aircraft Identification Rules for the East China Sea Air Defence Identification Zone of the PRC", Nov 23, 2013 at http://news.xinhuanet.com/english/china/2013-11/23/c_132911634.htm.
11. "The Yellow Sea Economic Basin—a sea of stars", at http://nederland.ipe.com/asia/the-yellow-sea-economic-basin-a-sea-of-stars_30583.php?articlepage=2

12. U.S. Extended Deterrence and Japan's Security, Yukio Satoh, Livermore Papers on Global Security No. 2, Lawrence Livermore National Laboratory, Centre for Global Security Research, October 2017.
13. Ministry of Foreign Affairs, 2011. Japan's Disarmament and Non-Proliferation Policy, Fifth Edition, available at http://www.mofa.go.jp/policy/un/disarmament/policy/pdfs/pamph1103.pdf
14. *Japan Times*, 2010. Secret pacts existed; denials 'dishonest': Deals reached on nuclear arms entry, Okinawa reversion: panel, May 10, 2010, available at http://www.japantimes.co.jp/news/2010/03/10/national/secret-pacts-existed-denials-dishonest/#.UePDxtJgf_Y
15. Ibid.
16. Ibid.
17. http://www.nti.org/analysis/articles/civilian-heu-japan/
18. https://www.globalsecurity.org/wmd/world/japan/missile.htm
19. *In Defence of Japan: From the Market to the Military in Space Policy*, Saadia Pekkanen & Paul Kallender-Umezu, Stanford University Press, 12 Aug 2010.
20. "Japan nuclear weapons program", http://en.wikipedia.org/wiki/Japanese_nuclear_weapon_program
21. http://www.mod.go.jp/atla/soubiseisaku/soubiseisakuseisan/2606honbuneigo.pdf
22. "Japan's Policies on the Control of Arms Exports", Ministry of Foreign Affairs at http://www.mofa.go.jp/policy/un/disarmament/policy/
23. https://www.rieti.go.jp/en/special/p_a_w/026.html
24. "Three Principles on Transfer of defence Equipment and Technology", http://www.mofa.go.jp/files/000034953.pdf
25. http://www.mod.go.jp/e/publ/w_paper/pdf/2016/DOJ2016_2-2-1_web.pdf
26. *The Diplomat:* Yuki Tatsumi, June 23, 2017, All About the Yen: Japan Begins Mid-Term Defence Planning, https://thediplomat.com/2017/06/all-about-the-yen-japan-begins-mid-term-...
27. *The Diplomat*: Franz Stefan Grady, May 2, 2018, Study: Japan's Largest Warship Can Support F35, https://thediplomat.com/2018/05/study-japans-largest-warship-can-support...
28. http://missiledefenseadvocacy.org/intl-cooperation/japan/
29. http://www.mod.go.jp/e/d_act/exc/vientianevision/
30. Toshi Yoshihara, " The Setting Sun, Strategic Implications of Japan's Demographic Transition" in Susan Yoshihara and Douglas A. Sylva, (eds.)2012, *Population Decline and the Remaking of Great Power Politics,* Potomac Books, Washington.
31. NATIONAL DEFENSE PROGRAM GUIDELINES for FY 2014 and beyond, http://www.mod.go.jp/j/approach/agenda/guideline/2014/pdf/20131217_e2.pdf
32. https://thediplomat.com/2018/03/japans-security-alliance-dilemma/
33. https://www.nytimes.com/2017/05/01/world/asia/japanese-warship-us-navy-ship.html

(Prerna Gandhi is an Associate Fellow at the Vivekananda International Foundation with a focus on Japan, ASEAN and Korean Peninsula. A doctoral student at Department. of East Asian Studies, Delhi University, she is a recipient of the Mitsubishi Corporation International Scholarship)

*

All time read: Civilisation

14

Sister Nivedita's Ideas on Indian Nationhood and their Contemporary Relevance

Dr. Arpita Mitra

"We are a nation, as soon as we recognise ourselves as a nation."

—*Sister Nivedita*

"...the love that Nivedita had for India was the truest of the true, not just a passing fancy. This love did not try to see the Indian scriptures validated in each action of the Indian people. Rather, it tried to penetrate all external layers to reach the innermost core of persons and to love that core. That is why she was not pained to see the extreme dereliction of India. All that was missing and inadequate in India simply aroused her love, not her censure or disrespect."

—*Rabindranath Tagore*

ABSTRACT

'Nationalism' has recently been a bone of contention in the Indian public sphere. An argument that surfaces often is that the concept of the Indian nation is a product of the nationalist struggle for freedom, and therefore, otherwise there is no historical reality to an Indian nationhood prior to colonial rule. In present-day India, issues of identity and diversity are also of particular import. In this context, Sister Nivedita's ideas on Indian nationhood assume even more importance. They shed light on many of the intricacies of the debate on Indian nationalism, like the idea of India, a pre-history of Indian nationhood, the dynamics between diversity and unity, and so on. Nivedita's conceptual contribution in this sphere has been largely ignored by the scholarly world. In the year of her 151st birth anniversary, the time is ripe to re-visit her ideas on Indian nationhood. It is also time to move beyond colonial legacies and think about a truly Indian narrative on 'nationalism' and the specificity of Indian nationhood, and to look at the phenomenon beyond its ideological dimensions, not restricting oneself to an exclusively political conceptualisation. Sister Nivedita's ideas point towards this direction.

Idea of Nationalism

'Nationalism' has recently been a bone of contention in the Indian public sphere, where a conspicuous section of the Indian intelligentsia has either questioned the very idea itself or criticised what they understand to be a particular version of nationalism. There is an argument that appears in different avatars in the works of many well-known social scientists of our times—the argument that the concept of the Indian nation is a product of colonial rule and the consequent nationalist struggle for freedom, and therefore, otherwise there is no historical reality as such to an Indian nation prior to the commencement and consolidation of British rule. In making such a claim, this group of scholars, notwithstanding the degree of sophistication in their arguments, join the British rulers who too claimed that India was a congeries of different races and not one nation. While present-day India battles crucial political conflicts based on identity in its North-Eastern states and in Kashmir and witnesses sharp identity-based ideological dissensions such as the case of Dravidian identity, the issue of nationalism assumes great importance and it is crucial that we understand the conceptual and historical issues involved.

Memorial plaque where Sister Nivedita lived   Memorial plaque at Sister Nivedita's birthplace

This paper is an attempt to present and analyse the nationalist ideas of Sister Nivedita (1867-1911), one of the foremost disciples of Swami Vivekananda (1863-1902), and a key figure in the intellectual and political life of colonial Bengal in the early twentieth century. The memorial plaque at her birthplace in Ireland describes her as a "writer and Indian nationalist," and rightly so, as she was one of the greatest champions of the idea of Indian nationhood. Her ideas on the subject are not only incisive but also particularly relevant in the context of many theoretical issues that plague us today. Given their relevance and given the fact that last year (2017) saw her 150th birth anniversary, it will be meaningful to re-visit her ideas on Indian nationhood at this juncture.

The Problematic

Is India a 'nation'? Is India *one* nation? Was there an 'India' before British rule created one? These are some of the questions that were the subject of much debate in late-nineteenth and early-twentieth-century India, where the interlocutors were Indian nationalists on the one hand and British imperial ideologues, on the other. When the British started ruling India, they invested resources in acquiring knowledge about India. Many were struck by the sheer regional diversity of the land, and found it difficult to conceive of India as 'one nation'; hence, the idea of Indian nationhood was dismissed as mere 'moonshine'. Denying the reality and legitimacy of Indian nationhood also served their imperial interests. They liked to claim that they were the ones who gave India a sense of cohesion or unity by setting up the administrative machinery, railways, connecting different parts of the land, and so on. The nationalist Indian intellectuals, on the other hand, claimed that Indian nationhood was a reality. They emphasised on the pre-colonial civilisational and historical basis of Indian nationhood.

At the root of the debate on Indian nationhood is the very concept of the nation in the first place. There is a particular history to the rise of nations and nationalisms in the world. Therefore, any discussion on whether India constitutes a nation should not be done without taking into account conceptual and historical issues related to nationhood. On the other hand, if one argues that Indian nationhood is a construct, it would be difficult to demonstrate in what special way Indian nationhood alone is a construct while other nationalities are not.

In the case of defining what a nation is, key developments in the history of the West (e.g., development of print-capitalism,[1] emergence of the public sphere, modern transport networks) have been considered as determining factors. This conceptual approach completely ignores factors specific to Indian history, like the well-defined natural boundaries, the busy pilgrimage routes and destinations spread across the length and breadth of the country, the political empires of the pre-modern era, common civilisational factors like much-cherished values and philosophical and spiritual ideas—all have contributed to the creation of a collective consciousness even before the modern Western-style public sphere emerged in India during colonial rule. One can concede that this consciousness was not 'national' strictly speaking; but it would be difficult to deny that there was already a kind of collective consciousness present in Indian society that served as a substratum for the development of later civic national consciousness. As pointed out by Sugata Bose recently—"Modern Indian nationalism, far from being exclusively derived from European discourses, drew significantly on rich legacies of pre-colonial patriotism and kept it alive through a constant process of creative innovation."[2]

Sister Nivedita is undoubtedly an important thinker in this context. The present paper proposes to examine her ideas related to Indian nationhood and their contemporary relevance.

Survey of Literature

There is relatively less academic work on Nivedita specifically, but there is a substantial body of literature on the discourse of Indian nationhood during colonial times. I shall first discuss the literature pertaining to Nivedita and then do a representative survey of the general literature.

In her book on cross-cultural nationalists, Elleke Boehmer mainly discusses the interaction between Sister Nivedita and Aurobindo Ghose.[3] All she mentions about Nivedita's ideas on Indian nationhood is a summary of Nivedita's key position: "The nation's unity and spiritual strength were 'self-born', and its future, concomitantly, should be 'self-determined, self-wrought': 'the one central fact is the realisation of its own nationality by the [Indian] Nation'."[4] There is no further deliberation on these ideas by Boehmer.

Amiya P. Sen has recently edited a selection of Nivedita's writings.[5] In the Introduction to the volume, Sen takes note of Nivedita's "persistent desire to disseminate the idea of a common nationality among Indians, to get them to believe in a common goal and a common destiny."⁶ According to him, however: "On several occasions…, her speeches and writings naively overlook or brush aside internal divisions or differences, and are clearly dismissive of the fact that in India, anti-colonial sentiments did indeed, produce a discursive nationalism that was not really backed by the shared sense of a common nationhood. Nivedita deliberately underplayed the linguistic, cultural or political differences that were progressively escalating in contemporary India; on the other hand, she took such idealistic projections to be potentially real."⁷

As we shall see in the discussion in subsequent sections, Sen's arguments are not justified. Sister Nivedita was well aware of the differences in India, but she argued that India was a nation not despite the internal differences, but precisely because of these differences (a nation is a *complex* unity). Secondly, it is wrong to claim that the discursive nationalism produced in India by anti-colonial sentiments "was not really backed by the shared sense of a common nationhood." Nivedita argued with evidence that the three pillars of nationality—"common home, common interest and common love"—have existed in India through centuries. However, one would be mistaken to look for elements that fit into a Western conceptual framework (which our postcolonial scholars continue to do).

Sen further writes: "…there is a utopian sentiment that pervades all her thoughts and writings, a utopia that rested on a passionate, if at times, also sentimental and uncritical attachment to India and Indians. What in contemporary parlance has come to be accepted as the 'idea' of India, might well have originated with Nivedita, but with certain trappings of superficiality."⁸ Sen, however, does not discuss his reasons for considering her 'idea' of India as imbued with "certain trappings of superficiality". One would like to argue that Nivedita was indeed and undoubtedly an idealist, but idealism is the basis of *all* nationalist thought. Without a degree of idealism, people would be self-centred and incapable of any kind of higher orientation. Furthermore, Nivedita's idea of India was not superficial, it was grounded in well-studied observations, some of which will be discussed below.

Now, we move on to a more general historiography of ideas of Indian nationhood. As is evident from the title of his article, 'The Imaginary Institution of India', Sudipta Kaviraj is of the following opinion: "India, the objective reality of today's history, whose objectivity is tangible for people to preserve, to destroy, to uphold, to construct and dismember, the reality taken for granted in all attempts in favour and against, is not an object of discovery but of invention. It was historically instituted by the nationalist imagination of the nineteenth century."[9]

In a recent publication, B.D. Chattopadhyaya discusses the issue of India's 'unity in diversity.' He analyses ancient sources in the light of questions such as: "what the meaning of 'unity' in the expression is, or what its limits are, implied by its juxtaposition with 'diversity'. In other words, if diversities are taken to constitute 'unity', at what stage do 'diversities' remain when the reference is to 'unity'?"[10] These are some of the questions the present paper explores with reference to Sister Nivedita's nationalist ideas as well, as they are closely related to the ideal of 'unity in diversity'. Chattopadhyaya rightly notes that R.K. Mookerji's *The Fundamental Unity of India* (1914) is one of the earliest historical statements of the idea of Indian unity. It should be noted that this book was a direct result of Mookerji's interactions with Sister Nivedita.

Sugata Bose's recent book on Indian nationalism[11] deals with the subject starting from 1917 onwards, as that is the publication year of Rabindranath Tagore's famous book *Nationalism* consisting of three essays, one of which is on nationalism in India. Since Bose's book takes off from the period 1917, he hardly discusses Nivedita. As is well-known, Tagore was a critic of the 'cult' of nationalism, and was more of an advocate of universal humanism. Nivedita had passed away by the time Tagore's book was published, and as is already known, although Tagore and Nivedita appreciated each other, their relationship was not free from undercurrents of intellectual conflicts.

The general drift of the literature is evident: a) It questions the existence of any entity that can be called an 'Indian' or a 'national' entity prior to colonial rule; b) based on the fact of diversity, it asks if India can be called *one* entity; c) taking a) and b) together, this discourse subtly questions the legitimacy of an Indian nationalism and Indian nationhood. None of these works discusses Nivedita's nationalist ideas, which can open up new and rich debates on Indian nationalism.

Research Questions

These are some of the questions that this paper will address:

- What were Sister Nivedita's views on the unique basis of Indian nationhood?
- How did Nivedita conceptualise the common grounds of Indian nationality?
- How did Nivedita conceptualise unity in diversity in the Indian context?
- How are Indian geography and history related to the formation of Indian national identity?
- What were the views of Nivedita's contemporaries on Indian nationhood?

Methodology and Sources

This is a work in the history of ideas. The principal sources consulted are original writings of Sister Nivedita and her contemporaries. Nivedita's writings which have been cited here were mostly written between 1909 and 1911. The writings of Aurobindo Ghose (later Sri Aurobindo) and Ananda Coomaraswamy cited here were also written around the same time—1907 and 1909 respectively. Swami Prajnananda's writings came out around 1913 and Tagore's 'Nationalism in India' lecture was written in 1916 and published in 1917.

Defining Nationhood

This section will deal with the concept of nation and nationalisms and discuss briefly the history of rise of nations and nationalism in the world.

The Rise of Nationalism

The twentieth century saw the rise of nationalism as one of the most potent forces in the world. (The twenty-first century has, on the other hand, seen a lot of assertion of ethnic identity, religious identity, linguistic identity and so on.) Nationalism was one of the key factors in the American and French Revolutions: "Many historians would agree that, as an ideology and discourse, nationalism became prevalent in North America and Western Europe in the latter half of the eighteenth century, and shortly thereafter in Latin America. The dates that are often singled out as signalling the advent of nationalism include 1775 (the First Partition of Poland), 1776 (the American Declaration of Independence), 1789 and 1792 (the commencement and second phase of the French Revolution), and 1807 (Fichte's *Addresses to the German Nation*)."[12] After 1792, the patriotic ideals of the French Revolution were exported all over Europe.

The territorial and economic basis of nation-states in Europe was already prepared by the late fifteenth century due to the rise of absolutist states and the failure to reunite Europe on the model of the Roman Empire: "The disentangling of 'England' from 'France' at the end of the Hundred Years War (1337-1453), and the rise of separate ethnically based states in Spain, Switzerland, Holland, Sweden, and Poland by the sixteenth century, broke the unity of Christendom even before the Wars of Religion and the Counter-Reformation, and forged an interstate system based on a complex web of alliance and balances of power."[13] To this was added commercial competition and wars between the states.

While the earliest nation-states were European, nationalism emerged elsewhere as well and became a truly global phenomenon. Thus, the world witnessed, for instance, the rise of Japan as a nation, following the Meiji Restoration of 1868; Arab nationalisms in the Middle East and North Africa; anti-colonial nationalisms in India and Africa, and so on.

Features of Nationalism

As discussed by John Hutchinson and Anthony Smith: "Nationalism was, first of all, a doctrine of popular freedom and sovereignty. The people must be liberated—that is, free from any external constraint; they must determine their own destiny and be masters in their own house; they must control their own resources; they must obey only their own 'inner' voice. But that entailed fraternity. The people must be united; they must dissolve all internal divisions; they must be gathered together in a single historic territory, a homeland; and they must have legal equality and share a single public culture. But which culture and what territory? Only a homeland that was 'theirs' by historic right, the land of their forbears; only a culture that was 'theirs' as a heritage, passed down the generations, and therefore an expression of their authentic identity. *Autonomy, unity, identity*: these three themes and ideals have been pursued by nationalists everywhere since Rousseau, Herder, Fichte, Korias, and Mazzini popularised them in Western and Central Europe."[14]

The French Revolution model is quite evident, albeit garbed in different wordings.

Sources of European Nationalism

European nationalism had its own antecedents. Millennial Christianity, the printing press, newspapers, an emphasis on civic virtue drawn from ancient Greek and Roman models like the patriotism of the *polis*—all contributed to the creation of the nationalist ideology in Europe. There were clearly theological influences as there were influences like "the doctrine of ethnic election which, originating perhaps with the ancient Israelites, became widely diffused in the Middle East, Europe, and East Africa…"[15] It is thus evident that European nations were not self-given entities, but products of long-drawn historical processes and influences of diverse kinds. Since the European nations properly speaking emerged only in the modern era, these were also young nations.

Kinds of Nationalism

Hans Kohn has differentiated between what he calls the organic 'Eastern' forms of nationalism, in contrast to the civic and rational 'Western' forms of nationalism prevalent in France, England, and the USA and so on.[16] Hutchinson and Smith refer to fusions and tensions when it comes to nationalisms in India and Africa: "On the one hand, a civic, territorial, anti-colonial nationalism, and, on the other hand, various ethnic and pan cultural movements…" They note: "The forms that nationalism takes have been kaleidoscopic: religious, conservative, liberal, fascist, communist, cultural, political, protectionist, integrationist, separatist, irredentist,

Diaspora, pan, etc."[17] An important question is whether nationalism is more cultural than political. They admit that one of the central difficulties in studying nations and nationalism has been definitional:—"the problem of finding adequate and agreed definitions of the key concepts, nation and nationalism." Clearly, there is no one model for nation or nationalism.

Concept of Nation

How is the concept of nation different from other forms of collective identity? "While it is recognised that the concept of the nation must be differentiated from other concepts of collective identity like class, region, gender, race, and religious community, there is little agreement about the role of ethnic, as opposed to political, components of the nation; or about the balance between 'subjective' elements like will and memory, and more 'objective' elements like territory and language; or about the nature and role of ethnicity in national identity."[18] As we shall see in the subsequent sections, Indian intellectuals of early twentieth century too had a lot to articulate about concepts like nations and nationalisms.

The Indian Context during Nivedita's Time

Swami Vivekananda with his Western disciples, Josephine MacLeod, Mrs. Sara Bull and Sister Nivedita (*left to right*)

Sister Nivedita, née Margaret Elizabeth Noble, had met Swami

Vivekananda in London in 1895, and the following year, she accepted Vedanta as her own ideal and Vivekananda as her spiritual master. Soon, she decided to take up the cause of serving India and arrived in Calcutta in January 1898. By this time, the rule of the British Raj was well-consolidated in India. Having absorbed the shock of the Revolt of 1857, the imperial government had made deep inroads into Indian society. The English education system that was introduced in the country, largely replacing the traditional system in India, did produce "clerks" as intended by its author Macaulay. But an unintended consequence of this system was also the emergence of a group of educated Indians who had started questioning the supposed benevolence of the imperial masters, especially from the point of view of economic exploitation. Peasant unrest in the country was a natural outcome of land reforms and agrarian policies under the British. One of the glaring manifestations of economic exploitation was large-scale occurrence of famine (in fact, Nivedita wrote on the sociology of famine as well).

The Indian National Congress (INC) was founded in 1885 in order to articulate the grievances of educated Indians against government policies. In course of time, there emerged a more radical section within the Congress who were dissatisfied with the petition culture of the Congress and were willing to undertake a more high-pitched struggle against the British. So, in 1898, when Nivedita arrived, Calcutta, the then capital, was the hotbed of politics and the rising tide of nationalism. However, as discussed earlier, the critics of Indian nationalist aspirations had an arrow in their quiver—the claim that Indian nationhood itself was the result of British rule, that a land as diverse as India could hardly be conceived as one nation, and therefore, the nationalist aspirations of Indians were not legitimate. Sister Nivedita's involvement in Indian nationalism is usually represented in academic works as an involvement in nationalist politics. However, as it will be evident from the ensuing paragraphs, Nivedita also emerged as a major theorist of Indian nationality. Her contribution to the discourse of Indian nationhood has been practically ignored by mainstream academia, despite the fact that she engaged with this issue in great depth and breadth.

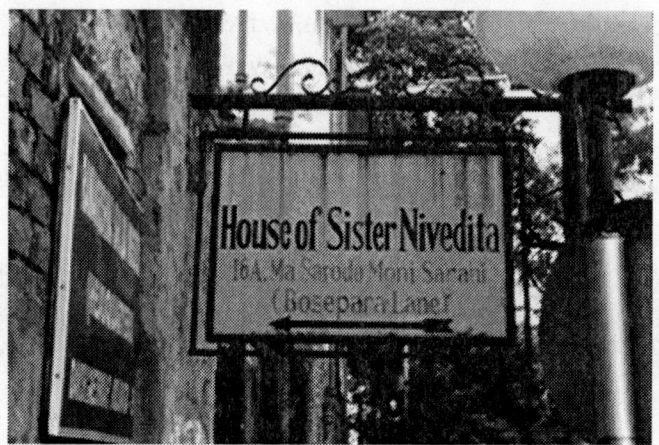

The house where Sister Nivedita lived in Calcutta (before recent renovation)

Nivedita's Contribution to Indian Nationalism

Sister Nivedita was indeed deeply involved in the Indian national movement. She was on good terms with INC leaders, cutting across political differences—for instance, Gopal Krishna Gokhale, who believed in legislation as a tool against the British on the one hand, and Aurobindo Ghose, who appealed for a more radical version of freedom for India, on the other hand. In fact, she was against any kind of split in the Congress (which finally happened in 1907), as she believed that unity was the need of the hour. She had especially close ties with Ghose. Soon, she was under British surveillance and narrowly escaped imprisonment.

In her writings and speeches, Nivedita exhorted Indians to develop a sense of civic nationalism—the idea that the nation was higher than the family. She was a prolific writer, who wrote on a variety of subjects ranging from famine in India to the role of art in shaping nationality. She contributed regularly to Ramananda Chatterjee's journal *Modern Review*. In 1910, when Aurobindo left for Pondicherry, at his request, Nivedita took charge of his paper *Karma Yogin* for a few months. She lectured at several places like Calcutta, Patna, Lucknow, Baroda, Nagpur, Wardha, Amaravati, Madras and so on. She has left behind five volumes of her complete works that include books, essays, lectures, reviews, etc. and two volumes of letters written to different people. An educationist by vocation, and a nationalist at heart, Nivedita was actively involved in the 'National Education' movement, pioneered by the Dawn Society under the leadership of Satish Chandra Mukherjee. In the short 13 years that Sister Nivedita spent in India, she led an active public life, dividing her time between writing, lecturing and serving India through plague relief programmes and running a girls' school.

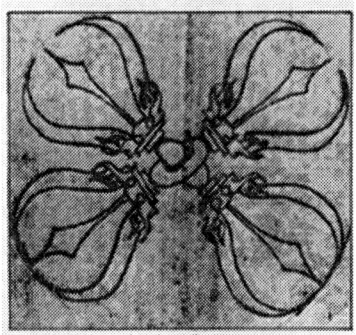

Vajra or Thunderbolt designed by Sister Nivedita

Indian national flag with *vajra* as designed by Sister Nivedita

A major work of service that Nivedita undertook in India was the care of plague victims. March 1899 saw a major outbreak of plague in Calcutta. She nursed plague victims even risking her own life. She also wrote appeals for plague relief funds in newspapers, initiated Plague Relief Work in Calcutta slums, gave lectures on plague and appealed to the Indian youth to sacrifice their comforts and come forward for the cause.

Following Vivekananda, Nivedita understood that the hope for India lay in the education and empowerment of women. On 12 November 1898, Nivedita convened a meeting to discuss the proposal for opening a girls' school. The next day, this "School for Girls" was inaugurated and blessed by Sri Sarada Devi, Sri Ramakrishna's spiritual consort, at Nivedita's residence, 16 Bosepara Lane, Baghbazar in Calcutta. Three little girls were the first students. Nivedita had a total capital of eight hundred rupees, gifted by the Maharaja of Kashmir. Being a *brahmacharini*, she had little resources of her own. In spite of that, she managed to provide even clothes and medical treatment to some of the students. It was not easy to get students for the school, as the then Hindu social customs were very rigid. Nivedita, however, went from door to door pleading with parents to send their daughters to her school. This school has grown into the present-day Sister Nivedita Girls' School in Baghbazar. According to Nivedita, an active involvement in the cause of the nation is vital for women's own regeneration: "To work, to suffer, and to love, in the highest spheres; to transcend limits; to be sensitive to great causes; to stand transfigured by the national righteousness; this is the true emancipation of woman, and this is the key to her efficient education."[19]

An area where Sister Nivedita made her invaluable contribution was the promotion of science in India. Vivekananda had heard Jagadish Chandra Bose's presentations in Paris in 1900. He got one of his disciples, Mrs. Sara Chapman Bull, to help Bose patent his discoveries. Nivedita met J.C. Bose in 1898. Later, she was to become a life-long friend of Jagadish Chandra and his wife Lady Abala Bose. British officials conspired to suppress Bose's scientific work. Nivedita tried to protect his interests and promote his work. She provided much-needed succour to Bose. She also assisted him greatly in the writing of many scientific books.

The present-day Indian Institute of Science (IISc) in Bengaluru is the result of a chance meeting between Vivekananda and Jamsetji Tata. They were aboard the same ship from Japan to America in 1893. Jamsetji was deeply impressed by Vivekananda's emphasis on the development of science and technology in India. Thus, in 1898, he offered to fund the setting up of a Post-Graduate Research Institute for scientific education and training. The British tried to foil these efforts. Lord Curzon was especially vocal in speaking against the feasibility of "Mr. Tata's Scheme". Nivedita spoke and wrote in favour of the scheme, met officials, and tried to garner support for the cause. The proposed institute eventually started functioning in 1911.

Nivedita interacted with all the great Indian stalwarts of the time and also influenced some of their ideas. She inspired Dinesh Chandra Sen to write his classic book on the history of Bengali language and literature. She equally inspired the cohort of young historians like Radha Kumud Mukherjee and Jadunath Sarkar to think and write about Indian history from an Indian perspective. She was a close friend of the veteran Romesh Chunder Dutt, whose writings on Indian history she found valuable for their perspective (she wrote a moving obituary for him). She supported the new Bengal

School of Art movement, spearheaded by Abanindranath Tagore. She wrote essays on the national ideals of art in India; collaborated with Ananda Coomaraswamy, the leading philosopher and historian of art of that time; mentored young artists like Nandalal Bose and Asit Halder and sent them to Ajanta and Ellora to discover the roots of Indian art. After her passing away, Rabindranath Tagore gave her the epithet '*lokmata*' (mother of the people).

Nivedita on Indian Nationhood

The Basis of Indian Nationality

In the context of emergent Indian nationalism, Nivedita's appeal to Indians was: "The duty of all who understand the Indian situation today, then, is to *realise* those eternal verities on which the cry for nationality is based."[20] According to her, this basis is both historical and social. She remarked: "It is a mistake to think that India has not in the past been a well-organised nation. Ashoka, two and a half centuries before Christ, Chandra Gupta Vikramaditya, four centuries after Christ, and Akbar and his immediate successors, have all been men who understood the idea of Indian Nationality, and loved and worked for it."[21] It could therefore be argued that although the Western concept of nationhood was a modern phenomenon, pre-modern notions of a politico-territorial unit that was more or less the predecessor of the modern nation was already operative in India historically at various points of time. Nivedita could clearly see that all the "smaller unities of the past" had prepared India to become a single giant national entity.

Secondly, as Nivedita pointed out, "Nationality is built on the common home, the common interest and common love."[22] There was a fund of ideas and ideals that were cherished by the inhabitants of the land across differences of creed, beliefs, regional characteristics and so on. She elaborated: "There is a self-organisation of thought that precedes external organisation, and [this brings about] the accumulation of characteristics in a single line.... In India, the distinctive stock of ideas rises out of her early pre-occupation with great truths. Neither Jain nor Mohammedan admits the authority of the Vedas or the Upanishads, but both are affected by the culture derived from them. Both are marked, as strongly as the Hindu, by a high development of domestic affection, by a delicate range of social observation and criticism and by the conscious admission that the whole of life is to be subordinated to the ethical struggle between inclination and conscience.... When Egypt was building her Pyramids, India was putting a parallel energy into the memorising of the Vedas, and the patient elaboration of the Philosophy of the Upanishads. The culture began so early, has proceeded to the present day without a break, holding its own ground and saturating Indian society with standards of thought and feeling, far in advance of those common in other countries."[23]

She then went on to elaborate on other social markers of Indian unity such as devotion to the family, and especially to the mother, the organic part played by the aged, and so on, demonstrating how 'Indian' mores are similar notwithstanding religious differences between the Hindus and the Mohammedans. In terms of more abstract values, she noted that "The old-time Dharma of the great sovereigns, the code of piety of kings of the Shanti Parva, represents the most beautiful product and expression of a nation's unity that the world has ever seen."[24]

Past and Place

The cry for nationality stands on two pillars—history and geography. Nivedita argued that both these factors provide ample basis for the constitution of Indian nationality. The role of history in shaping any nationality is undeniable: "…History is the warp upon which is to be woven the woof of Nationality."[25] Nivedita rightly pointed out—in her quintessential way—the part played by India's past in consolidating Indian nationality: "The work of Humanity is never lost. The nation that has been developing its civilisation during more than thirty centuries of sustained effort cannot fail to have won something not yet attained by those who have emerged within a thousand years from barbarism. That nation fears no ordeal. Is the struggle before it today, the first it has known? True, it is the struggle of a unification vaster and deeper than the past has dreamt of. But it is a unification for which the past has prepared it."[26]

She was acutely aware of the pitfalls of the history of India that was to be found in books during her times. Apart from the motivation of imperial interests that wanted India to forever remain a subject nation, it was also a question of unbridgeable differences in outlook and culture that informed the historiography on India of her days. She noted: "European scholars are blind and deaf to many of the problems and many of the lines of work that Indian history opens up in abundance."[27] History was the very site of contestation of power between the ruler and the ruled, the site of representation and identity formation. Nivedita insisted: "…there is nothing like knowledge of facts for dispelling fictitious self-hypnotisms. For this reason, a really valuable History of India presupposes a certain training in sociology. When definite knowledge is available, partisanship falls gradually into disuse. It is better, surely, to *understand* caste, than either to praise or to vilify it."[28]

Nivedita clearly stated that it was more important to understand than to defend or vilify, that is, an objective non-partisan approach is desirable over a prejudiced one. However, with her, objectivity of viewpoint did not mean dryness of approach. Without an intense engagement with the subject of study, no authentic scholarship is possible. On the other hand, this passion should not blindfold one to the demands of rigorous scholarship. Thus, she pointed out: "The tale of her own past that the Motherland awaits, must combine the critical acumen of the modern, with the epic enthusiasm of the ancient writer…. It must not only be critical, but also fiery, proud, constructive."[29]

The second important factor in the formation of nationhood is geography. Nivedita noted that India undeniably possesses to an extraordinary degree the first treasure of a nation—"geographical distinctness". Speaking about the fundamental laws of nation-birth, she pointed out: "Any country which is geographically distinct, has the power to become the cradle of a nationality. National unity is dependent upon place…. Complexity of elements, when duly subordinated to the nationalising influence of place, is a source of strength, and not weakness to a nation."[30] Nivedita was strongly influenced by the works of the Scottish town-planner and sociologist Sir Patrick Geddes, with whom she had even worked closely for some time. Geddes was in turn influenced by the French school of geography and sociology that accorded great importance to place in the making of human cultures. This influence is clearly noticed in Nivedita's remark: "...miracles of human unification are the work of *Place*. Man only begins by making his home. His home ends by remaking him."[31] In some of her other writings, she explained how place can influence history—as in the case of the desert people of Arabia or the fisher-pirates of the European coastline who catapulted to the stature of being the creators of empires by the sheer force of necessity as determined by the place of their habitation.

Unity and Diversity

"Today being the 30th Aswin, 16th October, 1905, Partition of the Bengali people is to be made by law. This day then, designed to be the date of our division, is henceforth yearly to be set aside by us, for the deeper realisation of our national unity. Having been made by this threat of division, overwhelmingly conscious of the essential oneness of the whole Indian Nation the heart of Bengal goes out to all parts of our common Motherland. Thus to you from us of Bengal, is sent today this thread of Rakhi-Bandhan, in token not merely of the union of Provinces and parts of Provinces but of bond that knits us all as children of one Motherland together. Bande Mataram."[32] Thus wrote Nivedita to Ramananda Chatterjee.[33]

The British left behind the curious legacy of both uniting and dividing the country politically. The process of political unification was an unintended consequence of British rule and was of course meant to serve their own expansionist interests. But they always claimed credit for this and refused to acknowledge that India was an organic unity in itself. Nivedita told Indians: "'India is One' is the formula of nationhood for her. A mantra means a great deal when it has *realisation* behind it, though without this, it is not even as good as a juggler's spell."[34] She could highlight the subtle dimensions related to the concept of national unity. Let us examine the issues one by one.

Firstly, it was claimed that India was divided along the lines of caste and creed and could not aspire for a common nationality. About communal tension—which was steadily on the rise towards the end of her lifetime—

she exhorted Indians to see it in proper perspective and not exaggerate its implications for national cohesion. In any body politic, some amount of tension and friction is natural and does not call to question the unity of the national fabric. She thus remarked: "What? Is a village riot so serious a symptom in the body politic? The child stole sour mangoes, as his mother worked over the cooking fire, but it is not therefore proved that the child has all the instincts of a thief! Courage, my friends, courage. Let trifles take on their true proportions. Turn we to reckoning our wealth instead of our poverty!"[35] This, however, should not be treated as an underestimation of the communal problem. She was rightly aware of it and tried her best to resolve these tensions and bring Indians together for a nationality that synthesised differences. She was very clear about her idea of future India as a civic national entity—a 'synthesis' of Hindu, Buddhist, Islamic and even British cultures, while upholding what is truly 'Indian'. Then came caste differences. In her quintessential way, Nivedita pointed out: "Is India disunited? She has so many castes! says one. And how could she ever be a nation, if she had not? Her castes are not her enemies. They are her children…"[36] She, in fact, saw differences as contributing to unity and not causing division.

She wrote extensively on the factors that have laid the basis of national unity. Pilgrimage circuits and trade routes that have been active in India since very early times, joining the north and the south, have contributed to Indian unity. So much so that revered *char dhams* of Puri, Badrinath, Dwarka and Rameswaram dot the four corners of the landmass thereby demonstrating their inextricable relationship with the historical geography of the land. Even the epics have served to unite India, despite the variations that have occurred in them across the length and breadth of the country. The epics are also testimony to the connectedness of the geographical landscape of the land. The pre-modern political empires, the ideals of the land—all have contributed to its unity. Even the common struggle against the British had been a basis of national unity.

Nivedita made a significant conceptual contribution by pointing out that a nation is a "*complex* unity" and rightly asked, "How shall there be a Nation without differences of social degree?"[37] Therefore, we need to rethink the concepts of unity and diversity and their relationship with each other. Unity and diversity are really two sides of the same coin. They are related concepts, one cannot exist without the other. If we did not have diversity, the concept of unity would be rendered meaningless. Secondly, unity does not mean homogeneity. The question of unity arises precisely where there is heterogeneity or diversity. Nivedita pointed out insightfully: "Many persons use the word unity in a way that would seem to imply that the unity of a lobster, with its monotonous repetition of segments and limbs, was more perfect than that of the human body, which is not even alike on its right and left sides."[38] And then she recounted an incident: "I cannot forget a French working man,…who came up to me some years ago, in a university-settlement in the West, and said, 'Have the people of India any further proof to offer of the oneness of Humanity, beyond the fact that if I hurt you I hurt myself, and the other fact that no two of us are exactly alike?' And then, seeing perhaps a look of surprise, he added thoughtfully, 'for the fact that we are all different is, in its way, a proof of our unity!'"[39] In this connection it may also be noted that she herself found "an overwhelming aspect of Indian unity in the fact that no single member or province repeats the function of any other."[40] They were all meant to be different in order to form a true unity.

Finally, Nivedita's idea of unity in the Indian context was that of 'synthesis'. Thus, she remarked: "…India is and always has been a synthesis. No amount of analysis—racial, lingual, or territorial—will ever amount in the sum to the study of India.... Perhaps all the parts of a whole are not equal to the whole."[41] The idea is that the whole is not merely a sum of the parts; the whole has an identity of its own which is distinct from merely a mechanical addition of the parts. Similarly, when one talks of India, one does not consider it to be a mechanical adding up of regions. As once again pointed out by Nivedita: "…apart from and above, all the fragments which must be added together to make India, we have to recognise India herself, all-containing, all-dominating, moulding and shaping the destinies and the very nature of the elements out of which she is composed. The Indian people may be defective in the methods of mechanical organisation, but they have been lacking, as a people, in none of the essentials of organic synthesis. No Indian province has lived unto itself, pursuing its own development, following its own path, going its way unchallenged and alone. On the contrary, the same tides have swept the land from end to end."[42]

Nivedita's Contemporaries on Indian Nationhood

The Basis of Nationality

Some of Nivedita's contemporaries like Aurobindo Ghose (1872-1950, later Sri Aurobindo) and Ananda K. Coomaraswamy (1877-1947) echoed some of her ideas on Indian nationhood. In 1907, Ghose wrote that the notion that the essential conditions of a nationality are unity of language, religion and race is a false notion. Hence, the argument that is put forward on this basis that India is no nation, is also a false argument. He wrote: "...because there is diversity of race, religion and language in India [one] thinks that there is no possibility of creating a nationality in this country. This is a very common stumbling-block, but is there any reality in it? Rather we find that every nationality has been formed not because of, but in spite of, diversity of race or religion or language, and not unoften in spite of the co-existence of all these diversities."[43] Ghose then discussed the case of the English nation that was built out of various races, and in which, till his day, the races which came later into the British nationality keep their distinct individuality, including their language.

Then he cited the "striking example of Switzerland where distinct racial strains speaking three different languages and, later, professing different religions coalesced into and persisted as one nation without sacrificing a single one of these diversities."[44] Ghose continued: "In France three different languages are spoken, in America the candidates for the White House address the nation in fourteen languages, Austria is a congeries of races and languages, the divisions in Russia are hardly less acute. That unity in race, religion or language is essential to nationality is an idea which will not bear examination. Such elements of unity are very helpful to the growth of a nationality, but they are not essential and will not even of themselves assure its growth. The Roman Empire though it created a common language, a common religion and life, and did its best to crush out racial diversities under the heavy weight of its uniform system failed to make one great nation."[45]

Aurobindo Ghose in Presidency Jail during the Alipore Bomb Trial Case

Then, Ghose posed the question from the other end: "If these are not essential elements of nationality, what, it may be asked, are the essential elements? We answer that there are certain essential conditions, geographical unity, a common past, a powerful common interest impelling towards unity and certain favourable political conditions which enable the impulse to realise itself in an organised government expressing the nationality and perpetuating its single and united existence. This may be provided by a part of the nation, a race or community, uniting the others under its leadership or domination, or by a united resistance to a common pressure from outside or within. A common enthusiasm coalescing with a common interest is the most powerful fosterer of nationality. We believe that the necessary elements are present in India, we believe that the time has come and that by a common resistance to a common pressure in the shape of the [Swedish] boycott, inspired by a common enthusiasm and ideal, that united nationality for which the whole history of India has been a preparation, will be speedily and mightily accomplished."[46]

Ananda Coomaraswamy

Coomaraswamy too reiterated more or less the same points as Nivedita and Aurobindo Ghose. He wrote: "What are the things which make possible national self-consciousness, which constitute nationality? Certainly a unity of some sort is essential. There are certain kinds of unity, however, which are not essential, and others which are insufficient. Racial unity, for example, does not constitute the Negroes of North America a nation. Racial unity is not even an essential; the British nation is perhaps more composed of diverse racial elements than any other, but it has none the less a strong national consciousness. To take another example, many of the most Irish of the Irish are of English origin.... Neither is a common and distinctive language an essential; Switzerland is divided among three languages, and Ireland between two.

Two essentials of nationality there are,—a geographical unity, and a common historic evolution or culture. These two India possesses superabundantly, beside many lesser unities which strengthen the historical tradition. The fact of India's geographical unity is apparent on the map, and is never, I think, disputed. The recognition of social unity is at least as evident to the student of Indian culture. The idea has been grasped more than once by individual rulers,—Asoka, Vikramaditya and Akbar. It was recognised before the Mahābhārata was written; when Yudhishtira performed the *Rājasuya* sacrifice on the occasion of his inauguration as sovereign, a great assembly...was held, and to this assembly came Bhīma, Dhritarashtra and his hundred sons, Subala (King of Gandhāra), etc...and others from the extreme south and north (Dravida, Ceylon and Kashmir).... No one can say that any such idea as that of a Federated States of India is altogether foreign to the Indian mind. But more than all this, there is evidence enough that the founders of Indian culture and civilisation and religion...had this unity in view.... Is it for nothing that India's sacred shrines are many and far apart; that one who would visit more than one or two of these must pass over hundreds of miles of Indian soil?... Or take the epics, the foundation of Indian education and culture; or a poem like the *Megha Duta*, the best known and most read work of *Kalidasa*. Are not these expressive of love for and knowledge of the Motherland? The 'holy land' of the Indian is not a far-off Palestine but the Indian land itself. The whole of Indian culture is so pervaded with this idea of India as THE LAND, that it has never been necessary to insist upon it overmuch, for no one could have supposed it otherwise."[47]

In the same vein as Sister Nivedita, Coomaraswamy too pointed out: "The diverse peoples of India are like the parts of some magic puzzle, seemingly impossible to fit together, but falling easily into place when once the key is known; and the key is that realisation of the fact that the parts do fit together, which we call national self-consciousness."[48]

Rabindranath Tagore

In about a decade, a powerful critique of nationalism came from none other than Rabindranath Tagore. He articulated this critique not only through his novels like *Gora*[49] and *Ghare Baire* but also a series of lectures that were published in the form of a book called *Nationalism* in 1917. Tagore's main objection to the cult of nationalism was this: "Our real problem in India is not political. It is social...Politics in the West have dominated Western ideals, and we in India are trying to imitate you.

We have to remember that in Europe, where peoples had their racial unity from the beginning, and where natural resources were insufficient for the inhabitants, the civilisation has naturally taken the character of political and commercial aggressiveness. For on the one hand they had no internal complications, and on the other they had to deal with neighbours who were strong and rapacious. To have perfect combination among themselves and a watchful attitude of animosity against others was taken as a solution to their problems...Each nation must be conscious of its mission, and we, in India, must realise that we cut a poor figure when we are trying to be political..."[50] Tagore was correct in his observations that the historical basis of society in the West has been politics and that it has not been the case with India. However, what he said in this context about the basis of developments in India (which he calls the social problem), to my mind, is not deep enough.

In response to his welcome address at Kumbakonam after his return from the West, Swami Vivekananda pointed out: "I have seen a little of the world, travelling among the races of the East and the West; and everywhere I find among nations one great ideal which forms the backbone, so to speak, of that race. With some it is politics, with others it is social culture;

others again may have intellectual culture and so on for their national background. But this, our motherland, has religion and religion alone for its basis, for its backbone, for the bed-rock upon which the whole building of its life has been based…religion is the one and sole interest of the people of India. I am not just now discussing whether it is good to have the vitality of the race in religious ideals or in political ideals, but so far it is clear to us that, for good or for evil, our vitality is concentrated in our religion. You cannot change it. You cannot destroy it and put in its place another. You cannot transplant a large growing tree from one soil to another and make it immediately take root there. For good or for evil, the religious ideal has been flowing into India for thousands of years; for good or for evil, the Indian atmosphere has been filled with ideals of religion for shining scores of centuries; for good or for evil, we have been born and brought up in the very midst of these ideas of religion, till it has entered into our very blood and tingled with every drop in our veins, and has become one with our constitution, become the very vitality of our lives. Can you give such religion up without the rousing of the same energy in reaction…? Do you want that the Ganga should go back to its icy bed and begin a new course? Even if that were possible, it would be impossible for this country to give up her characteristic course of religious life and take up for herself a new career of politics or something else. You can work only under the law of least resistance, and this religious line is the line of least resistance in India. This is the line of life, this is the line of growth, and this is the line of well-being in India—to follow the track of religion."[51]

What he meant by religion is the quest for the eternal, transcendental Truth, the true nature of man. This quest is so ingrained in the Indian psyche, by virtue of thousands of years of engagement with it, that it is difficult for anything else to have a deeper or more widespread appeal. And any effort at uprooting this and replacing it with something else will only cause damage. While "in other countries religion is only one of the many necessities in life," something incidental, it is the life-line for Indians. Each must grow according to one's own nature or law of growth and that is the path of least resistance for the person, because it throws up the least obstacles and instead facilitates the journey. In other words, the law of growth for India is not politics, but religion.

In his articles in *Udbodhan*, the Bengali magazine of the Ramakrishna Order, Swami Prajnananda[52] explained with great clarity and logical rigour that "if one analyses scientifically, it is difficult not to call the civilisational entity that developed in [pre-British] India a "nation", but it is for sure that such a nation did not develop anywhere else in the world."[53] Prajnananda clearly delineated that the historical development of the Occidental countries was such that the people who had cohabited a common territory for a long time, rallied and united around the common cause of politics; hence there exists a very Western concept of nation defined in political terms. But the basic parameter for determining nationhood, according to him, is whether a collective occupying a common territory has united around a common goal for a sufficiently long period of time so as to determine its own predominant tendencies. If this definition is accepted then both the Western countries and India have been nations, only the common goal has been different in the two cases. Following Vivekananda, Prajnananda argued that the common goal Indians have pursued for centuries is spirituality. However, if one insists that the common goal of a people has to be politics in order to justify the epithet of a nation, then, he writes, India was never a "nation", and will never be one. But this narrow definition of 'nation', according to him, would be thoroughly unscientific.

Swami Prajnananda

Coming back to Tagore, on account of the potential for aggressive tendencies within nationalism, he viewed nationalism as a "menace", a force that could lead people to "moral degeneracy" and "intellectual blindness". Tagore saw the ravages that nationalism could cause, for instance, World War I. Vivekananda could see that the root cause of war was materialism that also informed the Western brand of nationalism.

Vivekananda, instead, chose to emphasise the spirit of self-sacrifice embedded within nationalism. It matters which element one chooses to highlight. For example, having visited Japan, Vivekananda was quite aware of the Japanese efforts at expanding the army and the navy. But he never failed to appreciate the Japanese spirit of patriotism and extreme self-sacrifice for the nation (which is, of course, not the same thing as supporting the idea of war).

Thirdly, for Tagore, nationalism was too narrow an ideal that weaned one away from the greater ideal of universal brotherhood. Thus, he remarked: "Even though from childhood I had been taught that the idolatry of Nation is almost better than reverence for God and humanity, I believe I have outgrown that teaching, and it is my conviction that my countrymen will gain truly their India by fighting against that education which teaches them that a country is greater than the ideals of humanity."[54] Of course, universal humanism is a great ideal, but at the same time, every ideal has a proper place and function in human life and society. Nationalism also has its importance as an ideal. If one thinks in terms of graded progress from one ideal to another, then Sister Nivedita's views in this regard shed light on an important aspect and complement Tagore's views. She wrote: "Only by the love of our own people can we learn the love of humanity", and that one "cannot be a cosmopolitan unless one be a nationalist. And to become a nationalist, we must extend our narrow self."[55] Nationalism itself is a broad enough ideal that teaches one to expand the scope of love, to go beyond oneself and one's kin to embrace the *civitas*, the whole nation as one's own. It is indeed unfortunate that many consider this the end of the journey. But even for one who would love the whole of humanity, nationalism can be a necessary step.

The same point was made by Aurobindo Ghose in response to an article that appeared in *Bengalee* dated 29 June 1909, in which the author claimed that nationalism is the highest of all syntheses. Ghose did not agree with this view and replied thus in his article in *Karmayogin* dated 3 July: "[The author] even goes much further than we are prepared to go and claims for Nationalism that it is the highest of all syntheses. This is a conclusion we are not prepared to accept; it is, we know, the highest which European thought has arrived at so far as that thought has expressed itself in the actual life and ideals of the average European. In Positivism, Europe has attempted to arrive at a higher synthesis, the synthesis of humanity; and Socialism and philosophical Anarchism, the Anarchism of Tolstoy and Spencer, have even envisaged the application of the higher intellectual synthesis to life. In India we do not recognise the nation as the highest synthesis to which we can rise. There is a higher synthesis, humanity; beyond that there is a still higher synthesis, this living, suffering, aspiring world of creatures, the synthesis of Buddhism; there is a highest of all, the synthesis of God, and that is the Hindu synthesis, the synthesis of Vedanta. With us today nationalism is our immediate practical faith and gospel not because it is the highest possible synthesis, but because it must be realised in life if we are to have the chance of realising the others. We must live as a nation before we can live in humanity."[56]

Thus, it may be argued that Tagore's critique was true in its spirit, but it mistook the proper place of nationalism. Moreover, giving up national identities altogether would involve a completely different world order. So long as other nationalisms exist, Indian nationalism will and should exist. But we need to be careful nonetheless about the fact that the basis of Indian nationhood is not political, but moral and spiritual.

In Conclusion: Relevance of the Study

Sister Nivedita

The past two years have seen a spate of publications as well as impassioned public debates on Indian nationalism. The issue of diversity has been played up in contemporary identity politics to such an extent that it has come to threaten the very fabric of Indian nationhood. These issues are our inheritance from a colonial past, and have been perpetuated by a skewed understanding of the subject. The past two years have also witnessed a revival of interest in Sister Nivedita, as 2017 marked her 150th birth anniversary. As discussed above, her ideas on Indian nationhood can shed light on many of the intricacies of the debate on Indian nationalism that remains to be ironed out, especially with regard to issues such as the idea of India, a pre-history of Indian nationhood, the dynamics between diversity and unity, and so on.

Today, many scholars make similar arguments and their works demonstrate that what Nivedita had proposed was not a figment of imagination. For example, Shashi Tharoor makes exactly the same claims in his recent piece '*The Idea of an Ever-ever Land*' (2017). With reference to the prevalent view that the British gave India political unity, Tharoor argues that "throughout the history of the subcontinent, there has existed an impulsion for unity", which was manifest in the several overarching empires, like the Mauryas, Guptas, Mughals, even Vijayanagara and the Marathas—all of whom tried to build a pan-subcontinent kingdom. He further argues: "The same impulse is also manifest in Indians' vision of our own nation, as in the ancient epics the *Mahabharata* and the *Ramayana*, which reflect an 'idea of India' that twentieth-century nationalists would have recognised. The epics have acted as strong, yet sophisticated, threads of Indian culture that have woven together tribes, languages and peoples across the subcontinent, uniting them in their celebration of the same larger-than-life heroes and heroines, whose stories were told in dozens of translations and variations but always in the same spirit and meaning."[57] So much so that Tharoor even writes that the landscape the Pandavas saw in the *Mahabharata* was a pan-Indian landscape and "Lord Rama's journey through India and his epic battle against the demon-king of Lanka reflect the same national idea." He continues by invoking the cultural and geographical unity of India that is at least as old as Ashoka's empire. Tharoor even invokes the pan-India travel of Adi Sankara as an embodiment of the vision of Indian unity. If we look at more academic works on the historical and sacred geography of India, we would all the more realise the truth in Nivedita's claims and not dismiss them as uncritical sentimentalism.

It is important to recognise today that the fact that modern India is in a sense a product of colonial rule does not invalidate the reality of Indian nationhood. The underlying assumption of those who, on this ground, keep on questioning the validity of Indian nationhood, is that European nations are the 'original', therefore legitimate nations. It is too easily overlooked that even European nations had certain historical conditions as circumstances of their origin. Moreover, given the antiquity of the Indian land, it is well-nigh impossible that no sense of cohesion across large territories existed before the British arrived in India. In fact, Nivedita once stated that the British recognised the Indian nation all too well and that is the reason why they colonised India; had there not been the recognition of some kind of national cohesion or unity, they would have never thought of bringing disjointed parts into the same colony. The unintended and incidental contribution of the British in forging political unity in India does not take away from Indian nationhood its rightful legitimacy. Finally, given that a nation is always a *complex* unity, India's diversity actually contributes to Indian unity rather than being a divisive factor.

In conclusion, it may be pointed out that it is time to move beyond colonial legacies and think about a truly Indian narrative even on something such as 'nationalism', which is usually associated with the West. The lesson that India has to offer in the histories and pre-histories of nationalism is perhaps that one should learn to look at the phenomenon beyond its ideological dimensions and not conceive it exclusively in political terms.

NOTES

1. Benedict Anderson, *Imagined Communities: Reflections on the Origin and Spread of Nationalism*, Verso, London, 1991.
2. Sugata Bose, *The Nation as Mother and Other Visions of Nationhood*, Penguin, Gurgaon, 2017, p. 87.
3. Elleke Boehmer, *Empire, the National, and the Postcolonial 1890-1920: Resistance in Interaction*, Oxford University Press, Oxford, 2002.
4. Ibid., p. 42.
5. Amiya Sen, ed., *An Idealist in India: Selected Writings and Speeches of Sister Nivedita*, Primus Books, Delhi, 2016.
6. Ibid., p. 21.
7. Ibid., p. 21.
8. Ibid., p. 21.
9. Sudipta Kaviraj, 'The Imaginary Institution of India', in Partha Chatterjee and Gyanendra Pandey, eds., *Subaltern Studies VII*, Oxford University Press, New Delhi, 1999, p. 1.
10. B.D. Chattopadhyaya, *The Concept of Bharatvarsha and Other Essays*, Permanent Black, New Delhi, 2017, pp. 189-190.

11. Bose, *The Nation as Mother*.
12. John Hutchinson and Anthony Smith, eds., *Nationalism*, Oxford University Press, Oxford, p. 5.
13. Ibid., pp. 6-7.
14. Ibid., pp. 4-5.
15. Ibid., p. 6.
16. Hans Kohn, 'Western and Eastern Nationalisms', in ibid., pp. 162-165.
17. Hutchinson and Smith, *Nationalism*, p. 3.
18. Ibid., p. 4.
19. *The Complete Works of Sister Nivedita*, Advaita Ashrama, Calcutta, 1982, vol. 5, p. 27.
20. *Complete Works of Sister Nivedita*, Vol. 4, p. 288.
21. Ibid., p. 293.
22. Ibid., p. 205.
23. Ibid., pp. 265-266.
24. Ibid., p. 293.
25. Ibid., p. 307.
26. Ibid., p. 297.
27. Ibid., p. 310.
28. Ibid., p. 308.
29. Ibid., p. 311.
30. Ibid., p. 264.
31. Ibid., pp. 263-264.
32. *Letters of Sister Nivedita*, Advaita Ashrama, Calcutta, 2nd edition, 2017, Vol. 2, p. 47.
33. Pioneer of Journalism in India. Editor, *Prabasi* (Allahabad), *The Modern Review* (Calcutta)
34. *Complete Works of Sister Nivedita*, Vol. 4, p. 290.
35. Ibid., pp. 293-294.
36. Ibid., p. 291.
37. Ibid., p. 291; emphasis in original.
38. Ibid., p. 269.
39. Ibid., pp. 269-270.
40. Ibid., p. 270.
41. Sister Nivedita, *Footfalls of Indian History*, Advaita Ashrama, Kolkata, 1915, p. 16.
42. *Ibid.*, pp. 16-17.
43. *The Complete Works of Sri Aurobindo*, Sri Aurobindo Ashram Trust, Pondicherry, 2002, vol. 6, p. 642.
44. *Ibid.*, p. 642.
45. *Ibid.*, p. 642.
46. *Ibid.*, p. 643.
47. Ananda K. Coomaraswamy, *Essays in National Idealism*, Munshiram Manoharlal, Delhi, 1981, pp. 7-9.
48. *Ibid.*, p. 10.
49. It is well-known that the character of Gora was based on Sister Nivedita herself. Tagore had even discussed the character and the plot of the novel with her. But the final version of the novel was published years after Nivedita passed away, so we do not know how his conceptualisation of the character evolved over the years.

50. Rabindranath Tagore, *Nationalism*, The Book Club of California, San Francisco, 1917, pp. 117-118.
51. *The Complete Works of Swami Vivekananda*, Advaita Ashrama, Kolkata, 2011 (reprint), Vol. 3, pp. 177-179.
52. In his pre-monastic life, Swami Prajnananda was known as Devavrata Basu. He was active in revolutionary politics and swadeshi work. Along with Aurobindo Ghose, he was also arrested in the Alipore Bomb Case in 1908. They turned the prison into a veritable place for *sadhana*, as they spent most of their time in meditation and reading the scriptures. After his release from prison, Devavrata Basu received spiritual initiation from Sri Sarada Devi and joined the Ramakrishna Order as a monk. He was a contemporary of Sister Nivedita and his own sister later took up the work of the girls' school started by Nivedita. Prajnananda wrote extensively in the two magazines of the Ramakrishna Order—*Udbodhan* in Bengali and *Prabuddha Bharata* in English.
53. Swami Prajnananda, 'Prachin Bharate Nation-Pratishtha', *Bharater Sadhana*, Udbodhan Karyalaya, Kolkata, 1986, p. 4. This is my own free translation.
54. Tagore, *Nationalism*, p. 127.
55. *The Complete Works of Sister Nivedita*, Vol. 5, p. 244.
56. *Complete Works of Sri Aurobindo*, Vol. 8, pp. 84-85.
57. Shashi Tharoor, 'The Idea of an Ever-ever Land', in Nidhi Razdan, ed., *Left, Right and Centre: The Idea of India*, Gurgaon, Viking, 2017, pp. 212-213.

REFERENCES

Primary Literature
1. Coomaraswamy, Ananda K., *Essays in National Idealism*, Munshiram Manoharlal, Delhi, 1981.
2. *Letters of Sister Nivedita*, 2 vols. Advaita Ashrama, Calcutta, 2017, second and revised edition.
3. Swami Prajnananda, *BharaterSadhana*, UdbodhanKaryalaya, Kolkata (in Bengali).
4. Tagore, Rabindranath, *Nationalism*, The Book Club of California, San Francisco, 1917.
5. *The Complete Works of Sister Nivedita*, 5 vols., Sister Nivedita Girls' School, Calcutta, 1955.
6. *The Complete Works of Sri Aurobindo*, vols. 6-8, Sri Aurobindo Ashram Trust, Pondicherry, 2002.
7. *The Complete Works of Swami Vivekananda*, vols. 1-9, Advaita Ashrama, Kolkata, 2011 (reprint).

Secondary Literature
Books
8. Anderson, Benedict, *Imagined Communities: Reflections on the Origin and Spread of Nationalism*, Verso, London, 1991.
9. Boehmer, Elleke, *Empire, the National, and the Postcolonial 1890-1920: Resistance in Interaction*, Oxford, Oxford University Press, 2002.
10. Bose, Sugata, *The Nation as Mother and Other Visions of Nationhood*, Gurgaon, Penguin, 2017.
11. Chattopadhyaya, B. D., *The Concept of Bharatavarsha and Other Essays*, New Delhi, Permanent Black, 2017.
12. Hutchinson, John & Anthony D. Smith, eds., *Nationalism*, Oxford, Oxford University Press, 1994.

13. Reymond, Lizelle, *The Dedicated: A Biography of Nivedita*, New York, John Day, 1953.
14. Sen, Amiya, ed., *An Idealist in India: Selected Writings and Speeches of Sister Nivedita*, Delhi, Primus Books, 2016.

Articles
1. Kaviraj, Sudipta, 'The Imaginary Institution of India', in Partha Chatterjee & Gyanendra Pandey, eds., *Subaltern Studies VII*, New Delhi, Oxford University Press, 1999.
2. Tharoor, Shashi, 'The Idea of an Ever-ever Land', in Nidhi Razdan, ed., *Left, Right and Centre: The Idea of India*, Gurgaon, Penguin, 2017.

(Dr. Arpita Mitra has a doctoral degree in History from Jawaharlal Nehru University, New Delhi. She has been a Fellow (2015-2017) at the Indian Institute of Advanced Study, Shimla, where she had written a monograph on Swami Vivekananda's 'Neo-Vedanta'. Presently, she is Associate Fellow at the VIF, where she is working on different aspects of Indian history and culture)

*

15

MILITANCY IN KASHMIR: A STUDY

Abhinav Pandya

ABSTRACT

Today the State is at a very critical juncture. The movement is directionless and largely leaderless. It may take a blind turn. If it goes on like this, it may even lead to anarchy and Kashmir could become a hunting ground for barbaric Jihadi forces like Al Qaeda (AQ) and the Islamic State of Iraq and Syria (ISIS). The possibility of these pernicious forces capitalising on the existing youth unrest in Kashmir is further accentuated by the likely withdrawal of American forces from Afghanistan.

The recent Syria-styled Fidayeen attack on a Central Reserve Police Force (CRPF) convoy that led to the death of 46 personnel and the responsibility for which was claimed by the Jaish-e-Muhammad (JeM), involving a Kashmiri young Jihadi, is the most alarming indication of what lies in the future. Before the Pakistani "Deep State" and transnational terrorist groups spread their tentacles in Kashmir, India needs to get its act together. The solution has to be multi-pronged; political, diplomatic, psychological and spiritual and should involve multiple stakeholders and with multiple layers of engagement.

This study, based on interviews and casual interactions with a diverse range of people—youth from South, Central and North Kashmir, university, college and school students, security officials, NGO workers, artists, separatists, former militants, army government officials, religious clerics, mainstream politicians, youth leaders and ordinary civilians—covers a wide range of issues, including socio-political and cultural trends, perceptions prevailing among different stakeholders and the dominant intellectual and religious narratives. The primary focus is on trends emerging since 2016, after the encounter-death of Hizb-ul-Mujahideen (HM) leader Burhan Wani, which in many ways is considered as a watershed moment in the recent history of militancy in Kashmir.

Kashmir has had several significant watershed moments over the last three to four decades but 2016 is considered very crucial. The years preceding 2016 undoubtedly witnessed the silent sowing of seeds of the current discontent, the manifestations of which have come into sharper focus after the death of Burhan Wani. Significantly, this event has been invariably mentioned as the takeoff point for trends emerging since 2016. That is why this study is important for developing any suitable policy narrative and course of action for the future.

Kashmir's Politics in Drift

Recognising the widely prevalent view that the Kashmir dispute was primarily a political issue, any analysis of the situation must begin with a critical assessment of the current political scenario. The prevailing impression in the Valley is that politically, Kashmir is in a state of drift, heading towards a black hole. Mainstream political parties such as the People's Democratic Party (PDP) and the National Conference (NC) apparently seem to have lost their "connect" with the people. Their credibility has significantly eroded in recent times for various reasons. Commonplace Kashmiris accuse the mainstream parties of corruption, nepotism, atrocious governance and opportunism. College and university students generally maintain that during the PDP-BJP coalition rule, the high-class Saiyyids were placed in all prominent positions in administration, academia and other state bodies.

The PDP is perceived as having lost credibility and public support because of its alliance with the BJP. The latter is portrayed as a Hindu extremist party by active social media in the Valley, which is largely controlled and managed by elements based across the border. In South Kashmir, the PDP has been facing the ire of its core Jammat supporters for its alliance with the BJP. There is a perception in the Valley that by doing so, the PDP helped the BJP establish itself as a political force in the

Figure 1: Security personnel guarding the desolate roads of Srinagar after stone pelting, Courtesy: Adil Abbas

state, kick-starting debates such as tampering with Article 35 A and Article 370 of the Constitution.

Another significant reason for the ordinary civilian's ire against the now-dissolved coalition government and state administration in general, is their non-responsive attitude, extreme corruption, ineffective governance, and above all, allegations of arrogant and insulting behaviour by senior and district-level civil servants. Ordinary people are being made to wait for days on end for routine governance and administrative matters. In several interviews, Governor Satyapal Malik has categorically stated that "Corruption is the single biggest problem of the state. Those in power here, be it political, administrative or business power, live like Mughal emperor Jahangir. The poor youths who go with their ponies to earn a living during the Amarnath Yatra do so without even wearing warm clothes." (*Greater Kashmir*, February 25, 2019)

Thus, the state of Jammu and Kashmir is the victim of extraordinary levels of corruption, both at the political and the bureaucratic level. The pathetic condition of roads and other civilian infrastructure, inadequate sewage systems, half-constructed flyovers, shoddy execution of public works, insufficient public transport systems and primitive health and educational infrastructure, speaks volumes about incompetent governance, corruption, poor work ethics and administrative arrogance. People also hold earlier regimes led by the NC equally responsible for the abovementioned grievances. The feeling of resentment, alienation and hatred is deeply entrenched and mainstream parties are seen as working in tandem with Delhi, to pursue their selfish political interests.

It is not only the mainstream parties that have lost the connect with the people; the paramount and highly moralistic claims of the All Party Hurriyat Conference (APHC) to represent popular sentiment too hardly has any standing or relevance in present-day Kashmir. The National Investigation Agency (NIA) raids (*Economic Times*, July 13, 2018) have totally exposed the Hurriyat leaders as Pakistan-paid mercenaries with little concern for or connect with Kashmiri issues. The Hurriyat has been pursuing Pakistan's evil agenda on the one hand and exploiting India's fears on the other, all for an elusive dream of playing a dominant political role in the affairs of the state. Ordinary civilians, especially the youth, find it difficult to trust Hurriyat leaders, whom they accuse of corruption and nepotism. The widespread accusation is that the high-profile separatist leaders send their children to quality schools and colleges in India and abroad, manage high-salary jobs and elitist careers for their kith and kin, whereas the children of ordinary people are motivated and mobilised to participate in stone-pelting, become militants and die at the hands of security forces.

There are stories galore of Hurriyat leaders not disbursing monetary help to the stone pelters and their families and are siphoning off funds. After the refusal of Hurriyat leaders to talk with an all-party delegation (*India*, October 25, 2016) and the Yashwant Sinha-led delegation in the past, this belief has gained strength that the Hurriyat does not want the Kashmir issue to be resolved because they want to retain their perks and privileges from both India and Pakistan.

The Hurriyat is seen as a party in decline, suffering from internal frictions, lacking clarity of vision, motivation, and moral integrity. Syed Ali Shah Gilani's ill-health and frictions between Yaseen Malik, Masarrat Alam and Mirwaiz Umar Farooq have generated the feeling that the APHC is in perpetual decline, with no credible successor to the present crop of leaders.

Thus, on the political front, it is argued with conviction that present-day Kashmir lacks credible political stakeholders with sufficient popular goodwill and grass root support and this may pose a severe challenge in initiating any fruitful process of political dialogue/engagement. In the absence of credible representatives, the dialogue will be an exercise in futility. Additionally, this has also led to a definite disconnect with trends, narratives and events happening in Kashmir at the grassroots level.

The Disenchantment of Youth

The declining credibility of political parties and ineffective administrative machinery of the state has been contributing to the growing disenchantment among the youth. Besides, the disruption in the academic schedule due to frequent strikes, the law and order situation, students' agitation, etc., paint

Figure 2: Disenchanted youth of Kashmir pelting stones, on the pathway to militancy.
Courtesy: Adil Abbas

a grim future for them. In government colleges, student agitations on everyday issues like infrastructure can be effectively dealt with by the district administration, the college authorities and the vice-chancellor, but invariably ends up with the administration opting to march in the police as their first and only response! The police act in a high-handed manner, at times, resorting to the use of pellet guns. Often, one finds that people are demanding good governance and protesting to get electric transformers repaired, or issues of employment, water and electricity addressed, but by raising slogans of 'Azadi'.

On the question of jobs, it is alleged that even in the Public Service Commission recruitments, university recruitments and other appointments, mostly candidates close to powerful politicians and influential Islamist and anti-India pressure groups are selected and appointed. An applicant without political connections and financial strength stands very little chance. Many a time, the rejection of candidates happens because of the inherent bias against a particular region like hailing from an area considered a Jamaat-i-Islami (JI) stronghold, though someone with actual Jamaat support might easily get appointed!

The most significant reason for the disenchantment of the youth of Kashmir revolves around the presence of the army and other security forces across Kashmir. They complain that routine checking, barricades, ill-treatment, manhandling, sexual abuse, insult and humiliation inspire hatred against the security forces and the desire to seek revenge. They totally fail to recognise the reasons for the presence of the security forces in the militancy-affected areas. They also overlook the fact that all operations launched by the forces are against identified hardcore militants, and the civilians wilfully expose themselves to a confrontation with the forces by trying to obstruct their operations.

Youth Swayed by Militancy

Right from the initial days of militancy, going back to the early 1990s, the youth in Kashmir have grown up seeing a gun-wielding soldier or a militant. As a result, they have developed a mindset where the gun is perceived as the strongest and the only symbol of empowerment. This is very similar to another situation say, for example, in Uttar Pradesh or Bihar, for a rural and urban middle-class youngster, becoming an Indian Administrative Service (IAS) or Indian Police Service (IPS) or a politician is a strong symbol of empowerment. To the Kashmiri youth, living in an environment of conflict, it gives them a strong identity. The young boys are also fascinated by the thrill and glamour of gun-culture. They are lured by the smart military and commando-styled attires of the militants with their latest gadgets and weaponry. The pictures posted on social media attract the lay youngsters because such pictures give them instant fame and recognition in a state where there are hardly any other platforms for seeking recognition and respect. The heroism attached to young, handsome men dying for a cause creates glamour around militancy.

The rapid rise in the youth getting attracted to militancy since the Burhan Wani incident is not only in numerical terms. More importantly, there is a qualitative difference from the militancy of the 1990s when foreign terrorists primarily dominated militancy, with not much public support for terrorist attacks. However, today's militancy is mostly driven by 'home grown' elements, though Pakistan-based controllers and operatives continue to play a prominent role in weapons supply, funding and directing the broad narratives, strategy and agenda for militant organisations.

Militancy, these days is like a wave in Kashmir. The youth seem to be swayed by it. The youngsters seem to have lost hope with India because of the continuous failure of the dialogue process. They seem to suffer from an acute sense of despair, depression, and hopelessness. They don't see any future concerning good career, business, employment and quality of life. They do not have any expectations from the mainstream politicians because of the reasons mentioned in the earlier section. They are also highly critical of and disappointed with Pakistan because of the terror tactics used by the latter's proxies like the Jammat. Besides, they feel that Pakistan is unsympathetic to and insincere in supporting their nationalist aspirations.

One development of serious concern is that the youth seems to have lost the fear of death. Some see death as a pathway to glory and the Islamic concept of paradise. There is a kind of heroism being attached to gun culture. Militants are becoming role-models for the youth. Wallpapers of Burhan Wani and Zakir Musa are common on their mobile screens. They listen to the speeches of Masood Azhar and Hafiz Saeed. They listen to Arabic taranas (type of composition). Even art forms like rap music have themes of 'Azadi', with Islam and anti-India feelings very strongly embedded in them. Boys in the 8 to 14 years age group indulging in stone-pelting at the security forces during Cordon and Search Operations (CASO) are in the process, getting early exposure to militancy. The types of Zakir Musa, former Hizb-ul-Mujahideen (HM) leader and now the commander of Ansar Ghazwat-ul-Hind (AGUH)* have such a strong following that even boys of 8 to 14 years of age get themselves photographed in his style and post them on their Facebook and Instagram accounts. (*Since neutralised by security forces – Ed).

Figure 3: Radicalised stone-pelter of Kashmir.
Courtesy: Adil Abbas

The Islamic concept of the afterlife is a strong motivator for militants. The social system also gradually tends to support it. In villages, the graveyards have become revered places for social union and mobilisation. Funerals have emerged as places of community mobilisation. Such a scenario clearly indicates that in the near future Kashmiri youth may volunteer for suicide/Fidayeen missions. Similarly, stone-pelting also has a strong religious symbolism. In Islam, the concept of stoning Satan is very pious. The tactic of stone-pelting allegedly was picked up from Palestinian Intifadas. Credible sources have informed that CDs with strong religious-motivational lectures eulogising stone-pelting and displaying Palestinian videos were widely circulated in the Valley by separatist leaders in an organised manner in 2008-09 at the behest of controllers based in Pakistan. This kind of religious imagery is being used in a very disruptive manner to manipulate young minds.

The present generation of Kashmiri youth which was born in the early 1990s has grown up in this environment of violence, religious radicalisation and political turbulence. As a result, they already have a radicalised mindset to an extent. They have no memories of the common Pundit-Muslim syncretic social culture of Kashmir. With such a basic cognitive framework, they are not very much interested in Sufi practices.

Religious Radicalisation Contributing to Militancy

Religious radicalisation is another primary cause for the rise of militancy. Radicalisation is a fact of life in Kashmir. No Kashmiri can deny this. The debate on this is only limited to its spread and impact. There is a notion that 'Kashmiriyat' and its essence of Sufism will always act as a firewall against religious radicalisation in Kashmir. However, grassroot situations tell a different story. Shockingly, in South Kashmir, in a class of 40-50 students, 15-20 wanted to join militancy. They said they would even be ready to lay down their lives on one call of AGUH commander Zakir Musa. What should be a cause of genuine concern is the assertion that they want an Islamic Kashmir. They categorically reject the home-coming of Kashmiri Pundits. If these views are samples of the feelings of Kashmiri youth in general, there is much for our policymakers to worry about!

Between 2002 and 2008, the peace period, the JI strongly entrenched itself in Kashmiri society through proselytisation, ijtemas (religious gatherings), threats, terror and intimidation. Their ideology is that of a politicised Islam. In brief, the JI can be referred to as a South Asian cousin of Egypt's Muslim Brotherhood. They believe in an extreme version of Islam and implement the agenda of Pakistan-based handlers. The result of their activities was witnessed from the beginning of militancy in the Valley in the early 1990s and more intensely since the unrest re-erupted in 2008 and is continuing since.

The Jammat acts as the main conduit of militancy. Its cadres function as Over Ground Workers (OGWs) providing infrastructure support and the protective shell in which the militants operate. They also help in arranging logistics, weapons, shelter and facilitating movement. A large number of militants have a Jammat background. However, in rural areas, people are in a way 'scared' of the Jammat cadres. They fear that cooperating with the security forces or the civil administration will invite the wrath of the JI. Its militant wing, the HM, has once again resumed sending Kashmiri boys to Pakistan-occupied Kashmir (PoK) since 2012 for indoctrination and training, as they used to in the initial years of militancy.

In recent times, the young generation has become a little disillusioned with the JI. The reason for this is being identified as its deep involvement in terror in pursuit of the agenda of foreign players, ignoring the grievances of Kashmiris. The young intellectual class largely is not impressed with the ideology or the activities of the Jammat. Lately, the Jamaat has increased its outreach by inviting rural folk to participate in the Ijtemas. The JI is trying to strengthen its district-level set-up with a special focus on youth. It is targeting universities and colleges. Over the last few months, JI-controlled WhatsApp groups are being created in large numbers. It appears that some dominant long-term strategy is being designed to take ownership of the current youth unrest.

Copious amounts of literature on political Islam, books of Maulana Maududi, Syed Qutb and Hasan Banna are readily available in all bookshops. These books are widely read in universities and colleges. They are available in English and the quality of the printed versions is excellent. This unholy nexus between the bookshops, distributors, universities, colleges and religious organisations with their foreign-based donors and operators needs to be excavated to deal with radicalisation.

Radical Groups Competing for Influence

Notwithstanding the renewed efforts of the JI since 2010, a significant drift towards the Ahle-Hadith/Wahabi sect has been observed. Sufism, that was the essence of Kashmiriyat, is perceived to be dying a slow death. The Ahle Hadith, Jamaat-i-Islami, and Tableeghi Jammat reject the Sufi shrine worship and other syncretic rituals and practices. Their brand of Islam is fundamentalist in nature. The corruption in shrines and superstitious/dogmatic practices of Sufism are also substantial factors for the rise of the Ahle-Hadith and other fundamentalist Jamaats. Besides the robust petro-dollar funding, better infrastructure, educated religious scholars and global Islamism being essential reasons, Kashmiri youth feel that Ahle-Hadith gives them an empowering Islamic identity in a conflict environment. Where the dominant narrative is militancy, conflict and violence, the peaceful Sufi meditative religion does not align well with youth sentiment.

Though the majority of the population is still 'Etaqadi' (Barelwi local Muslims) but their roots in Sufism have lost spiritual essence. Only rituals like worshipping at shrines have remained with overtones of religious extremism and communalism, conditioned by the overall milieu of religious and political radicalisation. Once having a marginal presence in the Valley, the Ahle-Hadith now has around a million followers out of a total population of six million, and there are approximately 700 Ahle-Hadith mosques (*Times of India*, July 19, 2017). Their influence has substantially increased over the last decade. However, unlike the JI, prominent religious clerics and scholars of the Ahle-Hadith/Salafi sect do not discuss politics in their mosque lectures, preferring to stay away from it. They also consider militancy and JI activities as un-Islamic. They are busy establishing an ideological base for something even more dangerous, i.e., an Islamic Kashmir.

Thus, Kashmir is increasingly becoming a battleground for sectarian rivalries. Lately, some Ahle-Hadith scholars like Mushtaq Veeri have praised the Islamic State and its leader Abu Bakr al-Baghdadi for propagating the Caliphate Code in Kashmir. Mufti Shabbir Ahmad Kasmi (TOI July 19, 2017), a Deobandi (ideologically a close cousin of the Ahle-Hadith) has expressed support for Zakir Musa and his AGUH. Absconding Wahabi scholar Zakir Naik is very popular among youth groups of the Ahle-Hadith in Kashmir.

The JI and the Ahle-Hadith have a strong presence in the education sector and institutions. The Salafis are ahead of others in their non-religious social presence. They run orphanages, clinics, colleges, schools and madrassas. A lot of Salafi literature has been freely distributed in Kashmir over the last 30 years. However, with a home to 2.8 million mobile (TOI July 19, 2017) internet users, the spread of Wahhabi influence poses a greater danger through social media messaging platforms. This religious overdose is generating fundamentalism and exclusivism, eventually leading to extremist thoughts and actions.

It is pertinent to mention that the ideological justification of a global Jihad and sanctity for terrorism in Kashmir as Jihad is instrumental in generating public support for militancy and stone-pelting. They consider stone-pelting as their bare minimum contribution to the so-called Mujahids during CASO.

Such narratives have also raised fears among the Shias. Shia radicalisation is also on the rise in Kashmir. It has foreign roots. One can find a strong Iranian influence in the Shia community of Kashmir. It is very common to see hoardings of Khamani in Kargil and Leh. There is also a significant flow of foreign religious scholars and students to and from Iran.

Social and Mainstream Media in Radicalisation and Militancy

Social media is also playing a dominant role in radicalising the youth. Once a CASO begins, messages on WhatsApp groups mobilise people for stone pelting. Instagram posts of militants, fiery speeches of terrorists like Masood Azhar and Arabic taranas are widely circulated as well. The Youth Forum for Kashmir set up in Islamabad in 2012 by Ahmad Qureishi with the backing of the Pakistan Army has also played an influential role in fomenting youth unrest in Kashmir. They targeted universities and colleges.

Further, the coverage of Kashmir events in mainstream Indian media is acting as a major spoiler. Kashmiri youth maintain that mainstream Indian media portrays all Kashmiris as terrorists and Kashmiri politicians as being 'Pakistani'. The influential round-the-clock news channels indulge in bitter debates on communal matters, getting fanatic religious leaders on their shows that contribute to a highly polarised environment. Usually, such provocative journalism is taken very seriously in Kashmir. People even in the remote villages of Kashmir are well acquainted with names like Arnab Goswami, Major Gaurav Arya, and Subramaniam Swami. Some Kashmiri politicians and youth leaders go to the extent of attributing radicalisation in Kashmir as a reaction to Hindu extremism! They added that Hindu-Muslim dynamics in India has an enormous impact on the Kashmiri mindset. Therefore, unfortunate incidents of beef-lynching and communal riots create a feeling of insecurity among Kashmiris.

To an extent, this may be real, but religious radicalisation has its internal dynamics and it has been going on independent of happenings in the overall socio-political scenario of India. Furthermore, there is reluctance on the part of Kashmiris to accept that radicalisation might erode the *Tahreek's* international credibility by exposing strong Islamist undercurrents and diluting its supposedly secular and political nature. However, even the outer trappings of the movement are now a far cry from its much-touted secular credentials.

Despite this, one cannot deny that national media is projecting a highly biased and negative image of the Kashmiri people for small TRP interests. This is detrimental to India's long-term interests in Kashmir and therefore needs strong reversal through greater media self-regulation.

Civil Society and Human Rights Groups

Additionally, Indian civil society and human rights activists are playing a negative role. Incidents of beef-lynching are sporadic and certainly not a nation-wide phenomenon. Nearly 25 crore Muslims are living peacefully across India with all constitutional rights and privileges. Communal incidents are an aberration and given the sheer size of the country, their numbers have been minimal. Hindu-Muslim conflicts are mostly localised and arise out of non-religious reasons. However, civil society activists and political parties have been blowing things out of proportion for narrow interests or out of ideological hatred. There is hardly any rationality behind such narratives.

The oft-quoted narratives made rather irresponsibly for political gain ('rising intolerance', 'emergency-like-conditions,' 'government-being-controlled by Fascist and dictatorial forces') are having the worst impact on young minds in Kashmir. Deliberate and malicious attempts to portray the central government's dictatorial and extremist image is leading to a feeling that the Indian establishment is planning to effect demographic changes and dilute their autonomy. We all know that there is hardly any truth in such narratives but the repeated peddling of such lies is furthering the agenda of terrorist organisations and foreign-based actors. There is thus an urgent need for civil society and political parties to exercise rationality; otherwise it will severely hurt India's national security interests.

Impact of Developments in the Global Arena

Last but not the least, global jihad and the growing awareness of geopolitical happenings in Syria, Yemen, Myanmar, Pakistan and Iran may also be a contributing influence to radicalising Kashmiri youth. There are a few people who claim to have met Kashmiris who fought alongside ISIS fighters in the battles of Mosul and Fallujah. While the veracity of such claims is difficult to establish, this is not new. It may be recalled that the Arab Spring movement that started in Tunisia and rapidly spread across the Arab world, was closely followed in Kashmir with the youth agitation of 2008 being largely influenced by the happenings in that part of the world. In more recent times, the Baghdadi phenomenon in Syria-Iraq too found quick resonance in the Kashmir Valley. In visual terms, the black flag of ISIS has almost started competing with the green Pakistani one, not in terms of actual following of these symbolic displays but purely as an irritant against the authorities.

Having looked at the sporadic attempts to internationalise the Kashmir issue, it appears that the Kashmiri separatist movement is entering the next phase, i.e., its internationalisation. Such efforts can be seen in Turkey's rising involvement, which through its official online portal, TRT World, is leaving no stone unturned to blow the Kashmir issue out of proportion, fabricating and disseminating false information. One can also observe dishonesty in such attempts when the Islamist and extremist nature of the separatist movement is conveniently brushed aside. This discussion of attempts to internationalise the Kashmir issue deserves a separate and detailed commentary, which is beyond the scope of this report.

'Musa-Musa Zakir-Musa'

Any discussion on present-day Kashmir cannot be complete without a reference to former HM commander Musa, who now leads the AGUH which is ideologically affiliated to Al Qaeda. Musa represents a significant ideological shift in the thinking of Kashmiri youth. As opposed to supporting the old Hurriyat and nationalist doctrines of "Azadibaraye Pakistan" (Kashmir joins Pakistan) and "Azadibaraye Kashmir" (Independent Kashmir), Musa has come out with the idea of "Azadibaraye Islam" (Islamic Kashmir). He is immensely popular in Srinagar, Anantnag, Kulgam, Baramulla, Bandipura, and Gandarbal areas. Also, 80 to 90 per cent of his supporters are in the age-group of 16-24 years, but also include doctors and engineers. His focus is mainly on religious purity, bringing real Islam to Kashmir.

According to a young journalist who, as a student was a junior of Burhan Wani, martyred Indian Army captain Umar Faiyaz and Zakir Musa at the Navodaya School, 'Zakir bhai' was very religious even in school. He was reticent, stayed away from games, scolded girls for not covering their heads, was soft-spoken and an intellectual kind of a person who indulged in religion and philosophising. He emerges as a man with a clear and sharp vision for Kashmir. This clarity of mind projects him as a strong leader among the youth. Some young boys, who had participated in stone-pelting activities, said they followed Musa because 'it is the clarity of his mind which binds them to his narrative'.

Figure 4: A protester displaying the ISIS flag. Courtesy: Adil Abbas

Musa desires an Islamic caliphate in Kashmir that rejects Pakistan, India and the Hurriyat. He has a massive following among the youth. Class Twelve students from private schools are joining his organisation. Songs eulogising him are being sung during marriages! But his Kashmiri followers do not approve of the brutal methods of the ISIS. They find them un-Islamic. They prefer Musa's milder and convincing ways of establishing a caliphate. He connects through his compelling, lengthy and indoctrinating videos, heavy on Jihad and Islam narrative. His ideology defies the concept of nationhood.

However, there are worrying trends like mentioning the beef-lynching of Pahlu Khan and Akhlaq. His call to Muslims in other Indian states to rise, use petrol bombs and blow up government offices and police stations is aimed at trying to achieve an ideological shift in Kashmir. The youth following him are more passionate about Islam than the idea of an independent Kashmir. The process is of making a fundamentalist, puritan and extremist version of Islam the dominant narrative in Kashmir.

Understandably, his ideology is unacceptable to Pakistan. The HM and the JI are bitterly opposed to Musa. Pakistan-based actors are unable to comprehend the Zakir Musa phenomenon. Their think tanks, analysts and their OGWs are trying hard to understand Musa and his strategy. There are several conspiracy theories doing the rounds in political and security circles attributing his rise to the Indian establishment, but they lack evidence and are based on hearsay. Seeing his massive fan following, Pakistan is trying to 'accommodate' him through the HM and the Jaish. However, he is steadfast in his ideology and unwilling to give in to Pakistani pleas.

Presently, the AGUH does not have an organised cadre, funds or weapons. He is trying to raise his organisation and funds. He is very cautious in recruiting cadres. He asks them to snatch weapons and come back where his network finds them. More than 100 incidents of gun-snatching have been reported. He is also trying to woo HM cadres and rope in Islamic scholars. He convinced Abu Dujana to leave the HM and join him. He sees a high premium in recruiting engineers, doctors and people with IT skills. He has been trying to build his base in central Kashmir which is relatively a quiet area at present. Many AGUH sleeper cells are discreetly recruiting cadres.

There is an impression of complacency on the part of the security establishment in their denials of Zakir Musa and his tanzeem. Since he is driving a wedge between militant organisations and does not have an active organisation by himself, they do not perceive him as a major threat. The fact that the AGUH does not have a grassroots level cadre or organisation should not lull us into denial and complacency. Hypothetically, if he can manage funds and arms, he might raise an army ideologically motivated and highly radicalised. If they are trained in weapons and IEDs, then this may crystallise into an entirely new form of insurgency. Further, it seems he is likely to explore the option of cyber-Jihad.

By default, his ideological trajectory connects him to global Jihadi forces. His followers display a strong fervour for events in West Asia and broader geopolitical trends. With a role in a series of bomb blasts in Eastern Afghanistan, the Islamic State in Khorasan Province (ISKP) is already well established in that region and in the long run is likely to play into the hands of Pakistan's Deep State. Foreign fighters of ISIS returning to Central Asia may also see an opportunity in him given the declining fortunes of the ISIS in West Asia. They might want to stir things up in distant parts like Kashmir, given that the ISIS has declared Kashmir as the gateway to the caliphate in India.

Here, it may be added that the ISIS footprint is established in Kashmir. The area has beautiful Arab-styled Salafi mosques full of ISIS graffiti on side walls. ISIS flags during protests may be teasers with some symbolic value, but the caliphate ideology-IS mentality is finding ample space in Kashmir especially among the youth. Here, one is focusing more on the thinking and ideology and not on the actual organisational structure. According to a media report, (*Deccan Chronicle*, July 6, 2016), Mr. S. M. Sahay, a senior police officer of Jammu and Kashmir categorically stated that the youth bulge witnessed in Kashmir is very similar to the one fuelled in West Asia. Speaking at a seminar in New Delhi, he said, "Kashmir was beset by the same Islamism that had incited young Muslims to target Westerners in violent attacks." (*Boston Review*: "Kashmir's High Price for Demanding Independence," September 26, 2016).

Nadir Ali, President of the Centre for Peace and Justice, who works with pellet victims, organises interactions in remote rural areas of the Valley. He expresses serious concern about the rising IS-mentality among Kashmiri youth. His vast interactions reveal worrisome radical trends and notions of the caliphate and the Islamic Jihad getting deeply embedded in the Kashmiri subconscious.

Kabir Taneja, a senior analyst with the Observer Research Foundation, a think tank, in an article titled "Perils of Humouring ISIS in Kashmir (ORF June 30, 2018)", categorically rejects the presence of the ISIS in Kashmir, contending that it is the state police that is harbouring such a narrative for adopting a hard-nosed military approach in counter-terrorism easily. The basic premises concerning strategy and the organisational structure of the ISIS and their modus operandi needs more detailed exploration and can be the subject matter for another article. Here, it will suffice to mention that middle-level Kashmiri police officials with an in-depth understanding of societal trends and vast experience of CASO, generally agree that the ISIS mentality is slowly getting entrenched in the Valley.

Also, for a moment, even if we assume it to be a far-fetched situation that the current craze is primarily hyped around the persona of Musa and AGUH and could fade either for lack of funds or after his death, even then, the ideological shift which he is heralding in Kashmir will be pernicious to any attempt at a political resolution of the Kashmir dispute. The caliphate ideology will complete the circle of cultural alienation of Kashmiri youth from India. It will be impossible to have a dialogue with a generation that does not believe in international institutions, nation-states, elections, democracy, human rights and multiculturalism. The person may die, but the ideology will outlive him, and likely to get more rigid and intense after his death. If that happens, *Takfiri* (a Muslim who declares another Muslim to be an apostate, i.e., not believing in the essential tenets of Islam and therefore no longer a Muslim) extremism will be the next stage in Kashmir.

Many Sufi shrines such as those of Baba Hanifuddin and Dastageer Sahib were allegedly burnt in the recent past by Lashkar-e-Taiba ("J&K: LeT module behind Dastageer sahib shrine fire busted," Rediff.com, October 2, 2012). Senior Shia leaders, who are formally separatists, said in private conversations that Sunni extremism in Kashmir will make life difficult for Shias. They even suggested to this author that India should scrap Articles 35A and 370 to fully integrate Jammu and Kashmir with India and prevent the onslaught of Jihadi extremism against minorities like Shias and Sikhs. In many social, intellectual and political quarters of Kashmir, there are concerns of an intense sectarian war breaking out in Kashmir, besides lone-wolf attacks, and suicide bombings.

Since the AGUH does not have an organised command and control structure, even Musa admirers, in the interim, join other militant organisations. At the initial level, ideological differences do not matter much. The main thing is sentiment. So, they join whatever organisation they have access to or whichever is active in their area. In South Kashmir, most of them are joining the HM. Many others join Al Badr, Jaish and Lashkar, which are primarily foreign-terrorist (FT) organisations. They have highly trained cadres and are strictly controlled by and from Pakistan. The passion is so strong that in Central Kashmir alone it is said that 10,000 young men are waiting to take up arms. While this could be an exaggerated claim, the possibility of militancy raising its ugly head in Central and North Kashmir can be quite high in the coming months. The HM has strong local roots. It is not as harsh with informers as is the Lashkar and the Jaish. However, in future, if the AGUH can create an organisation and get access to funds/weaponry, then a significant chunk is likely to shift from the HM and other organisations to the AGUH.

In the near future, the HM and other established organisations are likely to continue posing a major security threat. According to informed sources, currently, the total number of militants in the Valley hovers around 300-310, not much as compared to 1990. The number of FTs appears to be just around 110-12, mostly located in north Kashmir, and the local terrorist element is around 190, mostly in South Kashmir. However, public support for militancy remains high and this is likely to continue. During CASO, thousands of people gather in no time for stone pelting. Mosques and social media platforms are used to incite people for stone-pelting. Militants, who die in the process, get tremendous respect and fame in society. People in large numbers attend their funerals, and their families acquire social prestige. The quick fame and glory for dead militants inspires many more to become militants.

These days FTs are using innovative psychological tactics like 'shadow militancy' to compensate for the lower number of actual fighters. In this, a terrorist named 'X' is introduced as different individuals in different names in different villages. So, when security forces neutralise a foreign terrorist, then someone from the other village will claim that he saw terrorist 'X' in his village and security forces lack the will or the strength to kill the 'other' terrorist 'X', lest they be accused of killing the wrong person. As a result, terrorist 'X' becomes a hero. Sometimes even divine explanations are also attached to that terrorist! It is profoundly demoralising for the security forces.

Changing Values; Crumbling Institutions

Amidst all these, the great sense of redemption in the idea of death as a Mujahid as a pathway to Jannat that could redeem them of all their worldly sins, still retains validity and emotional attraction in common perception. This attitude is strikingly similar to what French expert Olivier Roy has discovered about French foreign terrorists, many of whom have been found to be gays, drug addicts, hardly performing namaz and joining ISIS in search of an identity. Their social up-rootedness and lack of integration in Western society has provoked them to join the ISIS.

In Kashmir, a similar phenomenon could be happening. The new generation seems to be losing respect for old institutions of society. They do not respect elders and shrines, have no faith in institutions of family and marriage and indulge in promiscuity and drugs. Morals, loyalty and ethics in social, personal and political life have strongly eroded. The worst effect of the long conflict has been on the culture and traditions of Kashmir. Now in the absence of rootedness which the culture and social system provided, they are suffering from an acute sense of collective depression and hopelessness. As a result, they either take to drugs or seek new outlets for identity and anchorage in religion or rather an exclusivist and fundamentalist version of faith.

The Pakistan Factor

It appears that Pakistani controllers are finding it challenging to send weapons and militants across the border because of the increased vigilance and border fencing. India's aggressive response to the trans-border misadventures of Pakistani forces seems to have changed the perception on the other side. They believe that any misadventure will be met with massive retaliation. Further, they are facing global condemnation as a terror-sponsoring country and, are facing possible Financial Action Task Force (FATF) sanctions. The global mandate is against terrorism, so it is not as easy for them to stage major terrorist attacks. However, their strategy involves keeping a limited number of foreign terrorists active in diverse areas as catalysts. They keep the population on the boil, keep public passions high and abet people for stone-pelting.

Meanwhile, home-grown militancy seems to have filled the space rendering the pain of sending FTs partly superfluous. As a result one comes across many innovations in their strategy. It appears that in future Pakistan-based actors might stay more focused on strategy, planning and high-value logistics leaving the operational aspects to local actors. In the category of high-value logistics, they are inviting a group of 10-30 young Kashmiris to Pakistan to visit under the pretext of meeting relatives or other excuses and training them in the use of IED explosives. It is easier, cheaper and risk-free to undertake such missions. Also, the possibilities of being detected are fewer. They will continue to coordinate, act as an essential conduit, maintain discipline, and above all, punish any deviant behaviour. Further, Pakistan is likely to focus more on Fidayeen attacks because of the following reasons: 1) High-tech border vigil making infiltration difficult; 2) Large presence of home grown terrorists rendering risks involved with infiltration unworthy of being taken; 3) Emerging congenial socio-cultural and religious milieu in Kashmir making recruitments for Jaish suicide squads easier.

Recent trends also indicate that cross-border actors are interested more in raising human rights issues. To promote this, young people are being encouraged to study law, international relations, human rights and sociology. Cross-border actors intend to use such intellectual proxies for false propaganda, psychological war and to malign India's reputation abroad.

According to a veteran counter-terrorism expert, young scholars are invited to Pakistan on the pretext of attending seminars and youth conferences in universities. There, invitee scholars are arranged to meet prominent civil servants, diplomats, politicians and intelligence officials. Once they come back, they raise fictitious issues of human rights and their narrative is selective, biased and incomplete. In future, such activists are likely to be used to raise issues like the rights of people displaced by hydro-electric projects in the Valley.

Further, they are also focused on polarising and dividing the state on communal, religious and regional lines. Many prominent stakeholders, including mainstream politicians in Kashmir have been demanding a divisional status for the Pir Panjal and Chenab Valley, which geographically and in popular perception, are parts of Jammu region. Such demands smack of creating fractions in the Jammu region and infest it with a separatist insurgency. The Jammu region has so far been largely disconnected from the Islamist and separatist Kashmiri insurgency. Further, this author was also witness to nefarious attempts to usher in demographic changes in Jammu and Ladakh regions to make them Muslim-dominated and radicalise local liberal Muslims.

The Pakistan Government led by Imran Khan has made some initial gestures for peace, which is not unusual, but ultimately ends in nothing. However, public expectations on both sides of the border from the new government are high. The Kartarpur Saheb Corridor initiative did initially raise some feeble voices for some similar initiatives in Kashmir as well, but people do concede that in Pakistan, the political leadership only provides the façade; it is the army that calls the shots. Their overtures for peace have so far lacked sincerity and honesty so much so that a large segment of Kashmiris who are assumed to be soft towards Pakistan, do not trust them anymore. Also, if the prevailing perception of the Pakistan army drawing its sustenance from keeping Kashmir on the boil has even the least bit of substance, then there are sufficient reasons to find such peace overtures perfunctory and mere lip-service. Pakistan's insincerity is clearly evident in its lack of action against Masood Azhar and Hafiz Saeed, despite India's repeated requests.

The Way Forward

A prominent politician, when asked about the way forward in Kashmir, narrated an old Kashmiri story: "A lion comes to a field and a young boy asks his father to guide him. His father replies that now he does not need to do anything. Whatever has to be done will be done by the lion." He goes on to explain, "We Kashmiris chose the secular lion of India in 1947. Whatever has to be done has to be by India only." This story, true or otherwise, sums up in two sentences what Kashmiris expect of India and what India needs to do. However, it completely ignores the question, what Kashmiris need to do for themselves? Perhaps they know the answer but do not want to spell it out. Be that as it may, policy planners in New Delhi have to contend with this attitude and approach of the Kashmiri people and leadership.

Given this background, some observations/recommendations are being made on the basis of issues discussed in this study:

(1) While the phenomenon of a rising level of radicalisation, a strong sense of separatism, continuing alienation and anti-India feeling in Kashmir is a reality, yet these should not be the reason to conclude that things have come to a dead end. There are many layers to the prevalent sentiment of dissatisfaction and unrest. The anger of the youth is more about the trust-deficit which has intensified in the absence of a proper dialogue or engagement. Grievances with the civil administration, fears about dilution of autonomy, lack of employment and economic opportunities, near collapse of tourism and the handicraft industry, shoddy civilian infrastructure and basic utilities, poor academic infrastructure, corruption, nepotism and angst with routine discomforts arising out of their interface with the armed forces (including the use of pellet guns—since resolved, other forms of alleged or perceived military high-handedness) form a significant component of the youth resentment.

(2) The young shout slogans of "Azadi," but they have no clarity of thought nor any futuristic plans and strategy. This provides a ray of hope that in some ways and in some areas they can be engaged. The youth that expresses a strong sense of separatism surprisingly

softens down to show a genuine desire for dialogue and accommodation whenever mention is made of the efforts of former Prime Minister Vajpayee. The older generation and those who were involved in the militancy of 1990s have mostly become mainstream actors/citizens and they expect from the Government of India proper rehabilitation, peace and political dialogue.

(3) Local youth join any militant organisation for four important reasons, namely, hopelessness, revenge (mostly because of the atrocities by the armed forces), religious conviction and attraction for the gunas, a symbol of empowerment. Home-grown militancy and the public support for it is where we need a nuanced policy package that is a mix of soft and hard approaches. Indoctrination levels of local militants are low due to their strong cultural roots.

(4) Unlike a situation where people join militancy strictly out of intellectual ultra-leftist leanings while dealing with militancy in Kashmir, the emotional and psychological factor must be taken into consideration. Someone who has become a militant to seek personal revenge can always be brought back into the mainstream, or even the conditions that provoke an individual to seek revenge through the gun can be addressed.

(5) In the case of FTs who are highly radicalised and have a high level of anti-India agenda, our single-minded approach should neutralise them by force while crossing the borders or where ever else, in their hideouts or sanctuaries. They are enemies of the State and should be dealt with accordingly.

(6) Our primary challenge is not the number of militants but public support for it. The quantum and intensity of stone-pelting during CASO are reliable indicators of the level of public support for militants. Hence, we have to strike at the social and cultural constituency of militancy and bring the recruitment levels down. In the current phase, there appears to be a vacuum. There is no political, intellectual and spiritual leadership in Kashmir. The gun-culture has made deep inroads and the youth is directionless.

However, there are ample reasons for hope. In the course of discussions on youth unrest earlier in this brief, a number of suggestions and observations have been made. Along with them, it may also be mentioned that the youth in Kashmir are looking for a good career, joining the civil services, media, the modelling world and the film industry. There are many students pursuing master's programs in International Relations (IR). An interesting case is of a militant, fully trained in handling weapons and having participated in several encounters and getting converted into an ultra-Communist, now holding a Master's degree in comparative religions, and now pursuing his second masters in IR. Kashmiri youth are talented, sharp, and ambitious and looking for opportunities to study in foreign universities, get good jobs, and improve their quality of life. Presently, those opportunities are missing and it is important to try to create them.

Course of Action

Kashmir is at a very critical juncture. The so-called 'movement' is directionless and leaderless. It may take a blind turn. If it goes on like this, it may lead to anarchy and the region could become the hunting ground for all kinds of barbaric Jihadi forces like Al Qaeda and the ISIS. There are forces waiting to capitalise on the ongoing youth unrest. To deal with the situation, the following suggestions could be considered:

(a) It is imperative that before the Pakistanis or any transnational terrorist groups act, we get our act together and develop a new narrative acceptable to the Kashmiri people, built around finding a political, diplomatic, psychological and spiritual solution. The new narrative could also include the frequently heard demand for Azadi. We can redefine "Azadi" as "Azadi" from poverty, violence, nepotism, corruption, religious extremism and injustice. Against prevailing notions of "Azadi," our stand can be of "Azadibaraye aman-o-Ahatram" (peace with dignity). It has to be a multipronged approach with multiple layers of engagement.

(b) We need to have a long-term political and economic vision for Kashmir. We need to ask the right questions—what kind of Kashmir we want after 15-20 or 25 years and what is the roadmap for it. A committee of experts could be constituted to chart out a political, economic, educational, cultural and religious roadmap for Kashmir. It should define the underlying principles, objectives, the strategy and the steps ahead. There must be consistency in our approach.

(c) For some short-term gains, no compromise should even be thought of, with the core principles or our long-term interests and objectives.

(d) There should be no compromise with our policy of zero-tolerance to religious extremism and terrorism. A systematic crackdown on Jamaat-i-Islami must be strategically pursued, in all sincerity. Moreover, the effort must be undertaken on a sustained basis.

(e) CASO against militants must continue, ensuring minimum civilian casualties and discomfort. A strong force posture against militancy will strengthen India's state narrative and demoralise the cross-border sponsors.

(f) However, our approach needs to be nuanced. Overreliance on security narrative and use of hard power will not be very helpful in the case of home-grown militancy. If one militant dies, five others join the movement. Therefore, we have to address the challenge of recruitment and strike at the social, political, cultural and intellectual roots of militancy.

(g) OGWs must be dealt with a heavy hand. As regards other ways of eroding the constituency of militancy, some possible measures are discussed below in the section on youth engagement.

(h) As stated earlier, there is no clarity and logical consistency among the separatists and mainstream politicians regarding the political aspect of the issue. We need to strengthen the mainstream in Kashmir and institutionalise democracy as a spirit. We can strengthen mainstream politics by engaging politicians in dialogue and incentivising the joining of the mainstream.

(i) The mainstreaming process should include politicians, civil society, clergy, artists, writers, journalists, civil servants, academicians, students, panchayat leaders and the business class. Inviting mainstream stakeholders for lectures, seminars, discussions, and interactions across the country in universities, colleges, chambers of commerce, development institutions and by the different state governments will create the necessary goodwill. Engaging separatists will enhance their stakes in the peace process. It will create a friendly space to channel the political solution. It will be very helpful in mitigating the angst of people.

(j) The district administration should have an open-door policy. Cleanliness, electricity, road maintenance and other routine issues of public life will help in breaking the ice. The current disconnect between Kashmiris and administrative officials from other states working in Kashmir have led to a kind of stagnation. The district administration should have regular 'chaupals' in rural areas. This goodwill generating process has to reach the grassroots in Kashmir. District Collectors, Divisional Commissioners and other city administrative officials should visit schools, panchayats, mosques and other social forums in remote areas and engage the people in dialogue.

(k) Groups of Kashmiri teachers and students from rural areas can be taken to Delhi and other state capitals for informal interactions. Such outreach should avoid excessive media glare and politicisation of such events must be checked effectively.

(l) Youth engagement programmes have so far focused on employment generation. However, when the cause is psychological, such a narrow corridor approach will hardly serve the right purpose. Definition of engagement should be widened to include addressing their sense of alienation and the trust deficit. The key lies in the right way of communication and creating the right perception.

(m) Kashmiris by nature are scholars. Their natural skills in the softer aspects of life such as art, literature and emotions are very subtle and refined. We need to engage youth at that level where there is a meeting of minds. We need to create political, social and intellectual and cultural outlets for the young generation to express themselves.

(n) Youth forums can be platforms where political, social and cultural issues can be freely discussed. They should also be encouraged to interact with youth from other parts of the country. They can be invited to think-tanks, colleges, schools, and universities. The story of India covering freedom of expression, democracy, secularism, respect for diversity, multiculturalism and the liberty of pursuing various art forms, could sell well in this context. They should not see the gun as a source of empowerment. The alternative role models can be created in academics, sports, civil services, literature, journalism, and films.

(o) Kashmiri youth must be exposed to a course in critical thinking. The curriculum should focus on teaching diverse religious and ideological thought processes. It can have six schools of Indian philosophy, Western philosophy, and political philosophy, philosophy of religion, comparative religions and international affairs. The curriculum should also involve meditation, yoga and psychological counselling to generate positive thinking.

(p) The Kashmiri youth mindset needs to be internationalised and catapulted out of the perceived or real sense of victimhood. Sentiments of religious extremism and separatism are also strengthened due to lack of exposure to global developments. Through foreign exposure, they will have an interface with forces of post-modern globalisation, development and economic growth. They will see the fruits of economic growth, educational development, scientific advancement and technological innovation reaped by countries in the West and other nations like China, Thailand and the "Asian Tigers"; their mind, in all likelihood will venture beyond guns and religious obscurantism. Face-to-face with the new global revolutions in the field of artificial intelligence and space exploration, some of them will be able to perceive the futility of religious extremism and unrealistic notions of "Azadi."

(q) In brief, it can be said that the state should have a dominant presence in the academic space and not in the religious organisations as they mainly focus on "deeni-taleem," i.e., religious studies. In schools, the curriculum of Kashmiriyat and nationalism must be developed and taught. The young generation hardly knows anything about Nand Rishi, Lalleshwari, Lalitaditya Muktapida, Kalhan and the rich scholarly heritage of Kashmir. Such a narrative will go a long way in checking separatism and radicalisation.

(r) Easy availability of extremist literature must be given serious consideration. The youth must lay hands on non-religious literature. Literary festivals, music festivals and other literary events (by think tanks, development agencies, government bodies and non-government bodies) can be organised in Srinagar, Leh, Jammu and other cities of the state.

De-radicalisation

Moving on to other important issues, as stated earlier, there is an urgent need to take cognition of the growing threat posed by radicalisation in Kashmiri society. It is broadly agreed that the best guards against radicalisation are provided by India's family system and social traditions. Fortunately, in Kashmir, the family as a unit is still secure. Ordinarily, a radicalised person severs all ties with the family and old friends. However, in Kashmir, militants maintain their ties with the family, though for security reasons, physical contact might be few and far between. In families, girls and women are highly empowered. Kashmiri women, who constitute 50 per cent of the population, need to be engaged in the de-radicalisation campaign.

Further, efforts in the direction of reviving and preserving the Kashmiri cultural heritage in music, spirituality, arts, language, and literature can be undertaken. Since universities and colleges are emerging as significant centres of Jihadi radicalisation, these should be subjected to NAAC inspections on a regular basis. Apart from a quality upgrade, the NAAC should also keep track of radicalisation trends in academic institutions and submit regular reports on them. Prompt action must be recommended by NAAC to counter religious extremism in the academic world.

Also, there is a need for the Government to evolve a long-term de-radicalisation and counter-radicalisation policy for Kashmir. This would require detailed exploration by subject-experts, but it must be multidisciplinary in its approach, roping in religious scholars, experts in the philosophy of religion and politics, experts in cyber-jihad, psychologists, educationists, civil society members, geo-politics scholars, security experts, intelligence fraternity, sociologists, and other relevant actors. To begin with, the Government can launch a strategic, precise and an all-around effective crack-down on organisations like JI—the core constituents of the radicalisation infrastructure.

Business, employment and livelihood-business linkages of Kashmir and the rest of India, particularly in the traditional areas of horticulture, handicrafts, tourism and carpet industries, have always been very robust but for the last nearly three decades these links have come under serious strain on account of militancy. There is an urgent need to strengthen and further develop old ties. Tourism and carpet industries need a complete overhaul. New employment and business opportunities for the youth can be created in these sectors through specialised efforts. The existing schemes of the Government of India do not address the problems and concerns specific to conflict and post-conflict societies like Kashmir. For conflict zones like Kashmir, such schemes and programs need to be customised. For that, if required, even UN experts and international development experts who have worked in conflict zones could be co-opted.

Social Media

The narrative on social media needs to be challenged and replaced with an alternative. WhatsApp and Facebook groups run by Pakistan proxies like JI, global jihadi organisations and militant organisations are very refined and sophisticated in terms of quality of content and their logical rigour. Facts and figures are deftly manipulated and selectively presented to nourish a fertile ground for vulnerable minds which can be easy targets for Jihadi ideology and anti-India feelings. The quality and content of the videos are also quite evolved. India needs a very systematic, scientific and nuanced effort that reflects a sound understanding of Kashmiri sub-conscious while developing an alternate narrative. Here also, the task has to be assigned to experts in the field rather than left to the security and intelligence establishments on their own.

An alternative narrative needs to be created in universities and colleges of Jammu and Kashmir to counter the lies peddled by cross-border actors. Think-tanks, research forums, youth forums or inter-faith dialogue bodies and cultural interaction clubs can be created to challenge dominant narratives of Jihad and the hypocrisy of Pakistan in political matters. Pakistan keeps silent on the atrocities faced by Uighur Muslims in China but keeps harping on the grievances in Kashmir and India. Such forums can initiate debates on the conditions of minorities, state of civil rights and democracy in Pakistan. Rejection of religious extremist parties in the recent elections in Pakistan can also be the subject matter of such forums. These will be very helpful in demolishing the lies peddled by Pakistan and its proxies in Kashmir. They can organise discussions on strengthening democracy, merits of the liberal world order and the true meaning of Azadi.

The spiritual vision of masters like Sri Sri Ravishankar, Sadguru Jaggi Vasudev and others can be immensely useful in providing a healing touch to Kashmir. It may not be a well-known fact that the father of the deceased HM leader, Burhan Wani, spent several days in an Art of Living ashram after his son's encounter death. This fact puts a big question mark on the whole narrative of religious extremism in Kashmir. The Kashmiri subconscious still has sufficient space for the spiritual pathways of Tauhid and Vedanta. It is time we explored these domains.

The Pakistan factor in Kashmir affairs is a fact of life, and hence, it is important to engage Pakistan in a dialogue and peace process. However, there should be no going back on our firm stand that terror and talks cannot go together. Kashmiris have by and large now come to accept this reality. For any dialogue process to resume, progress and eventually succeed, Pakistan must cease support to and stop sponsorship of terrorism. In the meantime, the current robust kinetic posture against trans-border Pakistani activities in aiding and abetting terror activities, including financial support, must continue in a sustained manner. Since the Surgical Strike (Sept. 2017), people in Kashmir feel very enthusiastic about India's ability to respond in a pro-active manner.

For the future, if Pakistan does not show any substantial change in its stance, then the option of a sub-conventional/hybrid war should be explored. It also needs to be mentioned with special emphasis that India's strong and aggressive force-posture with Pakistan which in effect involves giving them a proportionate or even disproportionate response, if needed, plays an important role in clearing the smokescreen of confusion in a

Kashmiri mind. Call it a specific trait or a personal observation, the fact is that the Kashmiri sub-conscious is generally confused on various issues. Maybe several centuries of foreign rule has left its imprint on the collective psyche of the Kashmiris. In the Kashmiri mind, emotions are very dominant. However, the idea is not to generalise and the observations leave enough space for exceptions.

Coming back to the point of India's aggressive force posture vis-à-vis Pakistan, it must be mentioned that in the past, India's decisive victory in Kargil played an instrumental role in convincing Kashmiris that their future lay with India. But the best way to engage a Kashmiri mind is dialogue. That is the message coming out from all diverse stakeholders at formal and informal levels. The sense of political alienation is very strong. Cultural and religious alienation is also rapidly rising. Hence, a wide range of people feel that structured engagement will be helpful in generating trust and goodwill within a year. After that, the Government could come out with concrete political solutions. It would be desirable to approach the problem directly rather than taking a circuitous route by avoiding the political aspects of the issue. There needs to be clarity of vision for this, and in due course, concrete proposals need to be rolled out.

(Abhinav Pandya is a graduate in Public Policy from Cornell University. He has worked in political affairs, refugee rehabilitation, social capital and sustainable development in India and the USA. He has been a frequent contributor to the VIF on issues relating to radicalisation, and internal security affairs)

*

INDEX

Aadhaar Project, 86, 92
Afghanistan, 130-31, 141
Ahle-Hadith, 269-70
Al Khandaq, 133
Alan Greenspan, 7
Ali, Nadir, 275
All India Police-Population Ratio, 183
All Party Hurriyat Conference (APHC), 262
Altamura, Carlo Edoardo
    European Banks and the Rise of International Finance, 55
America First strategy, 204
Amina Mohammed, 142
Anti-war Sentiment, 135
Aranakyas, 34
Arthasastra, 37, 40
ASEAN, 221
Asia, Growth Shifts to, 62-65
Asian Development Bank (ADB), 211
Asian Financial Crisis, 62
Asian Infrastructure Investment Bank (AIIB), 211
Association of South East Asian Nations (ASEAN), 206
Asuravijaya, 40
Atharaveda, 34
Atharvaveda, 35

Baba Hanifuddin, 276
Balancing Sectoral Growth, 179
Ballistic Missile Defence (BMD), 182
Bank for International Settlements (BIS), 60
Basel Institution, 15
Battle Zone Commands (BZC), 108
Belt and Road Initiative (BRI), 211
Bhagavata Purana, 35
Bhagwad Gita, 35, 39-40
Bharat Net, 91
Bhattacharya, K.C., 30

Bhutto, Z.A., 119-20
Bilateral Coordination Mechanism (BCM), 206
Boehmer, Elleke, 230
Bose, Sugata, 232
Botnet Cleaning Centres, 88
Brahmanas, 34
BRICS, 76
Brig Bidwell, 120
Brig Malik
    Quranic Concept of War, 121
Brodie, Bernard,
    The Absolute Weapon: Atomic Power and World Order, 199

California Arabian Standard Oil Co, 49
Canada, 10
Capitalism, 2
Central Military Commission (CMC), 100
Chabahar Port, 138
Chattopadhyaya, B.D., 232
China owns US debt, 68
China Sea Air Defence Identification Zone, 210
China, 8, 18, 20, 24, 62, 67, 75, 138, 209, 211
China's Defence Expenditure, 13
China-Pakistan Economic Corridor (CPEC), 19-20, 138
Chinese Characteristics, 98
Claim for Parity, 116
Clean India, 75
CMC,
    Command Functions Restructured, 106
    Organisational Control Reconstructed, 104
CNIITMASH, 79
Col Gaddafi, 53
Cold War, 47, 130, 206
Combat Readiness State, 182
Commander Fleet Activities Yokosuka (CFAY), 204
Common Services Centres (CSCs), 85

Communism versus Generalship, 99
Comprehensive National Power (CNP), 174-76, 195
Comprehensive National Power, 174
Confidence Building Measures (CBM), 21
Confucianism, 29
Coomaraswamy, Ananda K., 30, 247-48
Council for Mutual Economic Assistance (COMECON), 48
CPC Politburo, 101, 104
Creating Usable Capability in Capital Acquisitions, 182
Crime and Criminal Tracking Network and System (CCTNS), 94
Current Account Deficit (CAD), 8

Danilovic, Vesna,
 When the Stakes Are High: Deterrence and Conflict among Major Powers, 200
Dastageer Sahib, 276
Daultana, Mia Mumtaz, 151
Decentralisation and Delegation, 193
Delhi Accord, 151
Demonetisation, 14
Deng Xiaoping, 175
Department of Posts (DoP), 90
De-radicalisation, 287-88
Dharmanibandhas, 36
Dharmashastras, 36
Dharmavijaya, 40
DigiLocker, 88
Digital Empowerment, 87
Digital Era, 82
Digital India, 75, 86, 90, 188
Digital India, Pillars, 87
Digital Life Certificates, 88
Diversified Trade Basket, 178
Dow Jones Industrial Average (DJIA), 60-61

East China Sea, 201
Economy, 176
Effective Water Management, 189
e-Money, 90
Enough of War, We Want Peace, 135
e-Sign framework, 89
Etaqadi, 269
European Economic Community, 50
European Recovery Programme (ERP), 47, 50

European Refining Capacity, 49
European Union (EU), 10
Eurosclerosis, 62
Exclusive Economic Zones (EEZ), 210
Expanding Base of Tertiary Education, 188
Expanding Economic Diplomacy, 193
Expanding Military Diplomacy, 193

Fed Open Market Committee, 66
Federal Republic of Germany (FRG), 48
Financial Action Task Force (FATF), 133, 279
Five-Nation Railway Corridor (FNRC), 138
Force Commander Northern Areas (FCNA), 121
Foreign Direct Investment (FDI) Growth, 62, 179
Foreign Direct Investment, 63
Foreign Policy, 192
Fred Hirsch,
 Controlled Disintegration, 57
Fukuyama, Francis, 5

G-20, 76
Gadgil, N.V., 151
Gandhi, Mahatma, 42
General Agreement on Tariffs and Trade (GATT), 4
Geopolitics, 11
German Democratic Republic (GDR), 48
Ghose, Aurobindo, 247-48
 Political Philosophy, 37
Gilgit-Baltistan (GB), 123
Global Current Account Balances, 54
Global Economy, Controlled Integration of, 57-61
Goods and Services Tax (GST), 14
Governance, 191
Great Leap Forward, 97
Gross Capital Formation (GCF), 178
Gulhati, N.D., 148
Gurumurthy, S., 30, 40

Haqqani Network, 132
Hassan, Javed, 121
Health Sector Allocations, 186
Heavy Engineering Corporation (HEC), 79
High Technology Exports Base, 187
Higher Education Mass and Quality, 188

Index

highly enriched uranium (HEU), 214
Host Nation Support, 204
Human Capital (HC), 184
Human Resources Pool, 180
Hydro-electric Policy of J&K, 166

Identity, 114
India, 1, 16, 18, 28-29, 33, 79, 82, 86, 116, 118, 120, 124, 164, 166
India, Multicultural Society, 40
India's Role in Afghanistan's Future, 139-40
India-Afghanistan Relations, 130
India-Japan Ties, 222
Indian Council for Cultural Relations (ICCR), 132
Indian Council of Agricultural Research (ICAR), 132
India-Russia
    Defence, 76-77
    Nuclear Power Cooperation, 78
    Terrorism, 80
Indo-Pak Dialogue, 122
Indus Drainage System (IDS), 143, 151
Indus River Basin (IRB), 145, 147, 149, 152-53, 155
Indus Valley Civilisation, 143
Indus Water Treaty (IWT), 18, 142-71
    Articles, 155
Inequality Reduction, 184
Information and Communication Technology (ICT), 82, 83, 186
Information Technology Enabled Service (ITES), 183
INS Arihant, 25, 26
Institutes and Research Pool, 187
Instrumental Implications, 39
Integrated Crop Area (ICA), 166
Integrated Joint Warfare (IJW), 98
Integrated Logistic System, 98
Inter Dominion Agreement, 154
Inter Services Intelligence (ISI), 21
Inter-Continental Ballistic Missile (ICBM), 215
Inter-Dominion Agreement, 151
Internal Security, 183
International Court of Justice (ICJ), 124
International Monetary Fund (IMF), 11, 47, 60
International North South Corridor (INTC), 138

International Peace Cooperation Law (IPCL), 207
ISIS, 275
Islamic State in Khorasan Province (ISKP), 275

Jamaat-i-Islami (JI), 264
James Akins, 53
Jammu & Kashmir, 162, 269-70, 278
    Kashmir Fixation, 118
    Politics in Drift, 261
    Youth, 265
Janapadas, 37
Japan, 9, 10, 14-15, 206-7, 219, 223
Japan's Defence Budget, 201
Japan's Defence Industry, 216
Japan's Missile Defence System, 220
Japan's Non-Proliferation Policy, 212
Japan's Nuclear Policy, 212
Japan-Russia summits, 222
Jayaswal, K.P., 37
Jinnah, Muhammad Ali, 147
Jinnah's two-nation theory, 115
Jones, Rodney, 38

Kartarpur Saheb Corridor Initiative, 280
Kashmir Militancy, 265
Kashmir
    Civil Society and Human Rights Groups, 271-72
    Disenchantment youth, 264
    Pakistan Factor, 279
    Social Media, 270-71, 288-90
Kautilya's *Arthsastra*, 36
Khan, Ayub, 120
Khan, Jenab Shaukat Hayat, 151
Khan, Liaquat Ali, 117
Khan, Wali, 115
Khyber Pakhtunkhwa (KP), 116
Kissinger,
    World Order, 39
Knowledge and Information (KI), 188
Kohn, Hans, 235
Krugman, Paul, 6

Lashkar-e-Taiba (LeT), 124
Leading Group for Reforms, 103
Libya, 53
Lilienthal, David, 142-43, 152

Literacy and Education, 184
Lobhavijaya, 40
Localised War, 98
Long-Term Capital Management (LTCM), 61

Madad (Help), 89
Maddison, Angus, 4
Maha Puranas, 35
Mahabharata, 33, 35, 40, 255
Mahajanapadas, 37
Make in India, 75, 86
    in Defence Sector, 182
Malhotra, Rajiv, 31
Manusmriti, 36
Maritime Domain Awareness (MDA), 222
Marshall Aid, 47-48
Marshall Plan, 47
Martin, William McChesney, 54
Marx, Karl, 2
Mary Kaldor,
    The Disintegrating West, 56
Mata Bhumi, Putro Aham Prithvya, 42
MGNREGA, Digital Boost, 88
Micro, Small and Medium Enterprises, 16
Military, 180
Military Area Commands (MAC), 99
Military Regions (MR), 99
Minerals, 190
MIRVs (Multiple Independently targetable Re-entry Vehicles), 26
Mission Mode Projects (MMPs), 84
Miyamoto Musashi, 199
Mobile e-Governance Service Delivery Gateway (MSDG), 85
Modi, Narendra, Prime Minister of India, 22, 25, 42-43, 75, 77, 81, 142
    visited Russia, 76
Mohammad, Jenab Ghulam, 151
Morgenthau, Hans J., 174, 194
Most Favoured Nation (MFN), 19, 21
Multilateralism, 10
Munshi, K.M., 30
Musa, Zakir, 266, 274-75
Musa-Musa Zakir-Musa, 273
Musharraf, Parvez, 20
MyGov.in, 89

Nakayamo Taro, 207

Nation, Concept, 236
National Broadband Network (Bharat Net), 86
National Command Authority, 26
National Defence Policy Guidelines, 205, 213
National e-Governance Plan (NeGP), 84
National e-Governance Service Delivery Gateway (NSDG), 85
National Intelligence Grid (NATGRID), 94
National Investigation Agency (NIA), 262
National Land Record Modernisation Programme (NLRMP), 94
National Optical Fibre Network (NOFN), 91
National Savings Rate (NSR), 178
National Scholarships Portal, 90
Nationalism, 228, 235
    Features, 234
    Rise, 233
Nationhood, 233
Natural Gas, 190
Natural Resources, 189
Nehru, Pandit Jawaharlal, 147, 151
Night Vision Devices (NVD), 182
NITI Ayog, 31
Non-Alignment Movement (NAM), 18
Non-Nuclear Principles, 200
North Atlantic Treaty Organization (NATO), 11, 48, 204
North Korea, 208, 219
    Crisis, 225
Nuclear Deterrence, 212
Nuclear Submarine, 25
Nuclear Supplier Group (NSG), 19
Nyaya, 36

Oil-Finance Cycle, 51
Olivier Roy, 278
One China Policy, 19
Online Facility for Firms to File Single Return, 90
Online Facility to Issue PAN Card, 90
Online Registration System (ORS), 89
Organisation for Economic Co-operation and Development (OECD), 4, 55
Organisation of Petroleum Exporting Countries (OPEC), 52, 60

Pakistan, 18, 20-21, 24-25, 114, 119, 127, 165, 166, 289